William Alexander Smith

From Occident to Orient

A record of a nine months' tour through Europe, Egypt, Holy Land, Asia Minor and

Greece

William Alexander Smith

From Occident to Orient

A record of a nine months' tour through Europe, Egypt, Holy Land, Asia Minor and Greece

ISBN/EAN: 9783337319557

Printed in Europe, USA, Canada, Australia, Japan

Cover: Foto ©Andreas Hilbeck / pixelio.de

More available books at **www.hansebooks.com**

FROM

OCCIDENT TO ORIENT.

A RECORD OF A NINE MONTHS' TOUR THROUGH
EUROPE, EGYPT, HOLY LAND, ASIA
MINOR AND GREECE.

BY

REV. WM. A. SMITH.

WITH AN INTRODUCTION BY

W. W. BARR, D. D.

Second Edition—Revised and Enlarged.

ILLUSTRATED.

PITTSBURGH:
UNITED PRESBYTERIAN BOARD OF PUBLICATION,
53 AND 55 NINTH STREET,
1897.

DEDICATION.

To the mother whose tender and prayerful interest has ever followed me through childhood's little griefs, the temptations of young manhood, the joys and sorrows of more mature years, and the perils of travel in foreign lands; as well as to the multitude of personal friends with whom we have been more or less associated in times past, is this little volume affectionately inscribed by the

AUTHOR.

AUTHOR'S PREFACE.

The literature of travel is so abundant in these days of multiplied facilities for easy and inexpensive travel, that we have hesitated to thrust before the public a second edition of a work that was never intended for anything but a limited circulation among the author's own friends and acquaintances. But the first edition has been so kindly received, that now, at the solicitation of friends, a second edition, enlarged and revised, is sent forth and committed to the tender mercies of a more public reading.

Careful as we have been to make our record, both as to historical fact and personal observation, as correct as possible, there will undoubtedly be found some errors, in regard to which the critical must be as lenient as though the authorship was their own.

Indebtedness is acknowledged to guide books, etc., for statistics, measurements, and general history. As for the rest we have relied on a good, full journal of daily events, kept as we went along.

It had been the life-long ambition of the author to see for himself those countries of the Old World, where history was made, particularly those portions of the Orient so intimately connected with the Book of books, so that by being able to localize place and event he could be clearer in his own mind and more useful to the public before which he must continually stand in his chosen sphere of teacher and minister. It was study then, and not pleasure alone, that gave motive to the nine months' tour of which the present work is a narrative. The journey was undertaken at a critical period of the author's life, at a time when it was specially calculated to be a renewer of health and spirits ; it was both in an abundant measure. The journey was a constant succession of delights from the beginning to the end. We have tried to make the reader feel that it was such, and to enter, as far as his imagination would permit, into the pleasure of the journey with us. It is hoped that some of those who may read our record, and who may afterwards make a similar tour in person, being limited in means, may find some hints as to economical traveling, which may be of some practical service to them.

W. ALEX. SMITH.

June, 1896.

TABLE OF CONTENTS.

	Page
CHAPTER I. ON THE DEEP	11
CHAPTER II. IN THE QUEEN'S CITY	19
CHAPTER III. HERE AND THERE IN LONDON	28
CHAPTER IV. THE GAY CITY OF FASHION	38
CHAPTER V. IN PARIS—SEEING THE SIGHTS	45
CHAPTER VI. SOUTHERN FRANCE; AND THE FRENCH AND ITALIAN RIVIERAS	53
CHAPTER VII. THE SEVEN HILLED CITY—JUBILEE WEEK IN ROME	65
CHAPTER VIII. RAMBLES IN AND AROUND ROME	77
CHAPTER IX. FAREWELL TO ROME—LIFE AROUND THE BAY OF NAPLES	88
CHAPTER X. IN THE LAND OF THE PHARAOHS	100
CHAPTER XI. UNITED PRESBYTERIAN MISSIONS IN EGYPT	111
CHAPTER XII. CROSS AND CRESCENT	129

CHAPTER XIII.
AROUND ABOUT CAIRO 140

CHAPTER XIV.
FROM CAIRO TO JERUSALEM 152

CHAPTER XV.
OVER THE HILLS OF JUDEA TO HEBRON, DEAD SEA AND JORDAN VALLEY 163

CHAPTER XVI.
WALKS ABOUT ZION 176

CHAPTER XVII.
EASTER DAYS IN THE HOLY CITY 191

CHAPTER XVIII.
THROUGH SAMARIA AND GALILEE 202

CHAPTER XIX.
FROM JERUSALEM TO ATHENS VIA. BEYROUT, SMYRNA AND EPHESUS 215

CHAPTER XX.
RAMBLES AROUND ATHENS AND CORINTH 223

CHAPTER XXI.
FROM ATHENS TO LONDON, THROUGH NORTHERN ITALY AND THE ALPS 236

CHAPTER XXII.
RAMBLES AROUND GLASGOW, EDINBURGH AND STIRLING 250

CHAPTER XXIII.
THROUGH REGIONS FRAGRANT WITH MEMORIES OF POET, NOVELIST AND MARTYR 262

CHAPTER XXIV.
WHERE PAT LIVES—OBSERVATIONS IN THE EMERALD ISLE 272

CHAPTER XXV.
HOMEWARD BOUND 280

INTRODUCTION.

By the Rev. W. W. Barr, D. D.

The prophet Daniel said more than five hundred years before Christ, as he looked with the seer's eye into the distant future, "Many shall run to and fro, and knowledge shall be increased." His prophecy is being fulfilled, at least in measure, in our day. Never was there such running to and fro in the world as at the present time, and never was knowledge so largely increased as now.

King Solomon said in his day, nearly a thousand years before Christ, "Of making many books there is no end." Did he live in this day he would repeat the declaration with an emphasis that he could not have given to his words when he wrote them. If he lived now, and contemplated only a single class of books, he would say, "Of making many books of travel there is no end." Perhaps he might add, "And much study of many of these is a weariness of the flesh." We are confident, however, that he would not say this of the little volume which it is now our pleasure to introduce to the reader.

The part of the world traveled by the author of this book, namely, from New York to Glasgow, to London, Paris, across France, through Italy, over the Mediterranean to Alexandria and Cairo, Egypt, then over to Palestine and through the Holy Land, then back to Greece and across the Continent through Switzerland to London, and again to Scotland and through Ireland, and by the Atlantic to New York, is familiar to travelers and to a large number of readers who have perused the volumes which they have written. On the whole there is no route of travel so interesting and profitable as this. A large number have realized its pleasure and enjoyed its advantages. A much greater number have only had it in their desire, or as a fond dream never to become a reality.

The best that these last could do has been to travel in thought and sympathy with those who have gone over the ground and have published what they have seen and experienced by the way. The pleasure and profit enjoyed by the volumes of travel that have appeared have been varied. Some of these have been delightful pen pictures and have been packed full of useful information; others have been commonplace, prolix, prosy and dull.

We do not hesitate to class with the former the volume that is now before us. The author traveled with his eyes and ears open. He went deliberately when and where the most important things were to be seen and learned. Places of less note and interest were passed by, or were seen hurriedly. He had with him for the most of the way a very pleasant and witty traveling companion, whom he designates as "H." Not infrequently he gives his readers the benefit of "H's" humorous and sage observations. On these the author sometimes comments, and exhibits a large degree of wit and humor himself. Often we seem to hear the loud laugh of these genial companions in travel, and we, though not with them, enjoy the fun. The book is much enlivened by this means.

It was our pleasure to go over, some years ago, the greater part of the tour made by the author of this volume. We have much enjoyed the trip again with him, and we are glad to testify in general to the accuracy of his observations and descriptions. The fault which we found with the book in its first edition was that there was too little of it. Often we wished that he had told us more. This was specially true of his trip through Egypt. We were disappointed that he did not take more time in that country, and especially that he did not tell us more of what he saw and learned of the United Presbyterian mission and missionaries in that land. This defect, however, is remedied in the new edition that is now issued by the United Presbyterian Board of Publication. Two chapters are here added: one entitled, "Cross and Crescent," and the other, "United Presbyterian Missions in Egypt." The value of the first edition, which was "intended rather to afford a little pleasure and recreation to personal friends, than as a means of adding to the world's store of knowledge," is greatly enhanced by these additional chapters. As at present published, the work takes its place among the most readable, pleasant and useful books of travel.

Philadelphia, August, 1896.

CHAPTER I.

ON THE DEEP.

AN ocean voyage to those who have often had the experience is not one of the most interesting things whereof to make a book chapter or a newspaper article. But it may as well be candidly stated at the outset that the chapters of this little volume are not written with the expectation that they will fall under the notice of, or to any great degree interest, those who from motives of business or pleasure have become habitual roamers of the great deep or countries beyond. To such, an ocean voyage presents little variety; always the same great expanse of sea on which days together may be passed without sight of sail or trail of smoke to indicate the fact that other fellow-mortals are anywhere within the sphere of your existence. To be sure, old Neptune will occasionally take pity on the voyager who longs for the spice of variety in his monotonous life, and raise commotion enough to satisfy the most eager hunter after variety. To those accustomed for the most part to land travel, or have passed the ocean but a time or two, an ocean voyage may be anything else than monotonous. Life on board the ocean steamship of the huge proportions and luxurious fittings as are most of the vessels belonging to the Cunard, Inman, White Star, and Anchor lines, presents a novel and pleasing feature to the traveler hitherto accustomed to the rattle and dust, and vexatious delays of railroad travel. What delicious hours may be enjoyed on the promenade deck, taking in the fresh sea air and watching the roll of the billows, or scanning the horizon for some other white-winged traveler of the deep! What recreation in some deck game with your fellow passengers, or amusement in watching the antics of the sportive porpoise! These are your day enjoyments; but the night has its own variety of sights for you.

For hours at a time we have stood at the stern of our vessel and watched the rolling balls and sparkles of phosphorescent light which the Titanic screw shot out over the vessel's foaming track like a thousand sparks from beneath a Vulcan's mighty hammer. Nor does this end the nightly display of Nature's fireworks. Look to the northward! Your landsman's eye never saw such auroral beauty as that. From the eastern to the western horizon that arc of electric colored light extends; and along its whole length, from both upper and lower edges, thousands of streamers are shooting skyward, many of them reaching to the zenith, and looking like giant comets' tails. There! like a great rocket, shoots up a brilliant streamer, whilst another one that has gone a moment before fades away, and so from one quarter of the sky to another the eye is drawn as these streamers in rapid succession shoot athwart the sky. A panorama of unequalled natural beauty is this display of ocean aurora.

Perhaps the reader into whose hands these pages may ultimately come will now be content to linger awhile on the ocean voyage, which commenced for the writer a pilgrimage of nine months, covering the larger part of Europe, Egypt, Holy Land, Syria, a part of Asia Minor and Greece. This simple record of our tour is made in the hope that it may interest those who never expect to see for themselves these lands of sacred and historical interest, as well as to furnish hints to intending travelers how such a tour as was made in this instance may be made to yield the greatest amount of enjoyment and knowledge for the least expenditure of money consistent with health and comfort. We may be pardoned, therefore, for a minutia of statement at times relative to the economies of the tour. Like most other travelers, we paid out some cash for experience, and those of our friends who may have the happiness of a tour through the Old World would doubtless prefer to have the benefit of our experience and retain their cash.

We were five Hawkeyes who resolved on widening the range of our mental vision by an eye to eye study and enjoyment of things beyond the water; and our capital for the enterprise was seven hundred dollars each. With this amount we hoped to journey leisurely through Europe, hastily through Egypt, with a month left us for Palestine. How we succeeded, and in what ways we departed from our itinerary of travel, will be seen as we progress.

Our passage is engaged by the Anchor line steamship "Furnessia," a fine vessel, next in size to the largest vessel of the fleet. We have decided on a first cabin passage, inasmuch as a special rate of forty-five dollars each is made for the company. Here we make our first mistake, as we afterwards find, in not taking a second cabin via one of the lines running direct to Liverpool and London. A quicker passage at a rate of thirty-five dollars would have been obtained in this way, with no loss of comfort.

It is a delightful day in the middle of October as we stand on the foremost part of the first cabin deck looking at the preparations for departure. There is the usual crowd of friends standing on the pier with ready handkerchiefs to wave their farewells to the departing ones. But we are friendless, so far as the great city is concerned; we are strangers going among strangers, and we are free to confess that, much as we had longed for this glad hour to come, we are almost as ready to use our handkerchiefs as many that we see around us. The bell rings out a warning, the whistle sounds, and the gang plank is drawn in, and two tug boats are at our vessel's side trying to drag her out into mid-stream. It looks like the babe trying to help the giant up, to see those two little tugs nosing our vessel around.

But how the ludicrous will mingle with the sombre! Just below us on the steerage deck is a young Italian who evidently hasn't grown rich in America, if we may judge by outward appearances, but whose heart is full to overflowing with the sorrow of the farewells he has just spoken. Just watch that dirty piece of linen in his hand as he makes a dip with it every few seconds at his muddy face! He is mopping the dirt all over that round face of his; and those awful facial contortions as he once more waves his soiled linen towards the shore! Will his countenance ever straighten out again? Poor fellow! he is performing a mission of which he has no knowledge; our own sad thoughts are chased away by the sense of the ludicrous in his appearance.

Down the North river we glide, past the Battery and the statue of Liberty. Just ahead of us is a fine French steamer, the "La Bourgogne," bound for Havre; and closely following us the fastest of the Cunard's line of steamships, the "Etruria;" whilst at our sides are the "Helvetia," and an Austrian Lloyd vessel. The "Etruria" steams proudly past us in less than half an hour.

Sandy Hook and Staten Island are already dimming in the distance when the steward's bell calls us to a new experience in our novel surroundings—our first meal on shipboard. Surely that must be a capacious side-board, we thought, from whence this multitude of dishes comes; and that larder must be well stocked that will stand such a strain as this upon it four times a day for the next ten days! But a friend at my elbow whispers something about seasickness, and we catch the idea that the steward's bounty may not require this sort of tax upon it very long. But the bar of the vessel is finding a liberal patronage thus early, if we may judge by the loose tongues that are betraying the spirit in a few of our fellow-diners. When night drops her sable curtain over the scene we are apparently alone on the great deep, for we have parted company with our consorts.

How beautiful this first night on our ocean journey! The sea rests in perfect quiet around us, and no sound disturbs the almost solemn stillness, save one, the great heart of the giant that bears us on over this watery waste. How it pants and throbs away down in the engine room, as if it would tear itself loose from the iron bosom that holds it! Its pulsations send a tremor from stem to stern, and with its labored breathings still in our ears we seek our berth and pass into dreamland. No mother's lullaby song could have wiled our infant spirit into a more placid mood, or introduced it into sweeter slumber, than did the throbbings of our vessel's great engines on this first night of our ocean slumberings.

Our second day out is the Sabbath; a quiet, pleasant day, with only one little incident to mar its pleasure. Death is the same everywhere, whether on sea or on land, a saddener of the spirit. At noon the body of a three-months-old infant is dropped into the waters at our stern. In the afternoon we enjoy sanctuary privileges in the saloon cabin, Rev. George B. Taylor, of Virginia, in charge of the services. Meet is it for us to praise the Lord on this, His holy day, for "They that go down to the sea in ships, that do business in great waters; these see the works of the Lord, and His wonders in the deep."

Nearly two full days has our vessel been on her way, and five hundred miles of sea lie between us and New York harbor. No sign of ocean life has been visible since we parted company with our consorts on Saturday evening until to-day, when a sail and steamer are sighted at some distance. Some of the cabin passengers amuse themselves at a game of shuffle board, whilst others enjoy the promenade deck in social chat with new-made acquaintances. Few have yet paid the usual tribute to Neptune, and consequently have not realized the truth of the Frenchman's remark, who was yet visibly under the influence of Ocean's forced tribute, when he said: "For plaisar I cross the ocean nevare"!

We have among our cabin passengers a certain number of Scotch and Irish young people who are homeward bound; and these same young people are not slow to perceive that our long deck and these moonlit nights afford opportunities for the cultivation of the tender passion such as coy maiden or gallant swain would seek for in vain on the land. And we have not the slightest doubt but that we landed passengers on the Irish coast, and carried others on to Scotland, who would not be long content to let the Irish sea separate their fortunes.

But even here on shipboard, as on the land, joy alternates with sorrow. Whilst the merry marriage bells are sending forth their most joyful peals, from another neighboring church tower the solemn death toll may be heard. Four o'clock of this, our second day out, and it is whispered that death is in the cabin. Yes, it is even too true, and that under the saddest of circumstances. A victim of the vessel's bar, from whom the fiery liquid should have been shut off early on the Sabbath, lies in the state-room in that sleep from which no earthly power shall wake him. Apoplexy of the brain induced by excessive drinking, and he dies drunk. A young mercantile runner he was, returning home to Glasgow, where a mother and sister were awaiting his coming. With the convivial nature common to his class, he gave himself up to the pleasure of the hour in company with two or three other kindred spirits. We missed him on the Sabbath from his seat opposite us at the table; but alas! we little dreamed that we should stand as we do to-night, a silent little company at the stern of the vessel with the wrapped and weighted body on a plank before us, waiting only for the solemn burial service to be read over him by the captain before sliding him off the plank into a grave two miles in depth. We have often listened to the Scotchman as he extolled the purity of Scotch whisky, and vauntingly declared that he knew how to take his drink in moderation; and we didn't know but what he was telling us the truth. But now we are ready to declare that if what we have thus far seen of the effects of Scotch whisky and of the Scot's moderation be not misleading, it is of a stripe similar to what we witness of it everywhere else.

On this, our fourth day out, the sea begins to roughen, and vacant places at the table are growing more numerous; and as you sit, strange, suspicious sounds from the surrounding cabins come to your ears, and we realize that we are in the midst of a new experience.

But, after all, this is only a gentle hint of the strange variety of life which old Ocean, in his restless moods, is likely to introduce on an ocean journey. Our next two or three days' steaming are days of pleasant sunshine and calm waters, with the passage enlivened with games, concert, song and dance. Our ninth day out and we have a dance of another sort in the dining-room cabin. The long, heavy sea swells of last evening gave us warning of an approaching frolic of the waves. How the dishes rattle and insist on moving around! The racks are put upon the table to keep them from taking independent journeys across the floor.

Early this morning, our tenth day out, the bold, northern cliffs of Ireland are discovered, and about three hours later we enter Loch Foyle and steam down to Moville, where we land our Irish passengers, about fifty-five of them, after having joined hands with them on deck in a parting song, "Auld Lang Syne." A cheerful, good-hearted crowd those Irish were, and it is with sincere regret that we give them a final wave of our handkerchiefs and turn our prow seaward again.

As we pass down the Loch, on our left we notice the ruined castle of an old Irish family of renown, the O'Doughertys. Those of us who have never been in this region before have no little interest in these bold, precipitous cliffs on our right as we pass along the northern coast, for here is the

Giant's Causeway, which has excited our curiosity since boyhood's days. And it is just a little bit exasperating to pass so near and yet not be able to visit it; but we console ourselves with the thought that we will see it on our return.

Along this rocky coast may be seen, as we stand on deck, the mouths of numerous caves, against which the sea, with sullen roar, throws itself in angry violence, and, breaking into a white foam, retires for a fresh onslaught. To our left is the "Mull of Cantire." Here is a light-house, the light of which is seen at a distance of twenty-two miles. Away in our front, rising up out of the sea like a huge bowl turned upside down, is "Ailsa Craig," or Paddy's milestone. It is a solid rock 1,200 feet high, the roosting and nesting place of countless numbers of sea fowl.

On our left is Arran, and to the eastward on the mainland, as we enter the Firth of Clyde, the town of Ayr comes into view. Near to Ayr the poet Burns was born, and in this region the muse inspired the production of "Tam O'Shanter," "Man was Made to Mourn," and the "Braes of Ballochmyle." But we will come into more intimate acquaintance with this region at another time.

The voyage up the Firth of Clyde, if made in daylight and in pleasant weather, is an exceedingly interesting one to the lover of natural scenery. It is already night when our steamer drops her anchor in the Grenock harbor, at the end of a ten days' voyage full of pleasant memories. A little delay with the custom officers, and we are off by train for Glasgow.

CHAPTER II.

IN THE QUEEN'S CITY.

OUR first impressions of Glasgow are not of the most favorable kind, as we take our first morning view of it from the windows of St. Enoch's. A drizzling rain is falling, and the smoke issuing from the tall chimneys of hundreds of foundries, manufactories and collieries spreads an air of gloom over things that come with depressing effect upon the spirits of our party, which have not yet fully rallied from the sea voyage. We hold a council and decide to remain over a day in the city, instead of moving on direct to London as we had planned. In this way we hope to renew our spirits and carry away better impressions of this, one of Scotland"s most prosperous and enterprising cities. But ere these wanderings are accomplished we expect to return and acquaint ourselves with the city more at our leisure. We find opportunity during the day to visit some friends, the old cathedral, and Knox monument. The next morning finds us busy in preparation for our London journey.

St. Enoch's station is a little world in itself. Not five minutes at a time throughout the entire day passes without either an incoming or an outgoing train; and you wonder as you meet the hurrying crowds sifting through each other in counter directions, where so many live, or what necessity of business keeps so large a part of the population in such a whirl of motion.

"These Old World people," remarks my friend, as we are noting some of the peculiarities of the rolling stock, "are a quarter century behind the progressive American in the skill, taste and luxury evidenced in the construction of their railroad rolling stock." "See that engine! No bell, no pilot; an uncouth looking machine, mounted on high wheels." "And these passenger coaches! Why, we could put two of them inside one of our Pullman or Wagner's, and no chance of heating them whatever." "People sometimes make mistakes," I answer, "in judging of the qualities of their pudding before tasting it. We'll get a good taste of British railway travel to-day in our four hundred miles of ride. Let us go and see if we can't have one of these compartments reserved for the exclusive use of our party." The proper official is seen, and our desire is granted without a murmur or an extra charge. "Note this as advantage number one over American railway accommodation," I remark, as our man plasters a notice of "Reserved" on a window of a second class compartment.

Our tickets are purchased over the Midland; second class fare to London, eight dollars. An official looks at the tickets as we enter our compartment, locks the door, and the guard toots his whistle and we are off. How we fly! Say what you please of the inferior rolling stock of British railways, the roadbeds are first-class, double railed, and complete in all the appointments necessary to speed and safety. We miss the warming apparatus of our American coaches on this cool morning. The only thing we have in lieu of it is a pair of galvanized iron cans filled with hot water, upon which we may place our feet. "No danger of fire in this coach," says H——. "Nor of the peanut, or yellow-backed literature man, either," another of the company answers. "And then," says the lady of the party, "we can brew our own tea, and have a delightful family spread all by ourselves, with no curious eyes observant of our motions." And so, with the aid of a little spirit lamp, and water obtained from the station pumps by the way, we do twice during the day.

If the traveler would see Scotland and England in their autumnal glory, and enjoy a ride through scenery the most picturesque, and over ground abounding in romantic and historical interest, let him take an early morning train from Glasgow, via the Midland, to London. He will be whirled along at the rate of forty-five miles an hour; now skirting the edge of some long chain of lofty hills, from which he can look down into valleys, green as in midsummer, alive with sheep and cattle; now flying through these valleys themselves, where he can obtain a nearer view of the low stone walls which cut the valleys into pasture fields so diminutive that one wonders whether they were not intended for garden patches instead of pasture fields. But we quickly learn that we are now in a country of small dimensions compared to the vastness of things on the other side of the water, and that every foot of ground must be utilized. As we approach the English border some one recollects that we shall get a glimpse of a little hamlet to which a rather romantic interest attaches, from the fact that, in days gone by, when the English law recognized the validity of the Scottish mutual declaration marriage custom, many an angry pater familias from the English side reached the burg just as the village blacksmith had finished the job of welding together two human lives. "Gretna Green!" Yes, here it is; but where is it? Too small to be seen. Yonder, doubtless, is the old inn at which so many modest couples avoided the banns nuisance, as well as the decided negative of the parental powers.

Darkness is already shutting out our landscape view when the flaming smoke-stacks of Leeds and Sheffield tell us that we are in the midst of the great manufacturing district of Yorkshire. We regret that we are obliged to make our entrance into the Queen's City under cover of darkness; be led, as it were, blindfolded, away from that which is familiar, and turned loose in the heart of a great unknown, without knowing whence we come or whither we shall go. We are landed at the Midland Grand Hotel about nine o'clock; and after a hasty consultation relative to the program for the morrow, we resign ourselves to the luxury of sleep.

A genuine London fog greets us this morning as we try to get a view of the great city. We have decided on a three weeks' stay, long enough to do the city in pretty good style, we think. Two of the party go out in quest of a suite of rooms, and soon return reporting that good accommodations have been found on Russel Square, consisting of three furnished rooms, at a cost, inclusive of breakfast each day, of sixteen shillings per week, with a cook and dining room thrown in for evening uses. After settling ourselves in our new quarters, we go out "Yankee Doodle" like to see the town.

That sense of vastness which we have before alluded to as giving place to a narrow, cramped condition of things on this side of the water, once more regains possession of our minds as we take our day's survey of the queenly city. Here we are met by such magnitudes both in respect to space, cost and material, that our American mind, used as it is to the almost limitless condition of things on the other side of the water, can hardly grasp the situation. "If this be London," said friend H——, one day after we had ridden around on the tops of tramways for hours trying to find the outer edge of the city, "where does England commence?"

We feel lost; shut up, as it were, in city, nothing but city, go where we will. Here are nearly four millions of people thrown together, the extremes of wealth and poverty. Here are men who own whole squares and streets, and who can at their pleasure put up the bars across the streets they own, as may actually be seen in more than one London street, and say to the public, "Hitherto, but no farther," and there are none to question the authority of the act. And the great question that is now perplexing the English as well as the American mind is, to what is all this concentration of power and wealth leading?

Right here in the heart of London on Trafalgar Square, during these days of our visit, gather thousands of the unemployed to listen to inflammatory harangues, and give vent to feelings and wrongs which they attribute, rightly or wrongly, we know not, to this domination of the upper classes. In some practical way the troublesome question must soon be settled or the Londoner will be witness to riotous demonstrations and troubles such as he has not seen for some time.

There is real want among the masses of unemployed; and men will fight for bread when they will fight for nothing else. This want reaches out even into the rural districts. The clergy of the Church of England, whose income is dependent in part upon certain land rents, have failed, owing to crop failures, to receive their rents; and many a poor prebendary is at this time sending home to the head of the church a cry of want. Business in London is depressed. The crowds of tourists have returned home, and certain lines of traffic have been closed. And yet in face of all this trade depression and want, London's annual folly, the induction of the new Lord Mayor into office, with all the usual reckless expenditure and public display of wealth, must needs go on. In the very presence of the riotous troubles in Trafalgar Square and Westminster Abbey all this is like a slap in the face to those who know not where the bread of the future is to come from. The mandate of prohibition went forth only yesterday from the office of the Commissioner of Police, forbidding all future gatherings and speeches in Trafalgar Square. How these things will be received we, of course, know not; but trust that London's peace may not be disturbed thereby.

To those who would see London at its best, we would say, do not come in the late autumn. Sunshine is too rare a luxury to be enjoyed in unstinted measure at this season of the year. Rain in abundance he may be sure of. And yet there are some compensations for the brighter summer season. The great rush of summer tourists is avoided, and one can see the sights at his leisure without the inconvenience of being jammed in with a crowd; and if he be economically inclined, he can find much cheaper entertainment in the autumn and winter seasons than at any other time. Thus far our experience is that we can live cheaper in Europe than at home.

Our first Sabbath in London is a bright, fogless day; and we hail it with gladness, for we would see London at her best on this, the best of days. We have each our favorite preachers that we are most eager to see and hear; and most of our party being clericals, we have looked forward with especial pleasure to this feature of the tourists' enjoyment.

Two of us start out early to hunt up Mr. Spurgeon's Tabernacle, hoping to be fortunate enough to hear this king of living preachers. In this respect we are favored, for we arrive early enough to procure a good seat in the body of the auditorium, and to hear the great preacher himself. The Tabernacle seats about five thousand persons; is double galleried all around to the pulpit. As we looked around over the vast audience we could see no empty seats. The Psalms are largely used in the praise service, and the music is led by a precentor. This praise service is one long to be remembered, for it was entered into with a hearty good will by the audience. We had often felt a curiosity to know whether Mr. Spurgeon would hear as well as he would read. We found the preacher in the pulpit to be still more charming than the preacher in print. He announced his text in Zephaniah III., 16, 17, 18. He deplored the degeneracy of the church in general; but whilst, like the faithful of ancient Israel, we are made to feel sad at the lack of zeal and true piety in the church, yet might we gather encouragement at Jehovah's words as contained in the 16th verse: "In that day it shall be said to Jerusalem, fear thou not; and to Zion, let not thine hands be slack."

Mr. Spurgeon and congregation have lately withdrawn themselves from denominational connection with the Baptist church, and have become independent. The sermon we heard contained throughout an undercurrent of apology for the withdrawal. This has proved to be our last opportunity of hearing Mr. Spurgeon, as goes to the south of France for the winter. These damp, cold London fogs begin to go hard with him.

In the afternoon we find our way to the historical old Westminster Abbey, and hear a sermon by the sub-Dean, Rev. George Prothero. It seemed like being carried back centuries to sit there in that grand, but gloomy, old Abbey, surrounded by marble busts, slabs and floor inscriptions, all reminders of the historic dead. The ashes of kings and queens, of heroes of bloody fields, of poets, historians, and statesmen, rest beneath our feet, at our side, and in every nook and corner of the sacred edifice. On the Sabbath previous to our visit a large number of the Trafalgar Square class attended the Abbey service and made a disturbance, and the presence of a platoon or two of police to-day is accounted for by the fear of a second disturbance of similar nature.

We are pleased with the outward respect at least which London shows for the Sabbath. As we have made our rounds to-day through some of the principal thoroughfares of the city we observe no signs of the ordinary traffic of the week. The back doors of a few restaurants and saloons are open. Oxford and Holburn streets, the great arteries of life in this city of wonders, through which we have more than once found it difficult to push our way, are still as an ordinary village street. A hush of silence has fallen upon the heart of the great metropolis as though it had heard the whisper of the Eternal commanding reverence for His holy day. Of course there is a hidden life behind the scenes, a restless demon that has withdrawn himself from public sight only long enough to mature his plans and recruit his energies for another conflict. What vice and wretchedness, what want and patient endurance of suffering, are covered up under this fair exterior, we care not to know, since knowledge of this kind only brings pain without a remedy.

Of this fact we have become satisfied, that exteriorly, London is on the Sabbath, one of the best ordered cities we have ever spent a Sabbath in.

We find a pleasure in our apartment life such as we are sure we would not find in the more public and expensive hotel life. Our genial hostess, Mrs. Christie, makes things just as home-like as possible for us. And how replete with rich experiences these days of ramblings are, sometimes as a company, oftener in pairs, and occasionally alone, in the highways and byways of the queenly city.

One of the most interesting of all historical spots of London to those who have any interest in the memory and deeds of those who lived to bless the world with religious truth and literature, is the Smithfield and Bunhill Fields quarter.

Mounting to the top of an omnibus at the Royal Exchange and going northward to Moor-gate street and City Road nearly a mile, we arrive at the Bunhill Fields Cemetery. It is a plat of ground containing about five acres, surrounded by a high iron picket fence. It was long since filled with those who sleep their last sleep. Here rest the ashes of Isaac Watts, Daniel De Foe, John Owen and John Bunyan. Over De Foe's remains the children of the Kingdom have erected a fine granite pillar. Taking a leaf from the

STATUE OF BUNYAN.

grave of Watts, we pass on to the spot consecrated to the memory of Bunyan. The place, so long marked only by a rude headstone, is now covered by a slab of stone about six inches in thickness. On this slab is placed a block of stone seven or eight feet in length, three feet wide, and two and a half in thickness. On this block lies, in the attitude of repose, a full length marble statue of Bunyan. Dead, but living he truly is, as no other purely human being lives, in the influence for good of his "Pilgrim's Progress." Hither come those of a Protestant faith who look upon the superstitious reverence paid by Roman Catholics to the dust and at the tombs of saints as sinful, to pay a venerated reverence to the last resting place of the wondrous dreamer. In times past those of a sterner Puritanic faith have begged with their dying breath that their coffins might be placed as near as possible to the coffin of the author of Pilgrim's Progress.

Just across the street from where these sleepers rest, is the chapel, house and cemetery of the Wesleys. Here the great pioneers of Methodism, the two Wesleys and Whitefield, preached, and here rest their ashes. Fox, of "Book of Martyrs" fame, is interred here also. Not far away is the old church of "St. Bartholomew the Great," in front of which the Smithfield martyrs suffered. London guards most sacredly these old cemeteries of the noble dead.

CHAPTER III.

HERE AND THERE IN LONDON.

LONDON'S parks are rather dull at this season of the year; but they are worth a visit notwithstanding, if for nothing else than to see how munificently the city provides for the free air pleasure of her children. We plan an excursion en masse to Regent's Park and the Zoological Gardens, situated in the northern portion of the Park. Regent's is the largest as well as the handsomest of the city's numerous and beautiful parks. It contains 472 acres, laid out in exquisite taste, adorned with sculptures, flowers, lakes and pretty villas. It contains a large botanical garden, around which runs a fine driveway of two miles in length. The Zoological Gardens are world-renowned; over 2,000 animals, birds and reptiles have here been collected together. One must take but a short nooning if he see in one day all the objects of interest in this fine park. We return a tired party at the close of this day's outing.

Hyde Park is the next in size and beauty. It contains 388 acres, and is abundantly supplied with shade, by trees which look as though they might have grown natively upon the spot. A fine lake called the Serpentine provides plenty of bathing accommodation in summer, as well as skating in winter. Joining it on the west are the Kensington Gardens; in reality a portion of the park, but which add 356 acres more to the park area.

At the southwest entrance to Hyde Park, near to the Apsley House, stands a colossal bronze statue of Achilles, weighing thirty tons. It was cast from cannon captured at the battles of Waterloo and Salamanca, and was erected, as the inscription says, to the "Duke of Wellington and his companions in arms by their countrywomen." To the left of Prince's Gate, on the south side of Kensington Gardens is the national monument of the Prince Consort; a Gothic structure 175 feet in height, with a base 130 feet square. It is a magnificent monument, and is said to have cost a million dollars. London has two other monuments that do her honor; Trafalgar Square monument, erected to the memory of Lord Nelson, and the London Fire column, situated near the famous Billingsgate fish market. The latter is one of Wren's executions, and from its height of 200 feet a fine view of London may be had on a clear day; we speak from experience.

We have been pursuing the policy of using damp or rainy days for visiting museums, art galleries and all under cover places of interest, reserving the bright days for out of door sights; and passing the evenings together talking over the events of the day and writing up our journals. It is seldom thus far that we have attempted to see London by gas light. But there are certain places of great interest which can be seen to advantage at no other time; and the reader will be pleased to go with us now on a night excursion to one of the city's most unique places of entertainment.

The cabman is called into requisition and we are soon landed at a large, brilliantly lighted hall. As we enter the door we seem to be among a throng of gaily dressed ladies and gentlemen, policemen, citizens and tourists. But we must be careful to whom we try to talk in this crowd. It is rather aristocratic in tone; and the chances are that if we make a blunder we will be regarded with a stare and contemptuous silence.

"Can you tell me, sir," I asked of a tall policeman by whom I happened to be standing, "who that pleasant old lady is sitting in the chair and every now and then quietly glancing around at the crowd?" My question is unheeded; thinking he was a trifle hard of hearing, I repeated the question in a louder tone, but still no answer; and beginning to feel a little vexed at the fellow's silence, was about to give his elbow a vigorous punch, when some amused smiles are discovered cast in my direction; and I awake to the fact that my policeman is a wax figure, like hundreds of others in the room.

It is Madam Tussaud's fine wax works exhibition that we are in. The figures are all life size, and natural as life. Here are some in repose, whose breasts are gently heaving as in the act of breathing. There are others in quiet curiosity turning heads and eyes around occasionally to see what is going on about them. More than once during the evening did we observe visitors trying to get some information out of these dummies. Here are kings and queens in courtly dress, representing both the living and the dead. Poets, statesmen, generals, from many countries, are here in grand assembly. If only they would talk! That is all that is lacking to make the whole brillant show a reality.

Passing out of this long hall, we enter another called the "Chamber of Horrors"; and truly the sights of this room are enough to give one the nightmare later on that night, if he find his bed at all. These are wax figures also. Here in his bath tub lies Murat, with the dagger driven into his side by the hand of Charlotte Corday, and a look of horrible agony in his face, as the life blood pours from the wound in his side. Decapitated heads of noted murderers, by the score, with gory necks still dripping. Here we find Guiteau in company with many other red-handed assassins. The guillotined heads of Robespierre, Louis XVI., Marie Antoinette, in another place, bring up sad memories of these unfortunate people. And here, too, is the very machine that did such cruel work in that awful Reign of Terror. "Wouldn't like to sleep with this crowd," said a visitor, as we were leaving the room for another, the Napoleonic Hall.

Here we find numerous relics of the great warrior; the bed,

with waxen image of Napoleon in it, on which he died at St. Helena; the carriage in which he sat and watched the burning of Moscow, and in which he traveled to the field of Waterloo. This latter is a relic of great interest, for it was Napoleon's state carriage while at Elba, and accompanied him on many of his campaigns. It was captured on the evening following the battle of Waterloo, and was sent to the Prince Regent, from whom it was purchased for exhibition purposes at a cost of $12,500.

A few days after our interesting visit to the Wax Works Hall, H—— and I find ourselves in St. James' Park. The day is bright and pleasant, and after touring around the park and Buckingham Palace grounds, we conclude to see a part of the city we have not yet been in. We have found out before this that the top of an omnibus, on a pleasant day, is one of the very best places imaginable from which to see the city. One can ride miles on one of these omnibuses for a penny. Climbing to the top of a bus which we are sure is going eastward some miles, we pass old Westminster Bridge and Parliament Buildings, over Westminster Road to its junction with the Kensington Park Road, thence by change of bus southward to Lambeth Road, and we have come within sight of the principal object of our search—the Bethlem Insane Asylum. On our side of the water its name, by an unwarrantable corruption changed to Bedlam, has become the synonym of all places where pandemonium reigns. But as we pass through this finely appointed and majestic lot of buildings to-day and observe the quiet that reigns, we resolve hereafter to speak a good word for the much maligned Bethlem of London.

Taking our usual position again on the top of a tramway car, four miles of riding over the old Kent Road brings us to Greenwich Park and Observatory, on the right bank of the Thames. The observatory is located in the park on a hill about three hundred feet above the level of the river. We make our investigations here, which do not result in the discovery of any new planet, or in learning why this particular observatory should be the central point from which the world's longitudinal reckonings should be made. Greenwich Station is but a small suburb of London, reached easily by excursion on the river, and worthy of a visit because of its fine hospital, world-renowned observatory and of its being the birthplace of Henry VIII., and his two daughters, Elizabeth and Mary. We return well satisfied with our day's ramble.

We devote another day to London Tower and Billingsgate fish market. At the tower we get a peep at the Crown Jewels, the blanket on which General Wolfe died when he received his mortal wound at Quebec; the Bloody Tower, where Richard III. murdered his nephews, and the Beauchamp Tower, where Walter Raleigh suffered his long imprisonment. Passing out of the tower into the central court yard, we come to a spot marked in the pavement where the tower gallows used to stand. Here Sir William Wallace, Raleigh, Anne Boleyn, Catherine Howard, Lady Jane Grey, with scores of other notables of the historic past, met tragic deaths. What volumes of history could these old towers unfold if they could speak out their secrets!

Our noonday lunch is taken on the fish market. Here is a new variety of London life which presents a novelty of feature comic enough to bring enjoyment to the most confirmed old dyspeptic. Fish! Fish! of every variety, in such quantities as we have seen nowhere else. And fishy people, too, whose evil inclinations are constantly making it necessary for them to possess the art of slipping themselves through the hands of the police, much as they do their own slippery wares into the baskets of their customers.

These days of our London visit are fast slipping away; and we might detain the reader here and there in the by-ways of many interesting excursions it has been our pleasure to make at different times. Parts of several days have been spent in the British Museum, which it were foolishness to attempt to give a detailed record of; for a volume in itself would be necessary to speak of the treasures which this marvelous depository of knowledge contains. Of the art galleries which we have visited, several of which London may well be proud, we have purposely refrained from speaking, for these will meet us in yet greater numbers and perfection as we ramble on through other lands. But there is yet one place of historical interest to which as a company we give one most profitable day; and thither the reader is now invited.

Said a lady friend to us a few days before leaving home, as she handed us a newspaper clipping, "Here is something descriptive of a place you may see while you are in London, and the reading of which may prove of interest to you now." It related to the Lollard's Tower in London.

To a person familiar with the history of the tower and the palace with which it is connected, it will prove of no ordinary interest to make a visit thither. There are difficulties, however, connected with a visit. We made two vain attempts to get inside the palace before we succeeded. A written order from the Archbishop of Canterbury must be obtained before the porter will open his wicket-gate to you. Lambeth palace, with which the tower is connected, has been for the last seven centuries the official residence of the Archbishop of Canterbury. It dates back to the twelfth century. In early times it was the residence of the Saxon kings. The Thames river used to splash its muddy waters against the sides of the tower, and when, in former days, kings and queens and other noted personages used to visit the Archbishop at the palace, they alighted from a boat at the foot of a pair of stone steps that led up to the palace entrance.

Now, this is all changed. First, next the river, comes the beautiful Thames embankment, a promenade for foot passengers, made of solid masonry and extending along the river on the south side from Westminster bridge to the Lambeth bridge. On the north side of the river the embankment extends from

Westminster bridge to the Black Friar's bridge. Next to the embankment comes a street, thus placing the Thames at quite a remove from the walls of the palace.

Queen Mary used to frequently visit the palace to see her favorite, Cardinal Poole; and thither also came Queen Elizabeth to visit Archbishop Parker. Elizabeth did not relish the idea of a church dignitary's infringement of the rule of celibacy; and it is related of her that on one occasion, after having been very hospitably entertained by the Archbishop's wife, upon her departure she said to her: "Madam, I dare not call you; mistress, I cannot call you; but whoever you are, I thank you." To this palace came, as a fugitive, the beautiful, but unfortunate, Mary of Modena, wife of James II., with her six-months-old infant in her arms. This infant became the future Pretender. In the crypt under the present palace chapel Queen Anne Boleyn, already under sentence of death, was induced by Cranmer, who had himself only two years prior to this solemnly sworn the clergy to bestow the royal succession upon the heirs of Queen Annie, to avow some just and lawful impediment to the marriage which had taken place with Henry VIII. She was beguiled into doing this under promise of life for herself that thus some reasonable pretext might be given for the bloody act already resolved upon. In three days from the time of this avowal she went to the block, and her maid, Jane Seymour, took her place as wife of Henry VIII.

We are conducted by our well-informed porter into the guard room. He tells us that in the feudal age this room was used as a banqueting hall for the retainers of the ecclesiastical lords who occupied the palace; and that in Archbishop Laud's time feudal armor enough to equip 200 men hung upon the walls. All of these evidences of feudal times are gone, and we see only the heavy oaken panels of the wall and roof, which had their origin in the days of chivalry. Passing into the chapel, which dates back into the thirteenth century, the first thing that meets our eye is a remarkable sarcophagus containing the remains of Archbishop Parker. In the times of the Commonwealth Cromwell's men, wanting to use the chapel as a dining-room and dance hall, and not liking their ghostly neighbor's contiguity, broke into the coffin, took out the remains and hid them in a dung-hill and sold what was valuable about the coffin.

Five hundred years ago Wicliffe met the charge of heresy in this chapel. As he stood all alone before his judges who were about to sentence him, suddenly the Lollards swarmed in around him, and these were immediately followed by Sir Lewis Clifford, who arrested the sentence about to be passed.

We are now led by our guide into the tower. In this tower, it is supposed by some, the Lollards suffered imprisonment. And we are shown eight iron rings fixed in the oak-lined walls, to which the sufferers were fastened. On the oaken walls are cut in numerous places inscriptions, sometimes consisting of scripture, and sometimes of other expressions of trust in God, and in several instances of devices of the heart. In one place we noticed where one poor fellow kept track of time by cutting little notches in the sharp corner of a piece of molding; and in another place we notice upon the wall a dark stain which by analysis is proved to be a blood stain. Our guide informed us that here these poor victims were oftentimes killed, and their bodies slid down through a sort of funnel into the Thames. There is a recess in the stone wall where it is said fires were built, and the victims suffered death by suffocation. It is proper to state in this connection that it is a matter of some doubt whether or not a Lollard ever suffered in this tower. The founder of Lollardism, Peter Lollard, suffered death at Cologne, as a political agitator, two years before Wicliffe was born.

There was a Lollard's tower somewhere, of which Latimer said: "I would rather be in Purgatory than lie in it;" and of which another victim said: "If I were a dog, you could not appoint me a worse or viler place." But it is asserted that this tower never was at Lambeth, for the great fire swept away all traces of Old London House, of Bonner's inquisition and dungeons, and that the traditions of the true Lollard's tower of London House were easily fastened to the iron ringed cell of the so-called Lollard's Tower of Lambeth. Be this as it may, one thing is certain, that the present Lambeth Tower was a place of misery and death to many of the saints in Bloody Mary's reign.

Admittance to the Parliament buildings was denied us, so we were forced to content ourselves with an outside view. The dynamiters from our side of the water have made it exceedingly difficult for a tourist to see many places he would like to see. A more imposing structure than the Parliament House it has never been our privilege to see. One gets the best view from the Westminster bridge or the Thames embankment, near to the Lambeth palace. It covers an area of eight acres, and its numerous turrets and lofty towers give it a sort of cathedral look. From its tall clock tower, "Old Ben," as it is called, 320 feet high, come the quarter hour strokes that tell us in musical tones of the flight of time. Close by, nestling as it were under its wing, is the St. Margaret's chapel, where Canon Farrar ministers. We had the pleasure of hearing and speaking with the Canon last Sabbath.

The day of rest was sadly disturbed by riotous demonstrations around Trafalgar square. The crisis between the authorities and the unemployed and the socialistic factions of the city was reached on last Sabbath. Sir Charles Warren had issued his mandate prohibiting the meetings in Trafalgar square, but in the face of this prohibition it was determined on the part of the leaders of this reckless movement to hold the meeting. On the part of the authorities it was determined to maintain the prestige of law, even if bloodshed was necessary in doing it. Early in the morning the square was taken possession of by a small force of police, which was augmented during the day, until at 2 p. m., when we passed the square, the major portion of the police force of London was massed in and around it. Later in the day it was still further augmented by a force of military. All was done in the way of remonstrance and silent endurance of taunts and insults that could be done on the part of the authorities to avoid bloodshed. But in several quarters blood flowed on both sides; two policemen were stabbed and carried off by comrades, and blows were freely exchanged, causing many bloody heads and faces. On every hand the mob was defeated, and on Monday quiet once more reigned on the streets.

There seems to be no remedy for this sad state of things save in the summary dealing out of justice to these firebrand fellows, whose wild harangues about liberty and equal property rights serve only to inflame the passions of a certain class too numerous in all large cities. There is needed, likewise, in addition to this measure of safety for the people, a careful, sympathetic consideration of the wants and woes of the people, on the part of the government; and in this particular the working classes of London deserve some sympathy. It is a government of the aristocracy, and in the interest of concentrated wealth. The Queen herself, with her court, seems oblivious to the distress of the multitudes of London. Her Majesty's recent Jubilee presents, now on exhibition in St. James' palace, London, of immense value, and as useless to her Majesty as old rags, if sold, would relieve thousands of London's starving poor, and make to herself a monument in the hearts of the people more enduring than the gold and silver of which these presents are composed. But perhaps we are wrong in suggesting this disposition of them at her hands.

CHAPTER IV.

THE GAY CITY OF FASHION.

THE three weeks of time allotted for our stay in this world of wonders has already passed its limit by several days, and the question of speedy departure is being discussed as we sit in our cozy parlor this morning.

The dreaded Channel! That is all that separates us from the French people, whose acquaintance we desire to make next. One member of the party falls into a meditative mood, and as we give his countenance a furtive glance now and then, it seems evident that some sorrowful recollections are coursing through his memory. "What may be the nature of your musings, friend H———?" we ask. "I was wondering if I should be compelled to lose as much grub in crossing the Channel as I did on the 'Furnessia.' Don't you think we could make the Channel by night? I'd like to steal a march on old Neptune this time, if I could." Our quiet man, W———, lifts up his voice in consolation, remarking that "We have choice of three routes, as well as a day or night crossing of the Channel. One daylight route via the London, Chatham & Dover railway to Dover; thence across the Channel 21 miles to Calais, this being the shortest of the three routes; time four hours from London to Calais. A second route is from Folkstone to Boulogne, a longer daylight journey of eight hours, width of Channel 29 miles. Then there is a third route from Newhaven to Dieppe, the longest of the three, but the cheaper, and will accommodate you with night passage."

The lady of the party, who also has had some sorrowful experiences on the "Furnessia," expresses her preference for the night journey; and although this is a little disappointing to some of us who already begin to think ourselves sea-proof, we give a ready assent to it, and roll out of London in the darkness, even as we had entered it. Two hours of riding and we are at Newhaven. The Channel steamer is in waiting, and we are soon stowed away in our berths, oblivious to the fact that 64 miles of dangerous waters roll between us and French soil.

What a night was that! But our recollections of it are as briny as was our friend's of his Atlantic experience. Let it pass; but ever after this we shall remonstrate against a 64-mile passage of the English Channel, when it can be made in 21. We are partially compensated, however, for the discomfort of the night, by a most enjoyable daylight ride through the Seine River Valley. There is something new and picturesque to our pilgrim eyes as we look out of our apartment windows over these gently rolling and well tilled plains of Old Normandy. We catch sight of many a thatch roof on the solid stone walls of the houses of the peasantry, but the better class are tile roofed.

Rouen, the capital of the province, is reached. We have a desire to linger a day or two in this old historic city, where the "Maid of Orleans" met her untimely fate at the hands of the English, but necessity pushes us on.

Shortly after leaving Rouen we have our first glimpse of snow. It puzzles us not a little at first to ascertain what it is that shines so white away across the valley on the distant hillsides. We are not thinking of snow, although the air is sharp enough to suggest it; for we had made up our minds to leave winter behind us on the other side of the water. But there the genuine article is, and the farther south we go, the more evident it is that quite a little fall of snow has taken place.

But there at last is the French capital coming into view. And now we begin to feel a sense of loneliness creeping over us. We have left our mother tongue behind us, and we know not who shall speak for us in this strange land.

"Parle vouz France?" said a cabbie as he rushed up to H———, apparently delighted to see him. "You're mistaken, friend; that isn't my name." "Oui, Parle vouz France?" persisted the cabbie. "No, sir! I tell you I am another fellow altogether," said our friend, as he gave the knight of the whip a lordly wave of the hand, indicative of growing impatience.

It being early in the afternoon, we have decided to hunt apartments at once, instead of going to a hotel. H——— and I, who have gained a reputation for ourselves in this sort of business by our success in London, are started out in quest of accommodations. We first seek a certain hotel in quest of an interpreter, whose name and address we had procured before leaving London. We fail to find our man, and try the job of apartment hunting alone.

"Maisons Meubles!" exclaims H———, glancing up at a yellow placard; "My sons—wonder what that other word is; French for dear, isn't it?" "Quite likely," I answer, "a Y. M. C. A. invitation to come up higher; let us do it." We do, and a madam with a white cap presents herself in answer to our summons. We use our best king's English, but all we could get in return was, "Non Parle Englaise, Monsieur; Parle vouz France?" Then we go through a series of pantomimic motions such as, if seen by our friends at home, would have led them to think that the journey was proving too much for our mental faculties. "Every one appears to be expecting Parle France to-day," said H———, as we found our way back to the street again. "Wonder who he is? Some distinguished Frenchman, I suppose."

We at least find a quarter where it seems reasonably sure we can be accommodated with such rooms as we desire, and post back to the Chemin de fer—we must call railway stations by their proper names in this country—get our friends and luggage into the care of a couple of hackmen, and go back again to the point where we expect to locate. Our hand baggage is deposited in the hallway of the house, and we pay our cabbies what we afterwards learn to be double the legal fare, but still they linger, angrily saying "pour boire." We cannot see that they look either boyish or very poor.

Alas! we are strangers indeed, in a strange land; we are perplexed, vexed, with these rascally cabmen. The madam who controls the house in which we have temporarily set down our luggage, and whom we have not yet succeeded in seeing, now puts in an appearance from down street, and immediately a breeze of another sort is blowing in our direction. Seeing her hallway littered with our luggage, she demands an explanation, and forthwith bids us depart, and likewise pours such a tempest of wrath upon our cabbies that they crack their whips over their horses and fly as though all the furies were after them. "And now what?" said the quiet man. "Hotel," we murmur in chorus; and hotel it is. Later in the evening we find our man, McDougall, who is engaged as guide and interpreter for a few days.

The Parisians take things easy in the morning; and it is nine o'clock next morning before our guide puts in an appearance. With his help we are soon domiciled for a two weeks' stay in a suite of rooms, comfortable and well located. Here we pay $7 per week for accommodations no better than those we had in London at $4 per week. Nothing is so cheap in Paris or in France, as in Great Britain. France is almost in a state of bankruptcy, and the government to keep itself afloat imposes a tax upon almost every article of merchandise. Paris, especially feels the situation, and groans under it.

The observations that we are about to make concerning this gay city of fashion are of a general nature, and, chronologically, would come a little later on in this record. But the reader may rest assured that they are the result, nevertheless, of a close observation of things that have come under our notice while in the city.

It seems almost incredible, but we have seen fine looking horses, doubtless crippled in some way, loaded up on carts and on their way to the slaughter house to be converted into meat for the dainty Parisian appetite. Horse flesh is a common article of food to be found in the meat stalls of the city. Even owls are found among the dressed fowls in the market. A good beefsteak will cost about twenty-five cents per pound in Paris. There is an internal as well as an external to Paris which differ from each other as day does from night. "What are your impressions of Paris?" said a Paris physician to us the other day, and we were nonplussed how to make a polite answer, for they are too low to sound well in a native's ears. Externally Paris is beautiful. With her stately palaces, flowing fountains, wide boulevards, trees, flowering plants and shrubbery, her triumphal arches and tall columns erected in so many places, all are beautiful beyond comparison. But religiously and morally, what aspect does she present? Much the same, we imagine, as Rome in the beginning of her decline. In Paris, no God is acknowledged save the god of Reason. No Sabbath is observed. All shops and places of business are open on the Sabbath as on any other day of the week. The houses of worship, even the Protestant, have but scattered congregations. Paris knows no rest either by day or night. The continuous rattle of carriages over the rough stone pavements is heard all hours of the night. Her people are a pleasure loving people, and the theaters are both numerous and well attended. The wine-shops are as thick in Paris as the dry goods and groceries are at home; there is a wine-shop for every fifty-seven of the population. "Eat, drink and be merry, for to-morrow we die," appears, to an outward observer at least, to be the unspoken sentiment of the average Parisian. The concealed vice of other large cities, here makes its appearance at the windows, and looks forth without the least thought of shame, as though it were the most worshipful thing in Paris.

The McAll Mission is the little leaven that is working in the midst of this great lump of wickedness. But it needs to multiply its stations an hundred fold to make an impression that will be visible to the casual observer.

France appears to be approaching a crisis of some sort or other; but what it will be, not even the most apt politician would dare to hazard a guess. The people are dissatisfied with a republican form of government. It is republican only in name, monarchical in practice. Even now during these days of our sojourn in the city, M. Grevy's Cabinet seems on the point of dissolution, and his own resignation is a forgone conclusion. Among people so excitable as the French, one knows not what to look for under such circumstances. If such a crisis were impending among the American people, we would have no fear but that they would come safely out of it. But we are getting out of our sphere when we try to discuss French politics.

Paris has few street railways, and no underground or elevated ones. Its street travel is accomplished largely by omnibuses and cabs—voitures, they are called. These swarm everywhere. There are second stories to the railway carriages in use on the suburban trains, in which one may ride and see the sights to good advantage.

The gilded dome of the Church of the Invalides, where Napoleon the First has found a final resting place, can be seen from almost every part of the city. It is among the first of the city's attractions for our company. On entering this church, which is in reality a mausoleum dedicated to the Napoleon family, we notice a circular marble balustrade directly beneath the dome, about forty-five feet in diameter. Looking over this balustrade down into a crypt some eighteen feet below the floor level, our eyes rest upon the red Finland granite sarcophagus in which the remains of Napoleon rest. The monolith of which the tomb is composed is porphyry, weighing 135,000 pounds. The cost of the monument, we are told, was about $1,000,000. Here rests in peace the great soldier who gave Europe no peace while he lived. In his will he expressed the desire that his remains might rest on the banks of the Seine, "In the midst of the people I love so well." It was a long while before the French people could obtain this boon from the English nation; but Napoleon III. at last accomplished it.

Adjoining the sepulchre is the home of the "Invalides" for old and crippled soldiers. It seems meet that the old veterans should end their days in peace under the shadow of the last resting place of the great military genius whose victories and exploits they love so well to dwell upon.

Our next visit is to the Pantheon, in the crypt of which temporarily rests the remains of the great French novelist, Victor Hugo. Opposite his tomb is that of Rousseau, and on his left the tomb of Voltaire. More interesting to us than all the rest, is the tomb of General Lafayette and wife. They rest in a private cemetery in the rear of an Augustine Convent. Admission is not given to the public, but a small gratuity to the attendant will procure an entrance.

We have only just begun our sight seeing in this gay metropolis, and we will let our next chapter give the story of our wanderings more in detail.

CHAPTER V.

IN PARIS—SEEING THE SIGHTS.

OUR hostess is a French lady, of course—it is the fashion to be French in this city—and not being French, we are out of the fashion, and must appear awful green to our neighbors, especially to our hostess, who understands no English. What a time we have with her, trying to make known our wants! And often in her perplexity she hurries off to a millinery shop adjoining for a daughter who speaks a little English. James, our guide, who lives somewhere in the region above us, often gives a helping tongue between us and our hostess. We are compelled, likewise, owing to our dependence on the said James for a tongue, to keep together in our excursions through the city.

We are going to take an out-door ramble to-day. James being a little corpulent, and filled with a pardonable pride in the fact of his exaltation as guide and interpreter to five distinguished (?) Hawkeyes, is not pleased with our economical habit of footing it so much; but he is informed that it would be entirely foreign to our ideas of things to do otherwise, save when it suits us; and so he yields to the inevitable.

On the Place Vendome we take a momentary survey of the graceful column that rises up out of the center of the square. It was erected to commemorate Napoleon's victories over the Austrians, and is cast out of the cannon captured from them.

In 1871 its predecessor, erected in 1810, was torn down by the communists. In this same square took place some of the fiercest fighting of that period.

Passing on to the Place de la Concorde, we notice on the Strasbourg statue—one of the eighty-five that adorn that square—a garland of flowers, and ask the wherefore of it. "You see," said James, "that mourning crown also; it is all in token of the French people's grief at the loss of Strasbourg, taken from them by the Germans in the late war. The French covet their lost treasure, and will never rest until they have it back." Before us is the Obelisk of Luxor, erected upon the spot occupied by the guillotine in the Reign of Terror, and where not less than two thousand persons were decapitated in that awful shedding of innocent blood. It was upon this spot that Louis XVI. and his queen, Marie Antoinette, were beheaded. It is now one of the prettiest squares in the city, and said to be the most beautiful in all Europe. It is situated between the garden of the Tuilleries and the Champs Elysees, and would need to be exceeding beautiful to excel these last named places. One would need to forget the tragic occurrences of the past, not to feel a thrill of pain mingling with his appreciation of the beautiful in the Place de la Concorde.

Opposite the Palace of the Louvre is to be seen another reminder of the tragic events that have taken place within the walls of Paris. "From the top of that church tower," said James, pointing to an old stone church across the street, "was given the signal for the Bartholomew massacre in 1572, and on that balcony"—pointing up to a balcony of the Louvre Palace—"stood the queen mother of Charles the IX. to witness the massacre."

Being so near the Palace of the Louvre and the Tuilleries, we conclude to end up the day in an investigation of the museum and halls of paintings which they contain. These Palaces were joined together under Napoleon III. They are solid granite structures covering, with the enclosed court, an area of sixty acres. The artist and the antiquarian will please

IN PARIS—SEEING THE SIGHTS.

exercise their patience a little longer, and excuse us a description of what we find in these grand old halls to-day.

Those who have read the history of the "French Revolution" will be interested in a visit to the place where stood in those days of terror the old Bastile. Taking a little steamer on the Seine, we run down the river a couple of miles to the Austerlitz bridge, and thence a short walk brings us to the Place de la Bastile. The tall Juliet column rising 155 feet up out of the center of the square marks the place of the Bastile from a distance. The old Bastile, where languished for years so many victims of French ferocity, no longer stands. The people becoming exasperated at the outrages perpetrated within its walls, finally rose up in July 1789, and demolished it. The column in the center of the square was erected in memory of the six hundred and fifteen who fell in the assault and capture of the Bastile; and in the crypt beneath are deposited the remains of those who perished at that time. One may ascend to the top of the column by paying the old veteran in charge a small fee; and it is well to do it, as we can testify from experience, for the sake of a very fine view of Paris.

Our quiet man astonishes us with the information that the ministry has fallen, and also that there are extensive catacombs under Paris. His first statement is a little alarming, considering that our company is four parts ministerial, and we look around to discover the Judas in our midst; but other statements follow which reveal the fact that it is the M. Grevy crowd that is meant. How serious this may prove we know not; but we are glad, at least, to know that our ministry still stands the test of Parisian wickedness.

"But the catacombs," says H———, "I'm interested in them." They are open to the public on the first and third Saturdays of each month; and this being the third Saturday, we may enter to-day. Our whole party is eager for this underground experience, for none of us had so much as dreamed that catacombs existed at Paris.

With our factotum, James, puffing along at our sides, we make for the river and take a little steamer up stream about a mile and land near an old Roman castle, the "Palais de Thermes," where we have planned to entertain ourselves until the afternoon. This old fortress, now converted into a museum of antiquities, dates back to the time of the Cæsars. It has undergone a renovation by some party anxious to preserve what was yet left of this relic of the old Roman occupation. In the court yard is an old stone-curbed well out of which, it is said, Roman governors had drunk. The whole building is now used as a museum of antiquities, pertaining largely to the 14th and 15th centuries. We become acquainted, by means of certain things we see in the museum, with some very peculiar and laughable customs of those feudal lords of the 14th and 15th centuries, which will not bear description in these pages.

And now for the catacombs! We must be on hand by one o'clock or be left out altogether, for there are many others besides ourselves to go in to-day, and the crowd will not wait. A hundred or more people are already on hand lighting candles for the journey, when we arrive. Government officials lead the way, and in Indian file we take our way down the long, winding steps. There are ninety-one steps in the descent. At the bottom, about forty-five feet below the surface we come to a long, narrow gallery, wide enough for two to walk abreast. Following this about ten minutes, we come to a hall where the roof is borne up by two pillars. From this hall we pass into a great charnel house of the dead. Here, stacked up on each side of the passage, in artistic shape, are the bones and skulls of six millions of dead. These were gathered during and since the Revolution from the various old churchyards around the city. To the right and to the left, as we pass along, other dark passages lead off, each with a chain stretched across it, to prevent wandering from the main passage way, and each walled up with the relics of the dead. We feel ourselves vastly in the minority in this dismal chamber, and behave ourselves accordingly.

Three-quarters of an hour brings us to another flight of stairs by which we ascend eighty-two steps to daylight again. Originally, these catacombs were quarries, from which much of the stone now in Paris buildings was taken. Abut seventy staircases in different quarters give access to the catacombs. They are said to extend under one-third of the city.

The famous tapestry factories, founded by Louis XIV., are well worth a visit; and we find it quite convenient to visit them on our return journey this afternoon. The carpets and rugs manufactured here are real works of art. Here we see the artist, in weaver fashion, putting pictured scenes into his work and making them look as fresh and beautiful as the painter does his work on canvas. There are one hundred and twenty of these artists, each one averaging not more than $1\frac{1}{4}$ yards per annum. These tapestry factories are still under government management, and the product of the looms is used chiefly for presentations to foreign courts. It would cost from thirty to forty thousand dollars to buy almost any of the specimens we saw. "Think I'll not patronize this factory when I order my carpets," said the silent man, who betrays his matrimonial inclinations in unguarded moments.

H—— has seen some military service, and, although a man of peace both by profession and disposition, he sometimes walks with a very martial tread and foe-defying look in his eyes, when the French soldiers are marching by with colors flying and a fine band of music in the lead. As we are taking a ramble one day outside of the fortifications we discover a fine opportunity to get upon the ramparts. It affords us a magnificent promenade, and we follow the works along for some distance, until we come to a point from which we can look upon the drill movements of a company of soldiers.

Watching them for a few moments, we make the discovery that our presence is causing somewhat of a commotion down below. We are evidently taken for an enemy, and an officer makes a charge; but my military friend is equal to the emergency, and gives the approaching official a military salute which "right about faces" him. "Now, then, as general commanding this scaling force, I order a retreat," says H———, and retreat it is.

TOMB OF NAPOLEON I.

Versailles is most easily visited from Paris, and as we are loth to leave the city without first seeing this most beautiful and interesting of all the suburban towns of Paris, we resolve on a visit thither immediately for we are now meditating a departure from the French capital. A distance of twelve miles, a half hour's ride on a suburban train, brings us to the palace and park of this old home of royalty. Before entering the palace, we pass on beyond through the wooded park to the Chateau of Marie Maintenon, a court mistress of Louis the XIV. Here are the private apartments of Napoléon I., with bed, furniture and bath, all as he left them, we are told. Here also the room in which Marshal Bazaine was tried and condemned on account of his conduct at Metz. A visit to the coach house follows. Here are kept the State carriages used by Louis XIV., Louis XVI., Napoleon, Josephine and Marie Antoinette.

Passing back again through the park, we view the gardens and wonderful fountains at the rear of the palace. The palace itself, exteriorly, is royal in looks as well as dimensions; a massive stone structure fourteen hundred feet in length. It was originally intended by Louis XIII. as a hunting chateau. Louis XIV. converted it into a palace for the kings of France. It was completed in 1672, after eleven years of toil upon it. The genius of man was forced to struggle against nature in the construction of the palace and gardens surrounding it. Rivers were turned from their courses that the waters might be conducted to the fountains. All the arts vied with each other in their zeal to carry out the design of a palace which should be the most splendid of all royal residences. Forty millions sterling—it is said—were expended in the work.

Louis XVI. with his queen, Marie Antoinette, resided here until the unhappy pair were taken to Paris at the beginning of the Revolution in 1792. It was Louis Philippe who conceived the idea of making the palace a great national art gallery of paintings illustrative of the military glory of France. Here, therefore, we find one of the finest collections of war paintings in all Europe. Eleven large halls are filled with them. The battle of "Abd-el-Keder," by Horace Vernet, occupies a space about 20 by 40 feet. Another painting representing the crowning of Napoleon and Josephine in Notre Dame, is alone worth the visit to Versailles, if one be as near as Paris. The painting is by David, and $20,000—it is said—was the price paid him for its execution. But it would far exceed the limits of this chapter if we were to tarry long enough in our description to tell the half of what is of interest to the student of history and art in, and around, this grand old palace. It proved to our company the most interesting day's tour of all those we had taken around Paris.

The contemplative man of the party has a mood on him to-night as we sit in solemn conclave touching the matter of routes on to Rome. He has suddenly taken it into his head to depart from the course of travel previously laid out, and take a short cut by night express to Rome, via the Paris and Mont Cenis railway. We object to night travel over such scenic routes, and moreover have planned to see southern France and travel over the Rivieras by the Lyons and Mediterranean Sea coast route. But our moody member must have his two months in Rome, whilst some of the rest of us are equally determined on only one month; and hence it comes that we leave Paris a divided company, for a season. We have yet some good company left us in H————, as we take our journey southward the next day for Marseilles. We are ticketed second class to Naples, our tickets allowing us to break the journey at any point we desire. The excursionist finds these circular tour tickets a great convenience. Our letters of credit have lost a value of one hundred and eighty-six francs each—about $36.25—by reason of these tickets. These letters of credit, too, are another of the traveler's great conveniences; he never has to carry much money with him. If robbed, he has his letter of credit, which would be useless to the robber, to fall back on.

CHAPTER VI.

SOUTHERN FRANCE; AND THE FRENCH AND ITALIAN RIVIERAS.

NOW, farewell, thou gayest of cities! We care not to know more of thee than what we see outwardly revealed; for we are fully satisfied that bitter misery and vice untold lie hidden in thy bosom. Farewell frost and snow! Ye must travel fast if we do not distance you now for months to come. Thus we think, as we roll out of the Lyons depot southward bound.

We have determined to break journey first at Fontainebleau, which is reached in an hour and a half. The forest, famous for its dark evergreen beauty, with an area of 64 square miles, is a part of our scenery for some time before reaching the town. Fontainebleau is a gem set in the midst of great beauty of natural surroundings. Like Versailles, it was planned for a royal residence, and used as such as early as the 12th century. The palace and surrounding forests are objects of general interest and we find ourselves thrown into the company of quite a large crowd of tourists as we leave the depot for the palace. A government official takes charge of the company as we enter the ground. He is French, we are not; and as we pass through the various departments we lose much of the information which he imparts to others—who are mostly French—touching the historical associations of the rooms. The obliging fellow does his best in a few words of English now and then for our specal benefit. We learn that there are nine hundred apartments in the palace, each of which is kept sumptuously furnished.

Much of interest connected with the life of Napoleon I. is centered in some of these rooms. There is the table on which he signed his abdication, covered over with glass to protect it from the relic hunter. In this hall the public first learned of the decree of divorce from Josephine; and here again is the room in which Louis XIV. signed the revocation of the edict of Nantes. In the principal court, called the cour des Adieux, Napoleon took his leave of the remnant of the old Guard who had followed him through all adversity up to the time of his departure for Elba. This scene is commemorated in a fine painting, "Les Adieux des Fontainebleau," seen in one of the galleries of the building.

A portion of the afternoon is spent in the forest park adjoining. Here are lakelets with waterfowl swimming around, flowing fountains of exquisite design and skill, and walks adorned with a profusion of flowers. The beat of the drum and the music of military bands resound through the forest, for the French are getting ready to whip the Germans for the insult to their arms in 1870.

We resume our journey at 11 o'clock p. m., and next morning, as we look out into the growing dawn, we discover that we are approaching Macon. At this point we strike the Saone river and follow the valley to Lyons, where the Saone unites itself with the Rhone. We pass now through the famous Burgundy wine region; and freight train and river boat alike are all loaded with hogsheads of wine. The valley through which we ride to-day is one vast vineyard.

"See," said H———, "the peculiar method of vine trellising. They have planted trees in regular order and clipt the tops of them, so that the vine does not lose itself in a mass of limbs and foliage. It's a novel idea certainly to hold an umbrella over your vine to keep the too fierce rays of the sun from spoiling your growing grape."

From our guide books we discover that the town of Arles, just ahead of us, has some interesting antiquities which are worth a visit. "Arles!" cries the gare man, and we are left standing on the platform while our train rolls on to Marseilles. There is only one passage out of these French gares, and that is guarded by the man who wants to see your ticket. Railway custom in this country is to see your ticket when you

AMPHITHEATRE, ARLES.

go to the passenger platform to take your train, and when you leave the platform to enter the station. The gares, or stations, are all fenced to keep out intruders.

We find a Frenchman who is familiar with our mother tongue, having been a soldier in our country during the war of the Rebellion, and with him set out to investigate the sights. Arles is the oldest looking town we have yet seen. It used to be the capital of Gaul, long years before Paris had an existence. A very ancient looking building on the banks of the Rhone is pointed out to us as an old residence of Constantine the Great.

Portions of the walls of the old city yet remain, and upon these have been built the newer walls of the modern city. Here is an amphitheatre said to date back to the time of Titus. It is quite a perfect specimen of an old Roman amphitheatre; and here on the Sabbath gather crowds to witness bull fights. The arena has the usual elliptical shape, sixty yards in length, and is possessed of wonderful acoustic properties. Sending our guide to the farthest end, we talked to him in the lowest possible tone, and were distinctly heard in all we said. In this very arena the gladiator has fought; and men have engaged in deadly combat with hunger-maddened animals. Yonder at the main entrance, on a level with the arena, are the open doors of the dens from which these animals rushed upon their human victims. Above the den corridors are the seats, ranged in terraces up to the height of forty feet, and accommodating about 25,000 persons.

The next day we take our leave of this interesting old town, and move on to Marseilles. "What are those dark green looking trees of which we see whole orchards?" I inquire, as we speed along; but I have asked too hard a question of my friend. The tree is a stranger to us both; but later on we find it is the olive. It gives an added beauty to the landscape scenery such as we have not before seen in France. Now for a distance we are swinging around the limestone cliffs, suddenly emerging into a plain and passing into a long avenue of evergreen trees, then a sudden plunge out of daylight into darkness, and a mile of tunnel brings us to the city by the sea.

Marseilles has the reputation of being the oldest city in France; founded, we are told, 600 B. C. by a Grecian colony from Phocea, yet it does not wear the appearance of such extreme old age. Poor Marseilles! She has been woefully afflicted in times past by her enemies. Hannibal, Cæsar, Visigoths, Burgundians, Ostragoths, Saracen, each in turn has had a bone to pick with her. Forty thousand out of her ninety thousand people perished by the plague of 1720-1. There was a mutual dislike between Napoleon and the city because his wars interferred so seriously with her commerce; and she was made to suffer the common fate of all who crossed his ambition. Since the conquest of Algiers in 1815, and the opening of the Suez Canal, Marseilles has entered upon a new era of commercial prosperity. Its population is not far from 400,000 at the present.

After a night of rest at the "Grand Marseille," we are ready to see what may be of interest about the city. "That hill," observes H————, "would be a good point from which to take our first view of the city, if we could only manage to scale it." The hill referred to was a tall cone rising up 550 feet or more next the sea, with sides so precipitous that it gave promise of some sweat of the brow before it could be made to yield us the desired vision. Crowning the top of the hill is the cathedral Notre Dame de la Garde, with a tower running up 148 feet with a colossal statue of the Virgin, 30 feet high, holding in her arms the infant Christ.

We are repaid for our toil in climbing this hill by the beautiful panorama of sea and city which lies spread out before us. There are two ports, one of which runs up into the city and out of which rises a forest of masts. The smaller sail vessels all crowd into this port. The large ocean steamers have a dock and port of their own farther out; a slice, as it were, cut out of the sea, and walled in by an immense stone breakwater, which forms a splendid promenade.

We visit an old church on our return, St. Victor. It stands, it is said, over the burial place of an old martyr. A priest in charge asks if we would like to go down into the crypt, and being answered in the affirmative, gives us lighted tapers and tells us to follow. He astonishes us with the information that Lazarus and Mary Magdalene are both entombed in these dark vaults, and points out their sepulchral chambers to us!

A Sabbath of rest in the city, and we are ready for another stage of our journey. What pleasure we anticipate as we move on eastward, halting here and there as suits our fancy, to enjoy the delicious climate, and see the luxury in which these southern Europeans are indulging themselves. A range of lofty limestone hills shuts off the sea view until Frejus is reached ; and now the railway closely hugs the sea shore, oftentimes plunging through a mountain of rock rather than separate itself from the water.

Toulon is reached; and now, delightful vision! We see the orange orchards, laden with their golden colored fruit, much of it ready for the market. Cannes, our first halting point, 120 miles from Marseilles, is a beautiful looking town of some 19,000 people. A hotel is found—the Louvre—which affords us substantial comforts at a dollar a day.

Our first ramble is to the top of Observatory hill at the back of Cannes. A fine carriage way, by innumerable loups, leads up the ascent of 800 feet. Past hotels, villas and pensions, most of them with orange groves in their front yards, the way leads; shaded here by resinous trees, adorned there by flowers in hues of every color, with as balmy an air as mortal need to breathe in. We were not astonished at our friend's burst of enthusiasm when he said, "Surely this is as much like Paradise as anything I will ever see this side of the heavenly one."

A magnificent view presents itself from the observatory. To the south is the sea, specked with sail and steam craft. Between lies Cannes, stretching for a mile and a half along its shore, beautiful with its villas and dark green orange yards. Out on the bay of Jouan is the Isle of St. Marguerite, with Richelieu's fort, where Marshal Bazaine was confined, and where also the "Man of the Iron Mask" had his prison home. To the north are the villages of Cannett and Grasse, famed for their perfumery manufactures. To the far northeast the white tops of the Maritime Alps cast down a frigid stare at this tropical luxury.

An afternoon ramble on the beautiful Corniche Road by the sea completes our sight-seeing at Cannes. In the evening we meet some American friends whose acquaintance we had formed at Marseilles. From one of these gentlemen, a press representative from Michigan and a personal friend of the American Consul at Jerusalem, we are kindly furnished with a letter of introduction to United States Consul Gilman, of Jerusalem.

Nineteen miles farther on is Nice, another winter resort for Europeans. We leave our train again at this point for a few days' touring. The population of these Riviera resorts varies according to the season. In the winter season Nice is said to have a population of 100,000. The season is just commencing, and visitors are pouring in by every train. Even consumptives from Illinois, Iowa and other western states are met with here.

Good pension board and lodgings may be obtained at two dollars a day in Nice. Our first ramble is with a crowd of ramblers on the Promenade des Anglais. This handsome drive and walk, 85 feet broad, stretches for two miles along the sea shore, and is the work of the English in 1882 in order to furnish work for the poor during a season of scarcity.

"What are those women killing?" said H——, as we noticed a number of them at the water's edge pounding something quite vigorously. "Trying to kill the dirt in their soiled linen," I answer, "judging from the victims already laid out on the pebbly beach." Sure enough! No washing machines here, save that which was created when Eve was fashioned. The linen is laid upon a smooth stone, soaped, hammered with another stone and then dipped into the sea, until the process is complete, when it is spread out on the clean pebble stones to be dried by the sun.

Three days of pleasant life are enjoyed in rambles along the river Paillon, among the olive and orange groves, and to neighboring heights; and we turn away regretfully, fearing lest we may not find as we journey on such paradisiacal towns. Nice is the native town of Garibaldi; and here, too, Lyte, author of "Abide With Me," has found a resting place.

Fifteen miles farther on is Mentone, the last of the towns on the French Riviera at which we shall have the pleasure of a stop. Monte Carlo, famous the world over because of its gambling hell, is passed, and we soon catch sight of the white villas of Mentone, as they rise up from the tops and terraced sides of the cliffs bordering on the bay of Mentone. The fine Corniche road clings to the sea closely all the way from Cannes to Mentone, and is often preferred to the railway by tourists, who desire to prolong that exquisite sense of pleasure which one feels in this region.

Mentone is both old and new. The old town sits upon the top of a rocky hill which juts out into the sea a distance, forming two bays. The streets of the old town are mediæval in look, narrow, filthy and crooked. It wears a shattered look, for it is hardly a year since an earthquake tried to get rid of the old town by shaking it off into the sea. But the newer portions of the town stretching along the sea for three-fourths of a mile on either side of the old, more than redeem, by their beauty, the uglier features of the old.

We have exhausted the week in the enjoyment of this pleasant semi-tropical climate and scenery, and we look about us to see what the Sabbath has in store for us. "Truly we are in luck," remarks H———, as he comes in from his inquiries with a beaming countenance. "Mr. Spurgeon, of London, is wintering here at the 'Beau Rivage,' and holds service for the few personal friends who care to visit him at his hotel." "But the service is not public, you say; only for personal friends, and we have not that honor," I answer. The difficulty is solved by sending a note to Mr. Spurgeon asking permission to attend the morning service, and a cordial invitation to do so is sent us. In the morning we find ourselves, with about a dozen others, in the parlors of the "Beau Rivage," and take a gospel feast from the lips of the great preacher. "The American brethren present" are remembered in his prayers, and are invited back to a communion service in the afternoon. This proves a day of sacred privilege to our souls, and one long to be remembered in the years to come.

"Surely," said H———, as we were toiling up the terraced side of the "Garavan," "these people are inclined to follow Scriptural injunctions in reference to their house building ; built upon rocks, and set high above flood mark, they certainly are." The morning is perfect, and a ramble of several miles out among the olives—now in the fruit season—and the lemon and orange groves, with the music of pouring waters rushing down from the Apennines to the sea, the songs of the birds in their leafy retreats, all in melodious harmony, fill our spirits with delight and make us wish to dwell forevermore just where we are.

But time moves, and so must we; and the next train bears us on towards San Remo, our next halting point, 16 miles distant. At Ventimiglia we cross the border between France and Italy; and here our baggage must undergo inspection.

San Remo in itself presents little of interest to the visitor. As a health resort it has some advantages over the other towns of the Rivieras, by reason of its sheltered position. Crown Prince Frederick, of Germany, is wintering here in the hope of final recovery. The chief attraction of our visit is the ascent of Mt. Bignone 4,235 feet above the sea level. A narrow cobblestone way leads by a gradual ascent for four miles to the village of St. Romalo, 1,700 feet above sea level. This part of the journey is made through a constant succession of olive groves, the way winding around like a serpent up the sides of the hill.

"What in San Remo is that coming!" said my friend, startled out of his usual composure by seeing a huge black bundle moving towards us. "That," I answer, "is a Mt. Bignone porcupine; see how his quills stick out! It will be wise to let him have the right of way, for he takes it all, anyway."

But as the bundle nears us, we observe a donkey's long ears sticking out and two pairs of hoofs close to the pavement. Yes, it's a donkey, with a great bundle of pine cones on his back, destined for the San Remo wood market.

A narrow path leads up from St. Romalo 2,500 feet higher, and after much sweat of the brow, we at last stand upon the top of our Pisgah as delighted with our view as ever Moses could have been with his view of the Promised Land. This view has been described by travelers as one of the finest in Europe. Seven towns are in sight; to the northward, with two lower ranges intervening, are the snow-crowned Alps, while a look in the opposite direction reveals a wealth of tropical vegetation. Winter and summer are each facing each other with this bald ridge as a dividing line. The vision, to be appreciated, must be realized in personal experience; for a traveler's description only mutilates the fair scene.

Genoa is our next halting place, and a few days of stay here results in an experience which renders the narrative of our visit altogether uninteresting to the reader. We would like to have seen the town of the "Great Christopher Colombo" under other and more favorable circumstances, but the Alps paid no heed to the pilgrim's desire and sent their sharp winds whistling down the Pass, sending him to bed for a few days.

Only one more halt before reaching Rome, we think, as we board our train at Genoa. We could not pass Pisa, of course, and therefore when our slow train comes into town at the edge of evening we sever company with it and take to a hotel.

Pisa! yes; guides by the score looking in upon us through the windows as we sit at our morning meal. Beggars! yes, a few; not more than a hundred at a time, each anxious to help you carry your superfluous wealth. We ask the landlord if there is not some back door way of stealing away from the impecunious crowd. "No"; he has put a high wall around his premises to protect himself from this same crowd. We sally

SOUTHERN FRANCE. 63

boldly forth and sling our noes and our—well, never mind—
to right and left, and finally reach the Leaning Tower, only
to be sold out by a fellow of another sort, who passes to the

THE TOWER OF PISA.

top with us under the pretense of making a company sufficiently
large to be allowed that privilege. Up a circular flight of stairs
of easy grade we go until we stand on the top, 183 feet from

the ground. If it were not for the knowledge that the old Tower has thus stood, eleven feet two inches out of its perpendicular, for over seven centuries, we would most certainly feel that we were on the point of coming down in worse shape than Darius in his parachute excursion.

The cathedral, next in order, is a work of the eleventh century, and is interesting enough to pay for a visit; but we will yet meet with others as interesting, and so pass on to the Baptistry. It presents some novel features of architecture. It is circular in form, with dome roof, in circumference $361\frac{1}{2}$ feet, in height only three feet lower than the tower. Its acoustic properties are its most marvelous feature. At a hundred yards distance the lowest tone of the voice may be heard. The most unmusical note or tone of voice seems to resolve itself into a symphony, and is caught up, echoed and re-echoed around the room and carried to the dome. Two hours of sight-seeing this morning in Pisa is enough, and we take a forenoon train for Rome. An eight hours' ride through an uninviting, marshy looking country, and under cover of night we enter Rome.

CHAPTER VII.

THE SEVEN-HILLED CITY—JUBILEE WEEK IN ROME.

"I am in Rome! Oft as the morning ray
Visits these eyes, waking, at once I cry,
Whence this excess of joy? What has befallen me?
And from within a thrilling voice replies,
Thou art in Rome! The city that so long
Reigned absolute, the mistress of the world."

SOMEWHAT of the poet's feeling takes possession of ourselves as we look forth from our window, on the first morning of our arrival, upon this once proud mistress of the world. The day is the Sabbath, bright and clear, and we take our way to the Scotch Presbyterian church to see if the "faith once delivered to the saints" is yet kept in its freshness and purity in this once ancient city, from whence emanated so much of the light that now illumines so large a portion of the Gentile world. The pastor, Dr. Grey, is now absent in America in the interests of his mission; but we heard from Rev. Mr. Purvis, who ministers in Dr. Grey's absence, one of those sermons for which the Scotch Presbyterian clergy are noted, both simple, pure and thoroughly orthodox, ourselves being the judge.

Besides this mission there are missions of the Baptist, English and American Methodists and Church of England, together with the Italian Free Church and Waldensian church. They are all but a drop in the bucket compared with the Church of Rome. She is dominant here with a vengeance. Her churches are both numerous and rich. The finest works of

THE PANTHEON AT ROME.

marble sculpture and paintings of the old masters are gathered together to adorn and enrich the hundreds of Romish churches in the city. She numbers her priests by the thousands, and just at present we might without exaggeration say, by the ten thousands, for the Pope's Jubilee festivities have gathered them in from all parts of the world. And more than this; she has planted here schools of learning for the youth of all nationalities, and is training in them a priesthood destined for all parts of the world. Next to soldiers and tourists, the most numerous class of people one sees on the streets is the black and red robed Romish student. The students of the different schools are distinguished by the color of their robes. The different orders of the priesthood are distinguished in like manner by colors of white, brown, blue and black; the purple is seldom seen on the street. With our strongly anti-Romish education we were not prepared to see any good in the Church of Rome; but in our peregrinations through her churches, and witnessing of her worship and influence upon the people, we are not so certain but that, partly purified as she is, her influence is manifold better than no religious influence. Indeed, we think that it is owing to her influence rather than any other that the city is as orderly as it is. One is ready to laugh at the superstitious feelings and beliefs of the poor people, but for all that there is a restraining influence in these same things that is a positive benefit to the community. The name of Christ is reverenced in Rome as nowhere else, and the different apostles, Peter and Paul more particularly, have shrines and churches almost innumerable erected to their memories.

Modern Rome is not the Rome of Paul's day. The gospel that he wrote and preached has left an ineffaceable impress upon the people. But God is worshipped through man, instead of being approached direct, and in so doing more or less of the worship cleaves to the man. No! Rome is not pure; nor is the Protestant church pure; it is only a question of degree, and the blacker of the two sheep may yet be made as white as the other by the cleansing power of the same Master. Rome presents a variety of contradictions. Founded about twenty-six hundred years ago, she presents a wondrously modern appearance. There is nothing to remind the visitor, unless he happens along at some of the unburied ruins, that he is in a city founded over seven hundred years before Christ. A new Rome has grown up over the grave of ancient Rome.

Under the beneficent rule of Victor Emanuel I., not only Rome, but the whole of united Italy, has entered upon a career of wonderful prosperity and improvement. Whole squares of beautiful buildings have been erected, and others are in process of construction. Even old Rome in her ruin is contributing to the present prosperity of the new by here and there unbosoming herself for the contemplation of the visitor, multitudes of whom are drawn hither by mixed motives of curiosity and study. The Roman art galleries are equaled nowhere else in the world. And where can one find such a stupendous ruin as the Coliseum, or one around which so much of tragic interest centers? Which "on its public shows unpeopled Rome." What sights have been here witnessed of gladiatorial combat, of bloody and unequal contest between man and beast, of the rending of innocent martyrs by hunger maddened animals!

But while we are making these general observations concerning Rome we are reminded that an expensive hotel may not be indulged in if we would protract our stay to a month. To see Rome in less than a month is to see her very imperfectly, and put a slight upon her that she does not deserve.

We are in as sorry a predicament in our attempt to communicate with the natives here in Rome as we were in the French capital; but we have been drilling ourselves in the object method and have made some progress in the art of pantomimics, so that when our tongues fail us we are not left without a final resort. Rome is so filled up with strangers drawn hither by the attraction of the Pope's Jubilee occasion, that it proves no easy matter to find accommodations in such a quarter as we prefer.

Our friends who have preceded us are comfortably located in a convenient and pleasant quarter of the city, but there is room for no more of us there. We prevail on one of our hotel waiters to go with us to some friends of his in the eastern part of the city, on the Esquiline Hill, where we succeed in settling ourselves quite to our liking. For a furnished room, with morning and evening meals for two, we pay thirty dollars for the month. Those who read this record, and who may, peradventure, visit the Eternal City, need not expect to be served with very elaborate meals at these rates, nor need they expect a central location in the city; but for ourselves we were abundantly satisfied in both these respects.

But, reader, there was one experience that fell to our sad lot in those humble quarters which, whilst it does add the spice of variety to a Roman pilgrim's life, is really not essential to one's happiness. The noisy creakings of H———'s iron bedstead during the night made me conscious that my fellow pilgrim was not enjoying the situation very well; and something in my own enabled me to keep careful vigil over my friend's movements.

"Friend," I at length ventured, "life in Rome does not seem to be agreeing very well with you. "True," he groaned, "Roman life, or some other kind of life, is proving a disturbing element to sweet dreams to-night. But," he added, as he sprang out of bed and proceeded to light a candle, "I'm badly mistaken if there is not more than one of us in this bed to-night; it feels lively enough to have a thousand of us, more or less." A careful search for his supposed bed-fellows revealed nothing, however, and he returned—not to rest—but to continued tossing. The sleeper in the other bed is keenly alive to the situation, and has planned a night attack on the enemy. With candle lit he awaits in silence the proper moment, and falls suddenly

INTERIOR OF ST. PETER'S, ROME.

upon the camp of the enemy, and joyfully exclaims as he attempts to seize a foe, "I have him!" "Can't be possible," comes from the other bed, "for he is still over here."

What a time we have with our Italian host, who speaks no English, to make him understand that the omnipresent pulce must be ejected at once, or we must abandon his room. With the co-operation of our host and a pharmacist of the city we put to flight our foe after a struggle of two or three nights.

It is not all sunshine in Italy, as we can testify from our experience thus far. There has been more of cloudy weather and rain than sunshine, until we begin to fear that even a month of stay will not suffice for the outdoor studies we are here to make. The rain has fallen in such quantities as to raise the Tiber to flood heights, and a portion of the city in the neighborhood of the Pantheon has been under water. But no serious inconvenience has been felt on acount thereof, for it is an old trick of the Tiber to which the natives have become fully accustomed.

New Year's day, however, comes and goes in bright sunshine. It is the inauguration day of the Pope's big show. For months past preparations have been making at the Vatican and elswhere, to make the week commencing January 1st a gala day for the Romish Church. The rulers of the earth have contributed of their gold and silver in pure coin, and in various other forms fashioned by the jeweler's art, enough to make the solemn Papal countenance wreath itself in smiles. If gold and silver can make a person happy, Leo XIII. must be very happy at the present time. The gifts which have been sent and brought in person are estimated at a value of $40,000,000; and he is in his 77th year. Poor man! We would not blame him to be very importunate for the return of his youth. High mass is to be said in St. Peter's this New Year's morning by the Pope in person for the first time in nineteen years. Being desirous of seeing and hearing as much of Papal doings as we possibly can during our brief sojourn, we turn our steps thither.

Alas for human hopes in this particular; we are doomed to disappointment! Everybody else in Rome appears to have this same object in view, and soon we are wedged in among a countless host of human beings in the great square in front of St. Peter's. A line of soldiers is drawn up at the foot of the steps leading up to the portico to prevent any farther crowding of the steps and portico.

The vast Cathedral is already full, and it accommodates 90,000 persons, allowing two and a half square feet to the person. A throng of people equally as large surged up and down the square and the two streets leading out of it, intent on gaining admittance to the great sanctuary. After lingering awhile in this state of turmoil, the line of soldiers in front gives way to the right and left, and then every solid foot of space in portico, steps and square in front is occupied. Another line of soldiers stand ranged close to the five vestibules leading into the church, and ingress is barred. The service within is concluded while the multitude yet linger on the outside.

And now comes the tug of war; those inside wanting out, and those outside still wanting in, the two multitudes stand facing each other. The tall red-plumed policemen. numerous as they are, seem powerless to do anything. At this point of affairs the military take matters into their own hands, and ranging themselves in ranks two deep across the whole end of the Cathedral, gently and good-naturedly push the entire multitude before them, until portico and steps, with a portion of the square, are cleared.

It was like a great wave of the sea, that mass of rolling humanity in its retreat before the glittering bayonets of the soldiery. Priest and plebeian, tourist and titled aristocrat, all jumbled up together, with a common feeling of respect for the bright steel in the rear.

So ended our vision of the Pope's high mass. But we try another experiment in the afternoon with better success. The New Year vesper service in St. John's Lateran is advertised to be of an unusually interesting character, and thither we go in time for a good position in this one of Rome's most beautiful churches. It is here that all the Popes for the last fifteen hundred years have been crowned. It is supposed to have the keeping of the heads of Saints Peter and John under its high altar, and lights are kept burning around the altar during the day in their honor. The vesper service proved of a highly interesting nature. The "Te Deum" in which the vast congregation joined at certain points was truly inspiring, enough so to raise even a phlegmatic tempered person into the third heaven of enjoyment. After vesper service we pass over to the "Scala Santa" building and watch the score or more of persons piously creeping up the stairs on their knees and kissing the steps in a very devotional manner. "Why all this?" you ask. Because these are the sacred stairs taken from Pilate's Judgment Hall, and down which our Saviour came after his cruel scourging and mock coronation; so, at least, we are told.

Martin Luther was once ascending these steps, and when about half way up he suddenly rose to his feet and walked down. He seemed to hear a voice, he said, whispering to him that "the just shall live by faith."

Everywhere we turn in Rome we are met by just such examples of credulousness on the part of the people of the lower classes. Illiteracy is the foundation upon which such credulity is built. St. Peter's has a most gorgeous high altar beneath which the headless relic of the Saint is said to rest. It is marvelous how the Romish Church succeeds in palming off such fictions upon the people. It is extremely doubtful whether Peter ever visited Rome or suffered martyrdom there; and yet

THE MAMERTINE PRISON.

place after place that we visit both inside and outside the walls of Rome is traditionally connected with some event in the great Apostle's life.

Portions of the old Mamertine prison of Paul's day are yet found at the foot of the Capitoline, on its eastern side. These cells are doubtless genuine, for they occupy the known site of the old prison in which St. Paul languished, and are both gloomy and far enough under ground to dispel all idea of fiction in the matter. In visiting these cells one day, with a monk as guide, we were shown the imprint of Peter's face in the stone wall, made, we were told with the greatest of gravity, by the jailer pounding the Apostle's head against the wall. "What barbaric methods of photography they had in those days," remarks H———. "And what a flinty face the fearless Apostle must have had, too," I answer, "to make such an impression as that upon the wall."

Epiphany day in Rome, a day of noise and a babel of confusion. Where shall we go to get out of it? The monarch of cathedrals on the Leonine side of the Tiber has not yet been visited under favorable circumstances, and we resolve to turn our faces in that direction for the day.

St. Peter's is, with one exception, Rome's greatest wonder. Its vastness of interior area is not fully realized on a first or second visit. Everything is of such huge proportions that it is only by a study of comparisons that we come to acquire anything like an adequate idea of the vastness of things. Look, for example, at that cherub with half-folded wings; it seems but the marble form of a lad two or three years old, as we view it from this short distance; but approach and measure by comparison with your own stature and you find it taller by two feet than yourself. As you stand at the portal, look down at the end of the nave to the high altar, and the men and women appear like small school children.

As we pass down the nave on this Epiphany day, about mid-way we notice a group of Catholic pilgrims, gathered around the large bronze statue of St. Peter, kissing the great toe of the Saint! That is the pleasant occupation in which all are most eager to take part. Just imagine the scene if you can. There sits the Saint in the pontifical chair with right foot extended, the great toe of which is kissed by each pilgrim, and then fondly touched by his forehead. The children are lifted up for their osculatory performances; the short-statured jump up on tip toe, while those of a somewhat finer mold and sensitive stomachic organization gently wipe with their handkerchiefs toe and foot before performing their own devotional act. "Surely that sort of thing would grow monotonous to the poor Saint if he were possessed of sensibility," remarks H———, as we turn away towards the high altar.

Over the high altar is a canopy supported by four twisted bronze columns fifty feet in height. This canopy is topped with a cross. The railing around the altar is adorned with 112 cornucopia, supporting as many silver lamps, which are kept burning during the day. A double flight of marble steps leads down to the reputed tomb of the Apostle.

We next take our way to the dome. The ascent is made from the interior by an easy grade of steps up to a height of 440 feet above the pavement. From this height we get the best possible view of Rome and surrounding country. The eye as it looks southward falls upon a wide stretch of Campagna presenting much the appearance of an Iowa prairie view, through which the yellow Tiber may be traced almost to its mouth. The city lies spread out in grand panorama to the east, and leading out in a southeast direction are the old and the new Appian ways, making towards the Alban Hills, which we see bordering our vision farther on.

Let the visitor who goes to Rome not neglect to view the city and its surroundings from the dome of St. Peter's. It was a happy experience with us.

CHAPTER VIII.

RAMBLES IN AND AROUND ROME.

EPIPHANY day, January 6th, is children's day in Rome. Toys and sweetmeats are dispensed in commemoration of the Magi's visit to Bethlehem and presentation of gifts to the Savior. Booths in great numbers for the display and sale of all articles that tickle the fancy or please the taste are erected in arcades and other available places on the day before. And such a display of this sort of goods we have never seen before.

The day is given up to enjoyment, and everybody and his friends go out in holiday attire to mingle their noise with, and feast their eyes upon, the gay crowds that are surging up and down between the long lines of gorgeously decked booths. If you want to know how much noise there is to the square inch in the average Italian, just present yourself in Rome on Epiphany day. The din of the shouting booth-keepers, the tooting of tin horns—and every small boy seems to have one—the beating of petroleum cans and characteristic loud talking of the people, all make a perfect pandemonium, lasting until after the midnight hour. In the matter of noise it is expected that on this day everybody may make as much as he pleases, with none to ask the wherefore of it.

The whole city has been in holiday attire for a week past, owing to the countless throng of visitors that are here to see and take part in the festivities of the Vatican. And truly the elements have been propitious, for this week alone since our coming has been in any degree pleasant for out of door touring. But now the excitement of Jubilee week is over, and as our fine weather gives promise of continuance, we can settle down to our usual occupation of sight-seeing.

The Vatican exhibition remained open for a few days and then closed in order to perfect the arrangement and classification of the Pope's presents. And now Pope Leo may drink his wine out of golden chalices, a new one each day, for the next five years. The numerous presents from the crowned heads of Europe, together with President Cleveland's remembrance, have served to elate him somewhat, if his utterances on this subject be sincere. He professes to accept it as an evidence that his supremacy is recognized by the world, and expresses the belief that the Holy See will soon regain its lost hold upon Italy. To us that day appears far distant when the Papal Church, in its present corrupt form, will regain its power over the minds of the people. The foolish beliefs which, for ages, it has palmed off upon the people, do not meet with the credence they once did. But, in its reaction from the papacy, Italy is fast coming into that state of no religion which has involved France in so much misery for so many years. The great need of Italy to-day is missionaries of the evangelical faith who can use the Italian tongue in public discourse. If such were planted, not only in Italy, but in the principal cities of Papal Europe, a great harvest of good, we think, would soon be the result.

Upon the Palatine hill we wander through the deserted halls, underground corridors and the once regal apartments of Cæsar, Tiberius, Caligula, Domitian, Commodus and Septimus Severus, and through various temples, the work of their hands, and remember that these majestic but melancholy ruins are all that is left of their builder's pride and might. Once these very halls through which our solitary feet are roaming, were thronged with the couriers of those who were called masters of the world. Here, on this spot, the assassin's dagger finished the career of Caligula. The whole hill, the one upon which Romulus founded his city, is given up to these historical ruins. Passing from thence to the Coelian, we find it largely given up to vineyards and tombs. Here we find the tomb of Tacitus, the historian, and but a short distance from it the tomb of the Scipios, which is one of the many catacombs in and around Rome. In the same vineyard with these tombs are two columbaria of special interest. The columbaria differ from the tombs in this particular, that they were designed to receive simply the urns containing the ashes of those who were burned, and consist of a number of niches cut in the walls for the urns. In these columbaria mentioned are found the names of several members of Cæsar's household who are mentioned by Paul in his epistles. The names are Tryphena, Tryphosa; Romans 16:12, Onesimus, Col. 1:7, Philemon, 1:23. From other inscriptions found in these columbaria it is certain that they were those used for the burial of the freedmen and servants of Cæsar's household; and Paul speaks in Philemon 1:13 and 4:22 of certain converts of the palace.

Not so certain are we of the next place we visit. It is the place, according to Romish tradition, where Domitian attempted to boil the Apostle John. A little round chapel just inside the walls at the end of the Via Latina marks the place.

In this connection it may be of interest to know that some frescoes of 14th century origin were discovered a few years since bearing inscriptions which when translated were found to relate to the Apostle John; one lengthy inscription being a letter from the Pro-Consul of Ephesus to Domitian concerning the heretical zeal of the Apostle, and his success in turning the people away from the "worship of the immortal gods," and asking the advice of the Emperor as to what should be done with the offender. Then follows this inscription quoted entire: "As soon as Domitian had read this letter, being enraged, he sent a rescript to the Pro-Consul, that he should put the holy John in chains and bring him bound to Rome, and there assume to himself the judgment according to the imperial command. Then the consul, according to the imperial command, bound the blessed John, the Apostle, with chains, and brought him to Rome and announced his arrival to Domitian, who, being indignant, gave command to the Pro-Consul that the holy John should be placed in a boiling cauldron, in presence of the senate, in front of the gate which is called the Latin gate, when he had been scourged, which was done. But, by the grace of God protecting him, he came forth uninjured and exempt from the corruption of the flesh. And the Pro-Consul, being astonished that he had come forth from the cauldron annointed but not scorched, was desirous of restoring him to liberty, and would have done so if he had not feared to contravene the royal command. And when tidings of these things had been brought to Domitian he ordered the holy Apostle John to be banished to the island called Patmos, in which he saw and wrote the Apocalypse, which bears his name and is read by us."

Passing out of the city at the Sebastian gate, we enter upon one of the most interesting rambles that can be taken outside the city walls. It is over the Appian Way, Paul's road into Rome when he came as a prisoner the first time. We were favored with a beautiful day for our ramble, and we passed over the road a distance of about five miles. The way is interesting, both because of its sacred associations and the ruins which line the road on both sides; but to Paul, if he were traveling the road at the present day, it would doubtless look gloomy enough.

Soon after leaving the gate we come on the left to the tomb of Geta, the murdered brother of Caracalla, and next on the right the tomb of Priscilla. These tombs are all either pyramidal or circular in shape, rising to a height of thirty or forty feet. Most of them have been standing for seventeen or eighteen centuries. Next of interest by the way is the church of "Domine, Quo Vadis," so called because a Romish tradition says that Peter, in fleeing from Rome, met the Saviour at this point and asked him, "Domine, Quo Vadis?" and was answered, "Venio Iterum Crucifigi," whereupon Peter returned to his doom. The exact spot (?) where the Lord stood is now marked by a round stone.

Passing several unknown tombs, we come to the tomb of the one supposed by some authorities to be that of the famous Raven which, in the reign of Tiberius, was so much of a favorite because of the homage he was accustomed to pay to the Emperor and Druses, that when killed by a shopkeeper near the Forum, received a very pompous public funeral. There are numerous catacombs both to the right and left of the road. They all present the same general appearance, underground chambers for the burial of the dead. In this respect they are unlike the catacombs under Paris, for these did not originate in quarries, but were made for, and were used only for, burial purposes. There are said to be not less than sixty different catacombs around Rome. The old Romans had a queer custom of burying their dead by the sides of their most noted roads. In Paul's day the Appian Way was the most celebrated road into Rome, coming from Brundusium, now Brindisi, and entering Rome on the south.

The most perfect of the tombs existing in the space we traversed are, first, the round fortress-like tomb of Cecilia Metella. It was erected in 79 B. C., and like the tomb of Hadrian within the city, has been utilized as a fortress in years gone by. It is a massive structure 70 feet in diameter and about 100 feet in height. Before reaching this tomb we come to the tomb of Romulus, son of the Emperor Maxentius, who died A. D. 300, and close to it are the remains of the circus consecrated by Maxentius to the memory of his son ten years after his death. To the right of the road, about a mile further on, are the three tumuli of the Curiatii, marking the place where the combatants fell. From this point on, looking ahead of us, the road makes its way straight as an arrow, until we see it climbing the western slope of the distant Alban hills. The author of "Rambles in Rome" claims that the site of the Appii Forum and the Three Taverns lies at the ninth mile stone from the Porta Capua within the walls. In this, however, he is contradicted by some other authorities, which locate it at the forty-third milestone. From this ramble we return to the city over the new Appian Way, crossing to the Latin Way to examine the Painted Tombs, a recent discovery.

Another day we take our way to "St. Paul's Without the Walls," not the largest, but withal the gem of all of Rome's beautiful and costly churches. The original church, destroyed by fire in 1823, was erected by Constantine to commemorate the martyrdom of St. Paul. It has been restored on a scale of magnificence almost bewildering. Internally it is one vast hall of marble work. The four pillars that support the altar canopy are of pure alabaster, and the altars at each end of the transept are of malachite, the gift of the Czar of Russia. A marble staircase leads down to the crypt under the high altar, where the relics of Paul and Timothy are said to be entombed. Outside the gable facing the Tiber is done in mosaic, occupying thirteen years in its execution, the work of the Vatican mosaic manufactory. It is one of the handsomest pieces of decorative art we have ever seen.

From this church we follow the Ostia road out a half mile, and turning to the left follow the Tres Fontanes road until we reach the place where, according to Romish tradition, Paul suffered martyrdom. The place is called Tres Fontanes, because when Paul's head fell to the ground it rebounded three times, and there sprang forth from the places touched by the head in its rebounds three springs. Whether the place is the genuine site of Paul's decapitation or not, it is, nevertheless, worth a visit. It is situated in a pleasant little dell in which is a triangular shaped garden, surrounded on its three sides by three old Romish churches, in one of which—the one at the far end of the triangle—are the miraculous springs, from which we took a refreshing drink, and with a pilgrim's devotional fondness, regarded the spot whereon Paul knelt to receive the stroke which gave him his glory crown. The Romish church possesses a wondrous knowledge (?) in reference to such places; it points out the place where Paul and Peter separated on their way to martyrdom, and has erected a large church upon the place of Peter's crucifixion.

A visit to Rome would be incomplete without an excursion to Tivoli and Hadrian's Villa. Tivoli is distant from Rome fourteen miles, and is reached by steam tram. The iron road leads us through the meadows once used by Hannibal as a camping ground. Tivoli being situated at quite an elevation above the Campagna, our iron horse is under the necessity of making the ascent by frequent tacks upon the hill slope, in doing which we pass through some fine old olive groves. The town is visited chiefly on account of its beautiful cascades. By reason of flood dangers the Anio was diverted from its own channel and led by a tunnel through the lofty hill on the slope of which the town sits, and left to throw itself down a precipice 300 feet in height. In its descent it strikes a rock which breaks it into spray. It is beautiful to look upon from the bottom of the gorge into which it is thrown; excelled in grandeur only by our own Niagara, and that alone in the volume of its water. There is a smaller cascade, also, and a half mile distant from the town the spacious ruins of Hadrian's Villa; all well worthy of a visit.

These pleasant, balmy, Italian days, how we enjoy them in our foot rambles in and around the city! We have an opportunity in a ramble to the north of the city to-day to see how rapidly New Rome is springing up outside the walls. There is more building going on at the present time, both within and without the walls, than in any of the European capitals we have yet visited. The old Mistress of the World appears to be rousing herself from her sleep of centuries, and rising again into somewhat of her former splendor and power.

Here and there in a dozen different places Egyptian obelisks are occupying church and public squares, numbers of which were brought hither and reared by Domitian, Constantine and other early Roman Emperors. Here on Monte Cavallo is an exquisite piece of workmanship by Phidias and Praxiteles; a pair of colossal horse tamers with their plunging steeds in marble, a present of King Tiradates to Nero. It is not certain whether they are intended to represent Castor and Pollux, or Alexander and Bucephalus. They stand in front of the King's palace on the Quirinal.

Here again is an elaborate work of art in the fountain of Trevi. The cooling waters of this fountain are drawn through the Claudian aqueduct, the arches of which we saw stretching out toward the Alban hills on the day of our Trivoli excursion. Fresh and sparkling do these waters look as they come gushing forth from the nostrils and mouths of Neptune's floundering steeds, as well as from a hundred crevices on all sides, and pouring over precipices in cascade form. Take a parting draught and throw in a sou, for the tradition is that then the traveler will return to Rome, no matter what obstacles beset his path.

Another place of pleasant resort and drive is the Pincio Gardens. We are reminded of Nebuchadnezzar's famous hanging gardens at Babylon as we stand at its northern or western side and look over the wall, a full seventy-five feet in height, down to the street below.

We spend portions of several days among the ruins of the old Roman Forum. There is too much of Roman history connected with this mass of ruins to give it only a casual study. The excavated area covers an extent of about nine acres. Here are great marble and granite pillars, erect and prostrate, of temples, palaces and senate halls; the triumphal arch of Septimus Severus, almost perfect, the Sacred Way, part of the pavement of which still remains, all of which carries us back to the earliest beginnings of Rome's checkered history. At this spot, on the northern edge of the Forum, stood the butcher's stall where Virginius seized the knife and saved his daughter's honor by her death. And here is the Curtian Marsh where, according to

IN THE FORUM LOOKING TOWARD THE CAPITOL.

the legend, Marcus Curtius and his steed made the wonderful plunge into the dark chasm as a votive offering to the gods; and close to it is Cæsar's tomb. And here again at the northern side is the site of the old Senate building, down the steps of which poor old Servius Tullius was hurled to his death.

Upon the side of the Palatine to the south of the Forum are visible the ruins of the Palace of the Cæsars, and farther east the arch of Titus, and still farther on, and to the south, we see the arch of Constantine, whilst at the extreme northeast corner of the Forum, Rome's greatest of wonders, the Colosseum, raises its huge proportions into view; "A noble wreck in ruinous perfection," one has said. What history gathers around the old walls! Could they speak they would doubtless tell us of the heartaches, sighs and tears of those captive Jerusalem Jews, as they labored in its construction; they would tell us of the times when they had held an hundred thousand people to witness some fierce gladiatorial combat or naval fight; for it was so constructed that the Tiber could send its waters into the arena. Or, they could tell us the story of that day when St. Ignatius was brought hither from Antioch and fed to the wild beasts in this very arena; or give a blood-curdling recital of how many others of the martyrs fought their last battles here and gained their glory crown. The Colosseum could give seats to 87,000 people and standing room to 13,000 more. There were eighty arches of entrance by which the building could be emptied in ten minutes. The Romans take a pardonable pride in the old ruin, and are constantly putting a clamp here, or a stone there, to keep time from wearing it out.

But there is yet an object of great interest in Rome to which we pay a visit. It is the ruins of Nero's Golden House. It is found on Esquiline hill, about a fourth of a mile from the Colosseum. Into the dark underground halls and apartments wandering around in the catacombs to find one's way through the long halls and rooms of this once sumptuous palace. There a small company of us are lighted by an attendant. It is like are numerous apartments yet to be excavated. Our guide lengthens out his bamboo torch and thrusts it up to the ceilings as we traverse some of the corridors in order that we may see the height and fresco colorings; the ceilings of the long halls are thirty feet in height, and the frescoings are in places as fresh as though they were but a few years, instead of many centuries, old. A triple portico, a mile in length, in Nero's time surrounded this vast palace, with a height sufficient to allow a colossal statue of Nero 120 feet high to stand in it. This statue was afterwards removed to the Colosseum, where its pedestal is still to be seen. The palace surrounded a large square containing a lake, vineyard, pastures and woods containing animals, wild and tame. In the palace itself the supper rooms were vaulted, and the ceilings were made to revolve and scatter flowers and breathe perfumery upon the guests.

It is worth while to wander through these now silent and deserted halls and remember their former glory, and the might and royal splendor of him who built them, and learn to what ruin all terrestrial glories, ourselves included, must finally be reduced; and then, if never before, resolve to lay foundations upon which a temple of holy character may be built against which the decadence of time shall have no effect.

CHAPTER IX.

FAREWELL TO ROME.
LIFE AROUND THE BAY OF NAPLES.

ERE leaving Rome we have yet a ramble or two in which the reader may feel some interest. It must not for a moment be supposed that we have attempted to bring within the compass of this brief record of a month's busy life in Rome all that was of interest to ourselves, or which might have proved of interest to the general reader. To have done this would far have exceeded the limits necessarily placed on this simple record.

We must yet see the interior of the Vatican, with its wonderful stores of art, as well as the old Castle of St. Angelo. For both of these places we must have a special permit, which will admit us on certain days of the week when the visitors are likely to be numerous enough to warrant the use of special guides. Let us halt a moment on this fine old bridge as we cross the Tiber to St. Angelo and the Vatican. It is now the oldest, as well as the finest, of the bridges in use at Rome. It was built by the Emperor Hadrian. Its parapet is decorated by the figures of ten angels in marble, almost black with age, holding in their hands the instruments of our Lord's passion. Just beyond the bridge is the Castle. With its white Paros marble covering and adornment of statues of gods and heroes, it must have stood par excellence in its original beauty. But now its beauty is a thing of the past. It is still majestic in its proportions, and interesting as a relic of Rome's palmier days. It was built A. D. 130 by Hadrian as a tomb for himself, and as such it was doubtless used. Sometime in the fifth century it was turned into a fortress, and is now used as a barracks. Crowning its top is a figure of Michael the archangel in the act of sheathing a sword; the tradition is, that at the close of a sore pestilence Gregory the Great saw the angel standing on the top of the fortress sheathing his sword as a sign that the pestilence was stayed; hence the figure on the top.

There is no beauty exteriorly in the Vatican building. It is a mass of scattered buildings resembling more a large factory or soldiers' barracks than the residence of the sovereign pontiff of the papal hierarchy. But its interior features will redeem its exterior ugliness. The visitor's approach is up a marble stairway of such length and breadth and beauty as to make us conscious that here, notwithstanding the deceptive appearance of things on the outside, are to be found palatial glories not excelled perhaps anywhere else in the world. Red-plumed policemen, the Pope's own, are scattered here and there in the halls and corridors to both watch and guide the visitor. When one remembers that according to the lowest estimate there are 4,422 rooms in the Vatican, he will see the necessity of some help in his wanderings through them.

Our first visit is to the Sistine chapel, famous the world over for the marvelous fresco paintings by Michael Angelo. On the ceilings, which occupied twenty months in the painting, are representations of nine Old Testament scenes pertaining to the creation, fall, deluge, and lives of Noah, Jonah, and other Old Testament prophets. Here also on the end wall is "The Last Judgment," Angelo's masterpiece, requiring eight months for its painting. To give anything like an adequate description of this fresco would require the half of this chapter. Eight rooms are devoted to the works of Raphael, in one of which we find his masterpiece, "The Transfiguration," multiplied a thousand fold in copies throughout the world. In the court of the Belvedere we find the Laocoon group, a wonderful piece of statuary, the work of three artists in combination. Here are long halls filled with busts, statues, etc., of early Greek and Roman art; Etruscan and Egyptian museums filled with vases, sarcophagi, and other relics of these ancient people. In a magnificent hall 220 feet long we find the Vatican library of 120,000 volumes, 25,000 of which are manuscript. But here we must find an end to the description of what cannot be described. It must all be seen, if a proper conception of the treasures of this wonderful palace would be had.

Leaving Rome at 8:05 o'clock a. m., we are at Naples at 2:30 p. m. "See Naples and die," I quote to friend H——, as we move out of the depot towards the "Belleview," where we have decided on a temporary stay. "I'll not do it," he answers, "for I want to see Egypt and the Holy Land yet, and—well, yes, I think I'd like to get as far back as home before I die." "As to seeing Naples, I'm glad I am here, for every prospect pleases, and"—dodging around as he spoke some dirty lazarones who lay sprawled out on the pavement sunning themselves—"only man is vile." Truly, there are few places on earth that can afford such luxury of scenery as this around the Bay of Naples. Under these sunny skies, and in the presence of a panorama of beauty nowhere excelled, life passes very sweetly, and we shall be loth to quit so pleasant a region for the dangers of the sea and the desolate dreariness of the sacred lands whither we journey. But there is a Neapolitan side to the one of natural beauty which this region presents, which is not so entrancing. Here the cabman flourishes in all his native duplicity. He is so concerned about you lest you weary your limbs with a little walking that he will follow you around with argument and entreaty, and having prevailed upon you, by fair promises and low fare, to take a seat in his trap, you are fairly caught, and will not get leave to go thence until he has extracted from your pocket double or treble his legitimate fare. He understands you perfectly at the beginning, but at the end he does non capisco at all. He is altogether in ignorance of the precepts of the moral law, and although in the presence of a constant reminder of how awful may be the pit of destruction in the other life for beings of his kind, he heeds not the warning of the smoking monster in view, but plies the next unwary pilgrim with the same sort of arguments, and opens his trap as complacently as though he was doing the most virtuous thing in the world. Avoid him if you can, for his ways are deceitful.

And yet we have another type of Neapolitan character to describe, and although described as of the masculine gender, be it understood that the description applies as well to the feminine. His name is "Legion;" you will find him at your elbow wherever you go, by night or day, in all the cities and towns which surround the Bay. The omnipresent Neapolitan beggar; his is a character unique and solitary. The boy and girl, the man and woman, old and young, of the middle and lower classes, think it no degradation to stoop to beggary. We are surprised at seeing the methods which some of the population, quite respectable in dress, adopt to get from you something for nothing. In fact, it appears to be regarded as the most proper thing in the world to do, to draw from the foreign tourist as large a portion of his supposed superfluous wealth as is possible by every means and pretext imaginable. Some of the boy methods are quite novel as well as amusing. Only yesterday in our tour across the Bay to the Island of Capri were we a witness to some of these novel methods. The boys in their row boats surrounded our little steamer before starting, and standing up in their boats with hats and hands extended, joined in some kind of a rattling song, at the close of which they would take up their collection, and then start off on another one, continuing this until the steamer pushed away from them. At Capri the same performance with an amusing variation was repeated. Two of the little fellows in nature's garb offered to plunge into the sea after any coins which might be dropped into the water for them; this they did repeatedly, seldom failing to bring up the coveted coin. The sea water of the Bay, standing as it does over a volcanic bed, is of such transparency as to render distinguishable objects at quite a depth.

Capri itself is the torn remnant of an ancient volcano. It is distant from Naples about eighteen miles. It is quite a resort for artists, because of its picturesqueness. The main object of our visit thither is to see a very remarkable blue grotto. The only way to raech it is by sea, the cliffs at this point being a full one hundred feet in perpendicular height. Our steamer goes to the spot and is met by a little fleet of row boats, into which we are emptied and taken into the cavern. The entrance is on the water line, and is so low that only in a calm sea is it possible for boats to enter. We lay ourselves flat in the boats to save our heads, and are carried in on the top of a wave into a spacious chamber, where a scene of marvelous beauty reveals itself. The water is a light indigo blue in color, and is so transparent from the rays of light streaming into the cavern's mouth that we can see far down into its depths. Our little fleet moves about hither and thither, the boats sometimes coming into slight contact with each other as we near the farther end of the grotto where the light is not so brilliant. At the far end of the cavern we notice a man in almost nature's attire standing statue-like upon some rocks, and beyond him a dark opening, which we are told leads to another interesting part of the cave. The whole scene reminds us of the classic description of the river Styx and its ghostly boatman.

From the cliff road leading from the Port to the town of Capri one of the finest panoramic views imaginable is unfolded. One only mutilates it by an attempted description. Directly in front of us, shining white in the sunlight, is the city of Naples, or Napoli, as the Italian would say, rising tier upon tier like the seats of a great amphitheatre, while to its right, almost at the extreme end next to Cape Miseno, is the village of Posilippo. In this region is the tomb of Virgil, and the slope of the hill looking eastward is said to have been his farm. It is now cov-

FAREWELL TO ROME.   93

ered with villas and vineyards. Around the point still further to the westward we come to the port and town of Pozzuoli, the ancient Puteoli, mentioned in Paul's travels to Rome. Just back of Pozzuoli is the Solfatara, the crater of a still smoldering volcano.

Let me stop long enough in my description to tell of our visit to this interesting place. The entrance is made through the court of a hotel planted square across a made entrance into a desolate basin-shaped plain of about ten acres in extent, the rim of the basin being the ragged rock upheaved edges of the old crater. At the far end of the plain a cloud of vapory smoke is issuing out of the hillside through an opening resembling a cave's mouth, whilst all around the vapory steam is issuing forth from every crack and crevice. Our guide crawls into the main entrance and brings us out samples of sulphur, arsenic and alum deposits. Essaying to do as the guide has done, viz., to creep in on our hands and knees and explore the mysteries within, we are forced to back out in a nearly suffocated condition. There appears to be a great cauldron of boiling sulphur water at some depth unknown, whence issues a strong current of scalding hot steam which one receives into his face if he lifts his head but a foot in crawling in, together with strong sulphur fumes which are suffocating. Tapping the ground in various places, a hollow sound is given forth which plainly indicates the hollow condition of things underneath the feet. Next to Vesuvius this is the most interesting object for a visit in all this region.

Coming back to our description of the Bay panorama as viewed from Capri, looking to the right of Naples, close hugging the shore, are the towns of Portici, Resina, Torre del Greco, Torre del Anunciato and Castelamare, and as a background to them all, old Vesuvius raises his smoke and vapor crowned summit. Coming on around to the extreme right, the villages of Meta, Vito Equense and Sorrento are all visible on the cliffs next the seashore. It makes a picture worthy of an artist's skill. Mrs. H. B. Stowe has made Sorrento an object of much interest to visitors by her book, "Agnes of Sorrento." It is here that she obtains her characters and scenery for her interesting tale. It is a beautiful place in itself, with its deep gorges, orange orchards, and cliff-crowned situation. It is celebrated also as the birth place of Tasso, the historian. Here Marion Crawford, with whose writings we are so familiar at home, resides. Sorrento and Castelamare are favorite summer resorts for the Neapolitans, by reason of their sheltered position from the sun.

We have made a pleasant addition to our party in the person of a young artist from Hamilton, Ont., who is enjoying our Naples rambles with us. The trio of us have pleasant, home-like accommodations with an English lady—Madam Story—who imparts to us much information concerning Naples and vicinity, and who furnishes us with all that is needful for the inner man at one dollar a day; and where dinner is taken elsewhere, at sixty cents a day.

From our room window at night we watch the flames as ever and anon they shoot up from the cone of Vesuvius. The desire has been growing upon us for several days past, as we have watched the old smoker and his nightly exhibition of fire works, to visit him. It is seven miles distant, as the crow flies, to the foot of the cone where the carriage way ends. We may go by carriage to the point just indicated, and then take an inclined railway up two thousand feet, walking from that point to the crater; or we may go by tramway around the Bay to Portici, thence on horseback or on foot in company of a guide up a very gradual ascent of two thousand feet. We choose the latter of the two ways as being far less expensive. We lose our artist friend in a crowd before we have yet taken a tram car, and supposing he has preceded us in another car, we lose no time in waiting for him. At Portici we are besieged by a score of guides, some with horses and others without. Selecting our guide, we commence our toilsome ascent.

FAREWELL TO ROME. 95

For a couple of miles our way leads through vineyards famous for the wine they produce. "Lacryma Christi"—tears of Christ—is the name given to the rare white wine here produced. Several times during the course of the ascent we are hailed by peasants with bottles and glasses who are ready to satisfy our thirst and curiosity by a draught of the precious beverage. Coming up out of the vineyard region, everything

STREET IN POMPEII.

wears a burnt, scoried look. These black rivers of lava that have poured wave after wave down the mountain side have left everything desolate in their course. Our sole leather suffers fearfully as we tramp on over the rough lava. Coming to the foot of the cone, an ascent of two thousand feet more at an inclination of about forty-five degrees through a loose black substance, like pepper grains, still lies before us. Here are men with ropes who want to pull us up; but we prefer to try our own muscle. Up a few hundred feet we discover the artist perched upon the shoulders of two men, who are exercising their muscle in the attempt to carry him to the top. But it is a sorry job for them. Our friend has heart disease, and is afraid to exert himself.

An hour of sweaty toil lands us on the summit, a ten minutes' walk from the crater. We halt awhile to rest and enjoy the panorama of sea and city spread out before us. "If the groaning monster beneath us should take a notion to heave, where would we land?" queried the artist. "It would be rather a rapid way of reaching kingdom come," said H——. Another ten minutes of circuitous climbing and we stand on the brink of the awful gulf where rage the fires which have caused all of this desolation around us. We peer cautiously over the edge to discover, if we can, the depths of this cauldron wherein the liquid lava is boiling and bubbling. The crater is filled with a vapory smoke, and it is only an occasional view that we can get far down the sides. At intervals of a few seconds there is a swell and a swish, and fire, lava and red hot stones are hurled up hundreds of feet into the air, most of it dropping back again into the crater with a noise resembling the air bubbles in a pot of mush nearly done. Oh the horrors of this pit of destruction! It makes us shiver as we stand looking down into its dark throat, where the panting of the restless monster is heard. If one would have a vivid idea of what horrors the pit of eternal woe may contain, let him contemplate the situation for a half hour amid the sulphurous fumes on the edge of the crater of Vesuvius. If all the furies of the pit had been at our heels we could not have made a more hasty retreat down the sides of the cone. Yes, it was undignified; but it had the merit of speed, and that, under the present circumstances, was more to us than dignity.

As we sit in Madam Story's comfortable apartments looking out at the flaming top of the old smoker we have been to see to-day, it occurs to us to compare expenses of the day's excursion with the artist. H—— and I find that our joint expenditure is a little less than two dollars, while the artist finds his to be $7.50. "So much for being able to help yourself," says H——.

Of course, like all other tourists who come to Naples, we must see Pompeii. A pleasant ride of an hour brings us to the place. Here we fall in with half a dozen Bostonians, and in their company set forth to investigate the silent city. We pay two francs each of an admission fee, which entitles us to a government guide. Here, as at Rome, there is a sort of premium put upon Sabbath sight-seeing, many such places of interest being free to the public on that day, whilst on week days a fee is charged.

A city, but no people; an anomaly among cities surely! One can hardly avoid the feeling as he passes into the deserted houses that he will be confronted by some of the inhabitants with a "Wherefore do you intrude" salutation. Its fine temples are no longer frequented by the worshiper; its beautiful palaces no longer echo to the tread of their owners; and the once crowded amphitheatre and places of amusement wait in vain for the lovers of pleasure. The little green lizards have taken possession of the ruins; and eye you as an intruder, or, scared at your presence, scamper off into crevice homes. The roofs being flat and made of wood, are all gone, broken in by the weight of ashes and pumice stone that buried the city. The walls and subdivisions of the houses remain in a marvelously well preserved condition. There are many fresco paintings on the walls as fresh in their colorings as though put on but a decade or two ago; many of them in rooms kept locked, which it had been much more to the honor of the Pompeians if they had never wasted time and debased art and soul in painting. Here in one room into which we look is the skeleton of a woman left by the excavators just as it was found. At another point we enter a bakehouse and peer into an oven out of which was taken, as late as 1862, eighty-two loaves of bread, reduced to a carbonized state, and now seen in the museums at Naples and Pompeii. In the kitchen of this same house a sucking pig was found in the stewpan; it also is found in the museum. "Surely," said H——, "although the Pompeians were evidently very wicked people, yet they had the 'straight and narrow way' among them; for most of these streets are only about six feet

BAKER'S OVEN, BREAD, AND FLOUR MILLS.

wide. There is one street eleven feet in width, not including the narrow raised foot-walk on either side. In the narrow streets the chariot wheels, running in the same tracks for long years have worn deep gutters in the hard lava pavement.

Thus passes the day at Pompeii; a novelty in the line of sight-seeing such as we shall not find anywhere else. We have enjoyed the company of our Boston friends, and together we journey back to Naples. Darkness has fallen over us before we make our start homeward, and the lamps of Posillipi, Naples, Torre del Greco, and Torre del Annunziata, in great semi-circle around the Bay, carry us back in memory to boyhood days, when the night fires on the prairies seemed to border the whole circle of our vision. It formed a picture worthy of the beholder's admiration. We have enjoyed Neapolitan life and climate immensely; but all good things come to an end, sooner or later, and we are now ready for the next stage of our journey over a thousand miles of sea to the land of the Pharaohs.

CHAPTER X.

IN THE LAND OF THE PHARAOHS.

THE traveler who goes to Naples—or Napoli, as the natives call it—and who desires a quiet English home for a couple of weeks or longer, will do well to look up Madam Story. For years she has given her attention to the entertainment of travelers who intend to make a protracted stay in the city. When we said our last good-bye to her she was located in a fine new building with a good sea view, at 190 Rione Amedeo. We have made some very pleasant acquaintances at Naples, among whom are Mr. Fletcher—an author of some note—and his lady; Rev. Irving, pastor of the Scotch Free Church Mission, and his excellent wife, in whose company many pleasant hours of converse and visitation have been enjoyed. Upon all these we turn our backs with regret when we board our vessel for Egypt.

Our divided company is again one, with an addition of three others, two ladies and one gentleman. Our steamer is the "Arabia," an Italian vessel of 3,000 tons burden, bound for Alexandria. We leave our artist friend at Capri. A delay in departure caused by the lateness of the mail from Rome, affords us another opportunity of witnessing the beautiful crescent of light that stretches to right and left around the Bay for miles. It is under a bright moon-lit sky, a glassy sea around us, and a light encircled Bay, that we draw anchor and put out to sea. Who that has ever left the Port of Naples under such circumstances can forget the scene? It is noon the next day when the Lipari Islands are sighted and a light vapory smoke is seen issuing from the top of Mt. Stromboli; the mariner's lighthouse it is sometimes called, for its red flame can be seen at night far out at sea, and gives warning of a near approach to the Sicilian coast. At this point we make the discovery that our famous countryman and poet, Will Carleton, and his wife, are fellow voyagers. They leave us at Messina for a few weeks of touring in Sicily. We have a few hours on shore at Messina, long enough to look the old town over and lay in a good stock of fine oranges for the voyage; they are very cheap here, about five cents a dozen.

Just after leaving Messina, to our left on the Italian coast, is the town of Reggio, the ancient Regium, to which Paul came after leaving Melita, or Malta. It is a bright looking town, as viewed from the deck of the steamer. A little later the smoking cone of Mt. Etna is seen in the distance, but it is long after nightfall before we enter the harbor of Catania, and we do not get as plain a vision, owing to darkness and clouds, as we would like to have enjoyed of this destructive giant.

On our second day out we are passing through the mingling waters of the Adriatic and Mediterranean, and we are tossed in rough waves. The promenaders are scarce; "All gone to bed," H—— says. It is certain we are almost alone on the deck. "It was in these waters," I remark, " that Paul's sail vessel was caught by the stiff breeze coming down the Adriatic and drifted southward to Malta and wrecked." A look of sudden intelligence shot athwart the clerical countenance of my friend as he exclaimed: "Now I know why Paul and his company fasted so long—fourteen days, wasn't it? All seasick, just like ourselves, couldn't eat;" and as the vessel gave a sudden lurch to one side, nearly throwing us off our perpendicular, he added: "This sea seems not to lose any of its power with age, for it is still strong enough to take the heart and stomach out of a fellow."

We come abreast of Candia, the Crete of Paul's time, on the third day. It was here that Paul desired his ship's company to winter. The island is a rocky, barren looking one from our point of vision. From the lighthouse on its eastern end we are just one day's steam from Alexandria, so the sailors tell us; but in our case at least we are several hours more than that. It is in the early morning of the fifth day that the feathery-headed palm trees stretching along the shore for miles southward of Alexandria are first sighted. Glad vision it is, too; for we have long had our hearts set on a visit to this land of the Orient. Pompey's Column comes next into view, and soon we drop anchor in the harbor of Alexandria. We must now introduce to the reader a fellow pilgrim whose acquaintance we have formed on the vessel; a Hawkeye like the rest of us, and of such a genial mold that we forthwith adopt him as a member of our party; and henceforth in this narrative he will be designated simply by his initial, R——.

What a novel scene presents itself to our Occidental eyes as the gang stairs are dropped for disembarkation. We are hemmed in on all sides by as comic a looking crowd as European ever saw around him.

There they are, those dark-hued natives of the soil, red-capped and turbaned, yellow, blue and white colored garments mingled up promiscuously, and some of them with little more than nature gave them to commence existence with. They want something, that much is very evident as we stand leaning over the rail contemplating the movements of the little row boat fleet. Down drops the landing stairs, and it is instantaneously evident that we are to be boarded and taken by storm. The top of the stairs is guarded by seamen who use with seamen's agility and energy a rope's end on the heads and bare limbs of the dusky crowd, but all to no purpose; some are halted, but others are aboard, and hand luggage is grabbed from our hands and dropped into boats, and the owner follows, of course, as soon as he can, and at the risk of an impromptu ducking must clamber from one boat into another until he forms a union with his captured luggage. Everybody is excited; the boatmen shouting and gesticulating for passengers, and the passenger shouting his inquiries, which nobody heeds. Just at our side an Arab hotel runner and a boatman are engaged in a hand to hand struggle over some baggage, which is finally secured by the hotel man and tossed into our boat. When we put foot safely on land we have time to collect our senses, and then understand plainly that the wherefore of it all is, that our Arab friends are very glad to see us, and the demonstration is in our honor. We feel gratified, but are very glad it is not to be repeated immediately.

A day suffices to see the sights of Alexandria. A guide who rejoices in the cognomen of "Liverpool Jack" engages a couple of carriages and pilots us to Pompey's Pillar; next, a drive along the Mahmoudiah Canal among the palm groves to a beautiful garden belonging to the Khedive's officers; next, to the catacombs, where some of the party enjoy the novelty of a boat ride on an underground lake; ending up with a visit to the Pasha's palace. Thus we pay our hasty respects to Alexandria, and are off next morning early for Cairo.

A railway 141 miles in length connects the two cities. Some of us are anxious to make a closer observation of oriental life than we would have opportunity of doing if we took compartment carriages, and so take third-class tickets, fare $2.50, and ride with the natives in a car with seats ranged lengthwise. "Look at these tickets," said H——. "They look as though the quails with their muddy feet had tracked all over the pasteboard out of which they are made." Our friend was alluding to the Arabic characters on the tickets.

It is only the middle of February, and yet these fields of white clover, favay and wheat, are within a few weeks of harvest time. Between the novelties inside and the strange oriental features outside, our eyes and senses have a rich feast all the way. The character of the country for the first thirty or forty

STREET IN CAIRO.

miles after leaving Alexandria is flat and marshy, but there is a decided improvement as we near the Rosetta branch of the Nile. "I would like to have one of those plows," said R——, who has been watching the fellahs in their rural occupations. "I would have all the museums in the country after it, for it is certainly the likeness of nothing else in all the upper or nether world." "We Americans," said H——, "could improve vastly on that method of plowing by turning a drove of swine into the field." See that white, long-legged bird following the fellah in his rooting operations! It is the white ibis, sacred to the god Osiris, and no fellah will harm him unless by accident. The people all appear to live in villages which thickly line the way; but for some reason they are afraid of the railway, and keep at a respectful distance from the stations. These villages are composed largely of low mud, or sun dried brick houses, and appear to have no order of arrangement.

Our near approach to Cairo is indicated by a sight of the Pyramids away to our right. How natural they look! just as we have had them pictured in our mind ever since boyhood's days. But our journey is accomplished after seven hours' ride, and we are dropped down in Cairo. And now we are face to face with another lot of our friends.

Carriage men are few, but hotel runners and donkey boys are almost as thick as frogs once were on a certain occasion in this stricken land. The donkeys are coming at us from all directions, not all of them headforemost, but backed in on us until we are completely captured and must mount one of the diminutive little creatures, or stand where we are. It is all done good naturedly, and we have not the ill grace to quarrel with the poor fellows who are doing their level best to earn their daily bread. In this particular they are ahead of their class in southern Italy, who prefer to beg it rather than to give any sort of compensation for existence.

R—— and self decide on a donkey trip to Heliopolis to see the ruins of the famous "City of the Sun." We go to a square where our friends, the donkey boys, are congregated, and as soon as our object is known the tail ends of a score or more of the little animals are pointed in our direction. We try to still the tumult long enough to make a bargain, but our friends are so enthusiastic at our appearance that they catch us up bodily and set us down upon the backs of a couple of the animals. R——, being the better looking of the two, is wanted by other animal owners, and is hauled off his animal and set upon another, whilst I, being a modest fellow, am covered with blushes at such unsought honors, and hastily dismount and seek the pavement as a refuge. R—— not liking his animal, does the same thing, followed by a half dozen donkey men. After a little parleying we essay once more to mount our animals, but again the donkey man, ever careful lest we over-exert ourselves, lifts us off our feet and sets us astride a couple of the animals, which are not the ones we want. Despairing of overcoming the enthusiasm of our friends by ourselves, we ask the aid of a policeman, and we are soon galloping off through a narrow and crowded street with a couple of the blue-gowned donkey men running behind us plying the rears of our animals with a stick. But at this stage of the journey R——'s donkey must needs make a somersault, causing our friend to make an unceremonious bow to the audience, not just the most graceful perhaps, but considering the haste with which it was done, quite overpowering.

As we journey out into the country we notice the process of water raising from the canals for irrigation purposes. There are three methods in use; the ladle, manipulated by two men with a rope, the well sweep, and water wheel methods. Look at that lean looking kine, hitched to the end of a sweep and going round in circles! You see him in use everywhere in this country. He is not the ordinary Egyptian steer, but Egyptian buffalo, a sort of domesticated animal which has existed in Egypt since the time of the earliest Pharaohs. He will not stop at the edge of a stream to drink, but will go down into it to wallow. Now we understand what Pharaoh meant when he saw in his dream the "Seven lean kine coming up out of the water." It was only in Egypt that Pharaoh could have had such a dream. And there goes the water carrier of Egypt!

WATER-WHEEL.

bending under the weight of a large goat skin filled with the Nile water. He looks as natural as he did years ago in his picture. Look at all these people, young and old, on the streets, along the highway, in the Arabic and Coptic villages, everywhere you meet the common class of people, all sucking at, and chewing sugar cane! It is one of the main articles of diet with the poorer people.

Six miles to the northward of Cairo is the site of the old "City of the Sun," On, or Heliopolis. The ride to it from Cairo is over a fine road beautifully shaded with acacia and mimosa trees. En route we pass the Palace of Koobah, built by Ismail Pasha for his son. In this region are some fine gardens and plantations filled with palms, vines, orange and lemon trees; everything growing in rich profusion, being kept well irrigated by the waters of the Nile close at hand. Next we come to the Virgin's Tree, an old sycamore under which, if we may trust the tradition, the Holy Family rested for a night in their flight out of Judea from Herod's wrath. A little farther on and we come to the obelisk of Heliopolis. Its mates—and there were many of them in the days when the sun worshippers paid homage to their god in the great temple—have all long since disappeared; many of them are in Rome, some in Paris and one in New York City. The obelisk now standing is said to be the oldest in Egypt. It bears the name of Osirtasen I., who was the second King of the XII. dynasty. It stands sixty-eight feet in height, six feet square at the base, made of one solid piece of red granite. The city itself, where Moses and Joseph, Plato and Heroditus, lived and studied, is only a heap of dust ruins, covering an area of twenty acres. The little mud village of Matareeyeh watches over the grave of its illustrious ancestor.

"I think I must be rapidly nearing Paradise," said H——, in an ecstasy of feeling, as we were taking a ramble in the Esbekiah garden one morning shortly after our arrival; "the climate and surroundings seem to indicate that perfection is reached in both respects; and this garden! did you ever see anything to equal it? Music and flowers, fairy grottos with pouring waters, lakelets, pepper and banyan trees, and trees with long pendant fruit like window weights, for which we cannot find a name. I never saw a man that was satisfied with the weather before, much less with his other surroundings, but I have nothing more to desire in these respects." "Alas, poor man!" said R——, who had seen some of the vanities of Cairo, and whose memory was full of donkey and dog experiences,

EASTERN WATER SELLER.

"I think you are growing a little too worldly minded, your mind —as it were—too easily captivated by the carnalities of this life. As for me, I'll take my Paradise where night is not made hideous by the eternal bark of these Cairo canines." "And you wouldn't mind leaving out the donkeys too?" I suggested. But R—— is a little sensitive on the donkey question, and so we make no further allusion to his humiliating experience.

In Cairo, as in other places, we have adopted the apartment method of living, with a little variation; we run our own culinary department. Our cuisine exactly suits us, for we can purchase anything we want on the market, and our little oil stove puts things into edible shape in good style. Here is a hint for the traveler who is possessed of more ambition to travel than he is of money to gratify said ambition. Hotel expenses in Cairo would be from three to four dollars per day; whilst we are enjoying all that is essential to health and comfort at an expense of seventy-five cents each per day. The little donkey with his large saddle and blue cotton gowned driver furnishes an easy and economical method of making numerous excursions in and around the city; and donkey and driver by the day will cost a dollar, more if you will give it; for an Arab is much like other folks in this respect, he will take all that he can get.

CHAPTER XI.

UNITED PRESBYTERIAN MISSIONS IN EGYPT.

WE are not long in Cairo until we make the acquaintance of the United Presbyterian missionaries, and with them pass a very pleasant Sabbath. We are conducted through the schools, and made acquainted with the details of the work. Their principal building is a fine stone structure facing the Esbekieh garden. Under the wise and zealous management of Drs. Harvey and Watson, and the devoted labors of their wives, the Misses Smith and Thompson, and other helpers, both native and foreign, the mission is proving a leavening influence that is felt not only in Cairo, but far up the Nile and over the Delta of lower Egypt. In the Cairo schools are gathered over four hundred scholars, many of them out of Moslem families, who are willing for the sake of better advantages which the mission affords to put their children under Protestant teaching. The missionaries tell us that there is a distinct understanding with the Moslem parents that their children shall be taught the cardinal truths of the Christian religion if they are sent to their schools. The natives distinguish between these missionaries and other so-called Christian sects by calling the former gospelers. They recognize the difference between a name and the living religious truth which the missionaries teach and enforce by their personal example.

UNITED PRESBYTERIAN MISSION BUILDING AT CAIRO.

In 1854 the United Presbyterians commenced mission work in Alexandria and Cairo with the view especially of reaching the large Coptic population of Egypt. The Copts are the real Egyptians. They have managed in some way, like the

Jews, to keep themselves distinct as a race from the alien bloods that have made Egypt so cosmopolitan in its character. These Copts, like the Armenians in Turkey, are distinguished for stronger intellectual force than the other native populations, and hence we find them occupying clerical and other positions of trust in the government, more numerously than the others.

Their religion is Christian in name, but it has lost, by reason of gross corruption, its vitality. It is more nearly Roman Catholic than Protestant. The higher orders of the clergy are forbidden to marry, the mass is recited in the ancient Coptic, which neither the priest nor the people understand. The priesthood of the church is composed of an ignorant, superstitious, and for the most part, an immoral class of men. But notwithstanding these lamentable deficiencies, it is a church which is more accessible to pure evangelical truth than any other of the oriental churches; and our missionary agencies have been most wonderfully blessed in the regenerating efforts put forth.

The wisdom of separating the denominations in their mission work in Turkey, Holy Land and Egypt, giving each a clear field, and avoiding the evil experienced in other parts of the orient, of confusing the mind of the oriental with the different shades of doctrine, practice and name, and all understood to be Christian, is very easy to be seen in the success that has attended the work in Egypt. It was surely the hand of an all wise Providence that led to the withdrawal of our missionary force in Syria, leaving the work there in the hands of the Irish Presbyterians, with whom it had jointly been undertaken, and concentrating in Egypt. It was not until twelve or thirteen years of missionary labor in Egypt, full of trial and hardship, but with bright signs of promise for the future, that this measure of concentration was effected.

The work then quickly expanded beyond the limits of the Delta, going up the Nile to the first cataract. The Fayoum, Beni - Souef, Osiout, Assouan, and Luxor, with a large number of other towns and villages, a litttle removed from the Nile on both sides, were visited by the missionary with his books, in particular the Scriptures in Arabic, from the Beirout Mission press, and the leaven of the gospel began to work not only among that portion of the people who could read, but among the priests, and other influential persons in one way and another connected with the government. The Khedive Ismail himself became so far influenced in favor of the mission that he gave it its present beautiful location facing on the Esbekiah square, with 35,000 dollars of cash in addition.

In 1860 a dahabiyeh called the "Ibis" was put upon the Nile for the purpose of itinerant work between Cairo and Luxor. Both men and means were lacking in order to the establishing of mission stations at strategic points up the river; in this boat the sick or wearied missionary of lower Egypt could take an up the Nile journey, carrying with him a stock of books, and scattering truth wherever he chose to halt, and thus keep himself active whilst recruiting his enfeebled body. Many thousands of Bibles and other books were scattered—sold—in this way. Competent persons to manage schools, and act as lay preachers, were converted and set to work in these capacities. Mission stations and schools grew on the hands of the missionaries almost beyond their ability to supply them, until in 1879 there was a force of 22 foreign missionaries, male and female, and 98 native helpers at work. Four central stations, and 35 out stations were occupied. Two thousand pupils had been gathered into the schools, and 1,000 communicants into the church organizations. And another fact in this connection which may well put to shame the benevolence of the richer membership of the churches in America, the contributions averaged more than $6.00 a member annually.

The statistics above given are for the sake of comparison with those of the present year, 1896, in order that we may understand how that the showers of blessing have continually descended upon this mission, making us almost to realize that the latter

UNITED PRESBYTERIAN MISSIONS IN EGYPT. 115

days are upon us, long foretold, when "Princes shall come out of Egypt; Ethiopia shall soon stretch out her hands to God."

The 22 foreign missionaries have grown to 42; the 98 native helpers to 401; the whole number of stations from 35 to 190. Out of 37 organized congregations, 25 of them have native pastors; two of these congregations are self supporting, and yet others will soon reach self support. The communicants have grown from 1,000 to 5,004; there were received on profession alone during the year beginning April, '95, and closing March,'96, 577. The average attendance at the Sabbath morning services is 9,729. The mission has now 125 Sabbath schools, with an enrollment of 6,222 scholars. There are 161 common and boarding schools, with 10,871 pupils. Over 62,000 books were distributed during the year '95-'96; of these 14,079 vols. were of the Scriptures. The total contributions by the natives for all purposes amounted to $47,244, an average per member of $9.44.

In their poverty, in a country where a day's wage for an ordinary laborer does not often exceed 20 cents, these people have given dollar for dollar sent to them from this country. At Assioot there is a theological training school, and at Cairo a theological seminary with eleven young men in training for the ministry. There is also at Assioot a medical dispensary, with Dr. V. M. Henry in charge. Over 14,000 cases were treated during the year. While the patients are in waiting a Bible reader reads out the gospel message, and thus healing for the soul as well as body is dispensed.

Now will the reader question for a moment that it was not the great Master's own voice who bid us enter this Egyptian field and thrust in the sickle into the ripening harvest? Or will the sceptic in regard to missions, whose eye may perchance scan the pages of this chapter, remain any longer in a doubtful mood as to whether foreign missions give any adequate return for the men and money spent upon them? We have only looked upon the surface, upon the visible results of this seed sowing of divine truth among a people that dig their rude plows into the richest soil on the face of the earth, and who would be as happy as any people on earth, if only they had the benefits of a Christian civilization and government. But who has mental vision keen enough to pierce the future and tell us what bearing upon Egypt's future the seed of the Kingdom now being scattered by so many willing, loyal hands is likely to have upon that fairest by nature of all lands?

If one could only see through the intricate problem of government, it would require much less of the keenness of mental vision to tell what is to come of all this. Egypt's rulers are not and have not been for centuries past in sympathy with their grand Master at Constantinople. They long for independence. It is humiliating to them in the extreme to realize that they belong, body and soul, to a tyrant who cares for neither, any farther than the mercenary use he may choose to make of them.

Beggared in his own domain, he sends his publicans down into the Nile valley to lay and collect a tribute which is heavy enough to crush the heart and courage out of a stronger people than the serfs of Egypt. He mortgages and pawns to foreign governments to keep himself from going into bankruptcy, and thus adds shame to humiliation in putting upon them the support of a foreign soldiery whose very presence is the token to them of serfdom and impotency.

This is their view of the matter; they long for the glorious days of Saladin, when the flag of a free and independent Egypt will once more float from the crest of their citadel crowned hill. Will Egypt be free? or will she become a part of the British empire? We hope the latter; for then our mission cause will have a protector, and Egyptian government in every way will be just, her native industries will be encouraged, and not taxed out of existence. Will the first be true? if so, will Islamism dominate and be the bitter foe to all that is Christian as it is in the realm of the Sultan proper?

Faith in the leadership of the great host of the Church militant must dominate in our own views of these perplexing questions; and faith, if it is anything, is rational. There are reasons why we believe that the conquering legions of the Cross will not end their work in Egypt until the great victory which will lay the whole of Egypt at the feet of our Prince be won.

In the first place, the axe has been laid at the root of Islamism in Egypt. It is dying in the presence of the more vital power of Christianity. Loyalty to Islamism there is none in Egypt, save among the Turks, who do not belong to the land. The Arab population hates too fiercely the oppression of Mohammedan rule to be very zealous in the faith of Islam. Education, knowledge of the Scriptures, and contact with our missionary agencies all through the land, have broadened their ideas, and tamed the Moslem fanaticism and prejudice towards the "infidel" which has characterized the race ever since the days of the Prophet. It is frequently said to the missionary, "Oh, you are a Protestant, I can believe you." "You believers in the Book will not lie like Christians. Ah! you are not Christians; you are Ingleze."

Said a Mahometan pasha to a lady principal of one of the Syrian schools shortly after the fearful massacres in 1860 in the Lebanon and Damascus regions, "Madam, such schools as yours, where you admit all sects, will make another massacre impossible."

Again, our cause, the cause of Christ, in Egypt must prosper because the land has been thoroughly prepared for it. English occupation, railroads, telegraphs, canals, and multiplied schools of a better grade, have stirred up the fallow ground of a country which, next to Greece, has stood well in the foreground of nations in its arts and sciences, its literature, philosophy, and the stronger qualities of character, courage and virtue. Its half effete systems of religion have had infused into them new life blood, the march of progress is onward and upward, and our missionary columns are in the very van of this movement, with the pillar of cloud, the evident token of God's presence, with them. The sinews of war, our sons and daughters, and our money, are ours to furnish; with our part done, why need we think of failure?

Fact is oftentimes more wonderful than fiction; and in the history of our mission work in Egypt it would be an easy matter to fill a volume with incidents having the variety of romance, adventure, the pathetic and ludicrous, all of which would be true in every detail. And we shall proceed to narrate one, the facts of which were given us by Mrs. Dr. Barnett, one of our earlier missionary ladies in Egypt, an incident which brought to our band of workers there, in days not so full of promise as they now enjoy, a fuller assurance that God was with them, working out His purpose of a blessing upon Egypt by ways and means which would never have entered their own minds.

It was early in the sixties, during the progress of the civil strife which very nearly rent in twain our national existence, that an Abyssinian woman and her little daughter were found living in Cairo, not far from the Shepherd hotel. The woman was dark as any of her race, but the daughter was fairer featured, and betrayed the European blood which ran in her veins. She was said to be handsome.

This woman, like Hagar of old, was set adrift with her daughter, her bottle of water and loaf of bread, when the fairer bride from over the sea took her place in the pleasant home in Alexandria.

The father's wish was still law with the cast off woman, and though much against her own inclination, each morning she led the little Bamba to the girls' mission school, at that time under the care of Misses Dales and Hart. She soon learned to read and embroider in gold and silver.

She heard the sweet story of old, how Christ came to help the helpless, and how His great love for sinners led Him to the cross and the grave, and her own hungering heart felt the throb of responsive love, and she yielded to the Saviour's claims upon her life.

She proved herself an apt, as well as gentle, scholar, and as soon as her attainments warranted it, she was given the

THE MAHAREEN BAMBA AND HER CHILD.

position of monitress in the school. Her mother easily became reconciled to the situation, and no obstacle to her continuance in the school was put in her way. She applied herself diligently to her duties, both as scholar and monitress. Her teachers often noticed with no small degree of interest their sweet-faced, intelligent pupil, and had expressed the hope to each other that they would be able to retain her in the school as a teacher. Their joy had been great when she first came to them and declared her faith in Christ.

In these oriental countries it is no uncommon thing for young native men to make use of their acquaintance with European ladies to forward their matrimonial designs by asking them to visit such and such places on a wife hunt for them. Sometimes their own lady relatives are sent upon the same mission. But Bamba was carefully guarded from such matrimonial dangers, for her teachers were bent on the accomplishment of a purpose of their own; they could not endure the thought of that blooming, gentle, young life being consigned to the dullness of harem life.

But whilst these good teachers were planning in the interests—as they supposed—of the mission, an all-directing Providence was planning better things for them. The widow of Runjeet Singh, the Lion of Lahore, king of the Punjab Province, India, came to England to visit her son, who was the pensioned guest of the British government, receiving $150,000 a year in lieu of his inherited sovereignty over the Punjab. While on her visit she died after making the Prince promise to return her body to India and have the royal funeral rites performed for it, which included its cremation. A rather reluctant consent on the part of the Prince was given to this, and he started from England en route to India via Egypt. His absence was only to be temporary, for he was in reality only a royal prisoner in England. His father, the Maharajah Runjeet Singh, came to the zenith of his power in the Punjab about 1838, but he died in the year following, and his kingdom gradually went to pieces, until in '49 it came under English rule. The now famous Koh-i-noor jewel was once the possession of Runject Singh. On the abdication of the Prince, Dhuleep Singh, it came into the possession of the English, where it now shines the brightest jewel in Victoria's crown. Prince Dhuleep Singh was brought, or came, to England. He was given rank next to the Prince of Wales, with whom he became very intimate, much to his detriment, as we shall see.

The Prince arrived at Alexandria, where he found himself compelled to wait the arrival of an Indian steamer. The route via Suez Canal was not then open. Whilst in waiting he visited Cairo. He had been trained in the Christian faith and believed himself a Christian. He was interested in the Christianizing agencies which he found at work in Cairo; and the operations of our mission did not long escape him. He called on the missionaries, visited the schools, and gave the mission a liberal donation. His spirit was under a shadow by reason of his affliction and his mournful mission to India. He found the mission rooms a pleasant place to while away some of his lonely hours; he went again and again. During one of his morning calls he startled Mr. H―― by saying that he wanted a Christian oriental wife, and did they not have in their mission some young lady of good family who would make him a suitable companion?

Mr. H―― rallied his confused senses enough to answer that girls of good families were taken away from their schools at an early age by fearful fathers lest wife hunters should find them out, their prospects in life be marred by gossip about their beauty or lack of charms, and after they had left the mission, they had little influence over them, unless happily the parents had become Christian.

"We have a little monitress," said Mr. H――, "in our school who is a jewel, but her parentage would not suit you." The Prince looked a little confused, for he had been taking some sly glances at Bamba during his visits, and he replied, "I want a wife from your school. I do not wish an English wife, nor do I want one from my own country."

The ever watchful Misses Dales and Hart had not dreamed of danger to their monitress from the Prince's direction, and when Mr. H—— hurried to them with the news, there was a little volcano of excitement; but they soon discovered that it was a wind which was wafting them good fortune, and they went at once to give the Prince the audience which he had requested.

The Prince did not need to ask, "Is she pretty?" for he had taken stolen glances enough to tell him this; but, "Is she a Christian? is she amiable, intelligent, and teachable?"

"She is all this," they answered, "and more; but she is a mere child, and unfitted to take upon herself such responsibilities as would fall to her lot as the wife of a Prince."

"All this that you have said," answered the Prince, "Is only so much in her favor, and I feel constrained to ask you to convey to her my request for an interview."

Bamba was requested to present to the Prince a piece of handsome embroidery, done by the girls of the school. With native grace she presented it, bending low and kissing the hand of the Prince. No suspicion of the state of the Prince's mind had as yet been given her, and fearing nothing from one in his position, her veil was not so carefully drawn as usual, and as she bent she disclosed the unsuspected loveliness of her face.

The Prince's heart had a true love smite, and he pressed his suit in true oriental style. The ladies were requested to make known to Bamba his wishes without delay. He left immediately on his voyage to Bombay. Bamba is soon informed that she has won the heart of a Prince. But she has no ambition to figure in such a romance; wealth or honors she craves not. She is contented in her humble sphere of usefulness until she can be better qualified for the life work she has in view. The ladies plead the Prince's cause as well as they were able, told her of the high honor the Prince was conferring upon her, of his Christian character, of the happy change it would make in her life, how unwilling they were to give her up, but that her interests would make them willing for almost any sacrifice. They did what they could to light the flame of love, but all in vain. Bamba listened to all, and then in her artless, simple style, made answer, "The Prince has honored me, but I cannot marry him, or even think of it. My life is consecrated; I wish to go to the benighted people of Abyssinia, my mother's country, and carry to them the light you have brought to us. I could not think of going to England, where

MAHMOUDIEH CANAL.

all is light. Oh, my ladies, I cannot do it, I cannot do it! I have prayed that I might live to accomplish some good work for my Jesus."

The Prince was detained in India, and the ladies plead on. It was explained to her that God had better ways of answering our prayers than in the ways we often wanted them answered;

that since it was in her heart to consecrate her life to her people's good, God was now opening up the way to wealth and position by means of which others better qualified to do this work than herself could be sent. Sometimes she would appear nearly won over to their way of thinking; and at other times would simply shake her head and say in a most pathetic manner, "It is all dark."

But at last the moment came when, raising her soft, tear suffused eyes to Miss Dales' face, she said, "I have decided to marry the Prince."

The Prince had given instructions that if she yielded to his suit, she was to be taken forthwith into the families of these ladies, dressed in European costume, servants should be employed, and everything arranged for her in a style befitting the sphere in which she should soon move. She must now eat with knife and fork; white bread, instead of the coarse brown loaf she had been accustomed to all her life, should be served to her. Her hair was to seek the top of her head; French heels and pointed toes were to be the style of shoes which should adorn her little feet.

The wealthy Alexandrian banker learned of the honor that had fallen upon his cast off daughter. He offered her the home she should have had from the first. Her mother urged its acceptance. Bamba accepted all these changes with modest grace, giving herself up like a piece of clay in the potter's hand to be molded as they saw fit. Her sweetness of disposition. without thought of conventionalities, made her manner and movements models of grace to the banker's family, and the society into which she was introduced. She had dropped into another world, a beautiful, sweet world, which seemed to have been made for her.

Prince Singh on returning learned with displeasure that she was in her father's home instead of being with the mission friends, as he had intended. Several weeks, according to the English law governing the marriage of foreigners, must elapse before the Prince could claim his bride. This interval he spent largely in the society of Bamba, teaching her English, and gathering a little Arabic from her. The wedding trousseau was being made by the most finished artists in Paris; whilst the most costly jewels were being got in readiness to adorn the person of the modest bride. The wedding day at length arrived. It was said the Prince was nervous, but the little bride went through the ordeal of a civil marriage first, and then the ceremony conducted by the English Episcopal minister, assisted by all of the American clergy, with a quiet grace and dignity as of one born to royal honors.

Partly out of interest in the good work our missionaries were carrying on, and also from a feeling of gratitude to the mission for the part it had taken in helping him to win his sweet young bride, the Prince on his wedding day gave to the mission a thousand pounds sterling in the name of his wife Bamba. A friend was won; and he was a friend who proved his worth in those years of need when the mission suffered from lack of funds occasioned by the civil war and the attitude of the Church on the slavery question. For many years in each balmy June month came the princely donation of $5,000. Here romance blends into beautiful history, where the hand of God can be distinctly traced. Since this first romantic episode in the history of the Egyptian Mission, there have been others of the mission school who, though bringing no such wedding fee to the mission, are proving remunerative investments elsewhere in the social and religious life of the orient.

The Prince took his wife to England. He had in some degree incurred the royal displeasure in marrying without counsel or consent of the Queen; but all was forgiven, and even the kiss of reconciliation bestowed upon the bride, when the Queen saw his fair Princess. It is said she loved her at first sight. On important state or social occasions with which the Queen and her household were connected, we are told that next to the Prince and Princess of Wales, position was given to our Prince of India and his wife. Our little Princess, in point of education, social culture, and general refinement, was all that her sphere and position required, for the Prince, when he asked "Is she teachable?" purposed to put these within her reach, if she had the talent of acquisition. She never forgot the dear friends of the mission, and ever spoke in deep gratitude that through their advice she had been enabled to realize her life ambition of doing good to her people in a far larger way than she had planned by herself.

The Prince, in addition to the annual gift already mentioned, sent out a printing press to the mission, besides loaning his dahabiyeh for use on the Upper Nile, so that the missionaries, by means of the printed page, schools, and preaching stations, might perchance open the gospel way clear into Abyssinia, and thus realize to the fullest the desire of their little Bamba.

It would be pleasant if we could end our story here by simply saying that these two lives so romantically blended together had lived on in their happy, peaceful and honored way, until the grim messenger had obtruded his unwelcome presence upon them; but we must follow them through trial and sorrow, even as we have followed them in their joys.

Sons and daughters grew up around them for a few happy years. The Prince was too intimate with the sportful heir to the British throne. He lost his fortune in gambling; and came to think himself harshly treated by the government. He brooded over his imaginary wrongs until, in an evil hour, he conceived the project of regaining the province which he had lost in India, and also of demanding the return of the Koh-i-noor jewel. He sold his personal effects, and with wife and daughters—his sons being in the English navy—sailed for India. He was stopped at Aden by an English man-of-war, and detained sometime. His wife and daughters were taken back to England, but the Prince went on to India. Here he renounced the Christian faith, and employed instructors in the Sikh religion.

It was his design to proclaim himself king, hoping to bring about a rebellion in his favor. His followers were few, and his project failed. England and Russia at this time were glowering at each other, and hostilities appeared imminent. The Prince hastened to St. Petersburg and tried to foment strife; in this also he was disappointed. At the Paris Exposition, 1878, he might have been found as a jewel merchant.

Battling with poverty and almost crushed with her misfortunes, not the least of which was her poor husband's apostasy from the Christian faith, the Princess was at length found by one of the Egyptian missionaries, who made known her destitute condition. Her wants were immediately supplied; but her health was broken, and she was soon at rest. Her faith wavered not, neither on her own account or her husband's. "I firmly believe," she said, "that my husband will return to the Christian faith, and will yet be saved."

The Prince married an American girl in Paris, after the death of his wife. But he tired of his exile, and made overtures of submission to the English government. He was forgiven, and his lands and income restored. One of his first acts after he returned to England, and after the restitution of his income, was the sending of £1,000 to the mission at Cairo in memory of the lamented Bamba, and with the gift the message, "I am yet a Christian." The Prince did not long enjoy his restored fortunes, but died, as it is said, in the Christian faith; thus reunited and exalted to positions even more honorable than those enjoyed on earth, they are safe from all dangers of apostasy, and evermore safe from the withering influences of misfortune.

Even as we write these lines comes the information from Cairo that Prince Victor, with his three sisters, son and daughters of Prince Dhuleep Singh and his wife, have made Cairo and the mission, during the last winter, a visit much enjoyed by the missionaries as well as themselves. It is to be hoped that they will take the same interest in the mission that their noble father and mother did.

CHAPTER XII.

CROSS AND CRESCENT.

THE observations we are now venturing upon do not belong, chronologically, at this point in our narrative; and lest the reader may think that we are venturing too prematurely upon reflections which our opportunities for observation do not warrant us in doing, it is well to state that it is after these countries over which the Sultan of Turkey holds rule have been traversed, and in the light of the bloody transactions that are filling the homes of oriental Christians with woe, that we have set ourselves to meditate upon these things.

Islamism and Christianity, nominal and real, are the two most potent factors at work in the Turkish Orient. They more or less dominate in all political questions. Church and State in the Turkish Empire are joined in a union that is indissoluble, save by the one force that dissolves all earthly ties. When the Empire of the Sultan meets the fate that it so surely deserves, and which must even now be at its very doors, then may we hope that the blunder so oft repeated in the history of nations, the effort to yoke Christ and Satan together under some form of state government, will be a thing of the past never to be repeated in the history of the future.

Islam would teach in its very name the duty of self-surrender to the will of Allah, but at the same time arrogates to itself the earthly representation of that will, so far as others are concerned. All other sects and religions must yield to Islam, for it alone is an embodiment of the will of Allah; "There is no God but Allah, and Mohammed is His Prophet." So the Romanist has said, practically, in the ages past, and enforced its doctrine in the same practical way, by force of sword, flame or dungeon. It commenced with a mistaken zealot, we might almost call him madman; his strength enlarged, his dominions widened, until with the very irony of history we might say of him, "That fortune favored the brave," for he had conquered an Empire larger than that over which Rome in its palmiest days of power had swayed its scepter. It commenced with the sword, it has continued with the sword, and, if the greater Prophet of Nazareth spoke the truth, it will end itself with the sword.

But what is this modern-day Islamism with which the Christian forces of the East must contend yet a little season? It still is what it has been from its very beginning, a scourge, controlled by the hand of God for some wise and holy end. It commenced its mission as a reforming element. Disgusted with the image worship of the corrupted Christian Church, it sought to annihilate them and rear upon the ruins a system more pure in the worship of one Supreme Being without the aid of the visible. But success turned the head of the Prophet; the lust of power enslaved him, until the spiritual gave way to the carnal. He must be the founder of a dynasty both ecclesiastical and civil in which, practically, not Allah but Mohammed must be the chief figure. Islam retains this feature of its founder until the present time. With all its fanaticism and fierce hate of everything that is not Moslem in faith, it holds the rod over the formal, effete, religious systems of the orient. It is God's scourge still to make purer and better those who bear the name of Christian.

But Islamism is not a unity. It is not in Egypt and the Holy Land what it is in the more northern parts of the Sultan's empire. It is divided into more sects than the whole Protestant Church; one Moslem authority says there are 150 different sects in Islam. There are two great divisions in the Moslem world, the Sunnites and Shi-ites, these again shading off into an almost infinite variety. The Mahdi and his followers of the Sudan are of the latter sect, and are in opposition to the Caliphate represented by the present Sultan, Abdul Hamid II. As has been intimated in a previous chapter, the native population of Egypt is not the bitter, fanatical, murderous, race that is found in the more northern parts of the empire. Islam has lost its sting there; it is not a conquered foe of Christianity by any means, but there are forces at work which bid fair to rob it of its power to harm. It is no longer an aggressive, but a passive, force; a waning religion that bows before the purer, more majestic form of a true Christianity. And this is said in face of the fact that the largest Moslem University in the world —the El-Ezhar—with 10,000 students, exists in Cairo.

Where the Cross was first raised there also the Crescent begins to pay its homage to the purer teachings of the Prophet of Nazareth. It is in large measure shorn of its political power in Palestine, and that is the backbone of Islamism. In Syria we find a weakened Islamism, weakened by educational and mission influences, as well as by a constant contact with European travel and commerce. It is loyal in outward form to the teachings of the Koran, and bemoans its apparent weakness in the presence of forces which it cannot banish or crush. Its spirit, its morality, differs not from that of the rest of the Levant; but its environments are restraining and destructive.

In this part of the Levant Islamism has come into touch with the civilizing influences of the Western world, and it is impossible for it not to realize that it is lacking in the vitalizing forces which it sees around it. In the Young Turkey Party, fast becoming an important element in Turkish politics, Islam is waking up to the fact that it has itself, like the effete Christianity of the middle ages, degenerated from first principles; and strenuous efforts are being put forth to regain this lost spirituality. That belief in the unity of God which, in the beginnings of Islam, was fundamental, has degenerated into pure and simple fanaticism. Predestination to good has taken a fatalistic turn. Islam, as a religion, has ceased to have any real spiritual force; it has become nothing more than a form of doctrine identified with aggression and despotism. A recent writer in speaking of Islam, says "That the great characteristic of Islam which is most manifest in the dealings of Moslems with each other and with the world at large, is the fact that it recognizes no moral obligation of any kind. Sin is merely transgression of statute; falsehood, deception, robbery, murder, have no moral quality whatever. The great mass of the Moslem community is utterly ignorant of what evangelical Christians understand by the sense of sin." No atonement for wrong-doing is possible except by punishment. Forgiveness in a Christian sense is unknown. "In its relations to Christianity Islam allows absolutely no apostasy. The death penalty is still existent in Persia, and while nominally forbidden in Turkey, it is at least exile and often death for any Turk to accept Christianity." It is strongly Jewish in this feature, and accounts for the few converts that are made from Islam to the Christian faith.

The Moslems of the Levant have taken alarm at the waning force of Islam as a religion, and as a result strong pressure is brought to bear upon the government from two opposite directions. On one side is heard the demand to restore again the austerities of the Moslem faith, to commence a policy of repression and extinction of the Christians in the empire. On the other side a progressive policy is demanded. "Islam has, and can still," they say, "adapt itself to varying communities and circumstances, and that there can be no reason why the highest results of European progress may not be appropriated by Moslems." And so we find in Syria and the coast regions Mohammedans opening schools for the better education of their boys and girls, demanding railroads, telegraphs, electric lighting, free press, wide-spread literature, freedom of thought and worship. But throughout the interior of his Empire we know only too well from recent events that the Sultan has decided on the brute policy of repression and extinction of all that oppose themselves to Islam. He has given free rein to rapine, murder and brutal lust, until the voice of an outraged Christian humanity throughout the Western world is raised in indignant remonstrance against such cruelties practiced in the name of religion. But the murderous fiend pursues his policy whilst hypocritically giving promises of gentler and more humane government. Surely there must be some truth in the old adage that "He whom the gods would destroy, they first make mad."

And so the struggle goes on between Cross and Crescent, and we anxiously look out for signs of the deliverer's coming. But how his feet do linger! whilst those thousands of God's poor, tortured, perishing children are crying "How long, O Lord, holy and true, dost thou not judge and avenge our blood on them that dwell on the earth."

Islamism is at a critical point in its history. It is on trial as it never has been before. A more vital force, regenerating and putting new life into the Christian organizations of the orient, has invaded its realm. In the presence of a weaker force, such as the nominally Christian religions of the Turkish empire have been, it has been able to stand, but in the presence of a stronger, it must go down. That fact is patent enough to the leaders of Islam, and in their frenzy and desperation, without any moral restraints in their religion to hold them back, they have gone like demons into the bloody work of extermination. We know what the result will be; for we can read the future in this matter in the light of the past. Islam gains no converts off its own soil; the self propagating power of love is not in it; it will perish where it is in the presence of the all-conquering power of the Cross. Woes untold may still be in store for the Christian Church, but the seed of the martyrs will yet bring forth a blessed harvest of good in the season appointed by the Divine Husbandman.

The tale with which we close this chapter, kindly furnished us by Miss Maggie Smith, of the Egyptian Mission, and which is narrated in her own language, is a prophecy of final things which will in a much broader, grander way gladden the hearts of those who follow the banner of the Cross in Moslem lands.

Ahmed Fahiny was of a very good family. His father had a good position in one of the government divans or public offices, and had only one wife, who was the mother of a large family. Ahmed attended our school for some time with an elder brother, but at the same time attended the Mohammedan University, El-Ezhar, with the expectation, if I remember correctly, of being one of their religious teachers.

In the autumn of 1875 he began to teach our new missionaries, Mr. Alexander and Miss Galloway, who were for a short time in Cairo. He became my teacher also. Besides reading other books we read a chapter from the Bible each day. Of this he afterwards said he tried hard not to think of the meaning, and if any argument was brought forward in favor of Christianity it irritated him very much, so much that one day he became angry and requested that nothing more be said to him on the subject of religion. The only recourse was now to prayer. The chapter each day from the Bible was read without comment. After many months he began to ask questions, often bringing a list of questions which he had prepared. Finally he was satisfied as to the truth of Christianity, but did not dare to mention it to any one. Prejudice, too, was hard to overcome. He afterwards expressed his feelings in this way, "I was like a man cast into the midst of the sea; near me was a ship in which I knew I could find safety, but I felt that I would rather perish than be saved by that ship, which is Christ." He would rise at night to pray when all were asleep, and he would imagine his brother's eyes were looking at him.

At this time he was in great conflict of soul, on the one side fear from his family and friends, the terrible disgrace he would bring upon himself and his loved ones, for he dearly loved his parents, brothers and sisters. The terrible persecution and perhaps death that would follow; the hate that must take the place of fond love in the hearts of those most dear to him. On the other side there was the love of Christ, and salvation through him alone. So the decision was made to take Christ as his portion, remembering that he would receive an hundred-fold in this life with persecutions, and in the world to come life everlasting.

He wrote out a confession of his faith in Christ, with Scripture reasons for becoming a Christian, but even then he carried this confession with him for many days before he could get courage to hand it over and thus make known to us that he was a Christian. He had gathered quite a little library of English books, many of them second-hand, and he prized these books very much indeed; he determined that though he must lose all, yet he would save these books, so he began to bring some of them each day when he came to give the lesson, sometimes bringing one of his father's slaves to carry some of them. Finally all were brought; then he wrote a letter to his father telling him that he had become a Christian, giving his reasons for so doing, and begging him to examine into the truth of the Christian religion.

Ahmed could not return to his father's house after this, but was taken into Dr. Lansing's family. The girl's boarding school and home of the single ladies and the lower chapel were all that had 'been built at that time of our now large, commodious mission building, and Dr. Lansing lived a short distance away. We were warned that there were spies about, waiting to kill the young convert, and every precaution was taken to preserve his life. He felt it to be his duty, however, to come to church on Sabbath, at which time he was accompanied by the missionary gentleman, and was wrapped up in such a way as to disguise himself. On the 26th of November he received the solemn rite of baptism. It was indeed a day of rejoicing, but mingled with fear. Our lesson, which now consisted in Bible study and prayer, was taken at Dr. Lansing's, but as nothing was heard from his people he became more bold and ventured over to the mission house for the lesson. One Thursday evening he was returning, after the lesson, and as he stepped under the colonnade of the house to which he was going he was surrounded by a number of his relatives, disguised in the dress of laboring men, who caught him and thrust him into a closed carriage, and he was quickly driven away. Some time passed before he was missed; search was then made for him. Those who saw what was done were told that it was by order of the government, and no one would tell if they knew about it.

What a time of sorrow and suspense and constant, earnest prayer! But days passed before we had any tidings about him. He was taken to his father's house, where every effort of bribes, threats and tears was tried to make him recant. A noted infidel was brought, named Gamal El Dien (or Dean). This man had been banished from Persia and afterwards from Turkey, and, I think, finally from Egypt, where he had quite a following. He had once come to Dr. Lansing's to talk with Ahmed, and we were all astonished at the way Ahmed maintained his part of the controversy, and we felt that God was indeed verifying to him His promise, "It shall be given you in that hour what ye shall say." This man was brought to his father's house to shake his faith in Christianity, and even, if possible, to make him an infidel, which to them would be much less disgraceful than becoming a Christian. The first day after his capture eight hours were spent in controversy with this man; the second day six hours. The third day, although he was ill, he was dragged from his bed to argue with the infidel again, but after several hours he was unable to go on. At this time his mother sent for him. She seemed to be dying, and begged him for her sake to repeat the Moslem creed, "There is no God but God, and Mohammed is the Apostle of God," saying, "Say it with your lips if you cannot say it with your heart." He was led to do this, when they quickly presented a paper which they had prepared as a recantation, and forced him to sign it. Then it was made known to the Mohammedans that he had forsaken the Christian religion and returned to the faith of his fathers, and a great feast was made in honor of the occasion.

When the missionaries heard of his recantation they demanded that he be brought before the English consul and have an opportunity to declare whether he were a Christian or Moslem. When he came his brothers were with him and were armed, having threatened to kill him and any who would try to protect him, if he still confessed himself to be a Christian. Dr. Watson and Dr. Lansing went to the consulate and when Dr. Lansing said, "Ahmed, have you returned to Islam?" he replied, "Yes," seeming not to realize that by so saying he was denying Christ. They sent an officer to demand his books. In one of them the writer inclosed a letter in which was set forth in strong terms the terrible sin of denying Christ. Ahmed did not feel that he had denied his Saviour, and the letter seemed to almost break his heart, as he said they had asked him to say it with his lips though he could not say it with his heart, and that they knew he was a Christian at heart.

After this he continued to be a prisoner in his father's house, never being allowed to go out, except when accompanied by his brothers, who kept a strict watch over his movements. After some time he found opportunity, with the help of a slave, to whom he gave a piece of gold, to go out, promising to come back soon. He made his way to the missionaries and told them that he was still a Christian, and a prisoner, and then returned to his father's house where he was kept in close confinement until he finally made his escape, and this time he came to us with no earthly possessions but the clothes he then wore. Once or twice his brothers, with others, visited him to try in every way possible to get him to return, or at least to go out with them for a walk, but he knew it would not be safe to trust himself to them. His favorite brother, Mohammed, had sworn to kill him, even if by so doing he should himself become a beggar. The native brethren warned him, telling him not to go to the balcony or even to look out of the window lest he be shot. They all had learned to love him, and were very much distressed, as they could realize better than we how cruel Mohammedans are, especially for such a crime as becoming a Christian.

Soon after this when the missionary gentlemen were away at a meeting of Presbytery, there came a letter from Lord Aberdeen, now the Earl of Aberdeen, and his lady, who were then taking their wedding trip on the Nile. They had just read of this case of persecution in an English newspaper, and wrote to ask if they could do anything for the persecuted one. They hastened back to Cairo and were told by the English Consul that Ahmed was not at all safe in Egypt, and they offered to take him to Scotland, I think Lady Aberdeen paying his expenses from her own private purse.

Judge Barringer, the American judge who then lived in Alexandria, who has done much to help our mission, sent money which was used to procure an outfit for Ahmed, and he was soon ready for his journey to Scotland. Lord and Lady Aberdeen came to the house to take him with them, Lady Aberdeen telling me that they would do all they could to make him comfortable and happy; and indeed they were the very kindest of friends to him. He was carefully guarded by soldiers from the consulate until he was safely on board ship the next day, when Mr. J. Giffen sent us a dispatch telling us that he was safe.

After reaching Scotland he was placed in the care of the Rev. Burton Alexander, with whom he studied for some time, and afterwards Lord and Lady Aberdeen sent him to the University of Edinburgh, where he completed his course, and then studied medicine, graduating with honors.

He afterward married a Christian lady and was sent by the London Missionary Society as a missionary to China. In a letter from the foreign secretary of that society he writes of

Ahmed: "Dr. Fahiny is doing earnest and faithful work at Chiang Chin, and seems from all I can learn to be a thoroughly devoted and true hearted Christian missionary." I hope that some day Ahmed, or Dr. Fahiny, as he is now called, may be able to work where he so longs to, among the Moslems of his own loved Egypt.

CHAPTER XIII.
ROUND ABOUT CAIRO.

THE intellectual trend in Cairo is upward. The English protectorate and the multitudes of Europeans and Americans who make Cairo a winter residence are modernizing influences which are telling powerfully on the orientalism of the city. The scholars in these mission schools of Cairo are taught the English language, and we hear verses of Scripture and recitations in several of the rooms as we make our tour of inspection; and hence it comes that we are at little loss for our mother tongue in Cairo, for guides and a host of others who derive a profit from the traveler's visit have enough English at command to answer all practical purposes.

To-day we had the privilege, seldom accorded a Frank of ordinary rank, of visiting several Zenanas and conversing, through an interpreter, with the occupants. The privilege was obtained for us by Miss Maggie Smith, of the United Presbyterian mission at Cairo. In making these visits we come in contact with two mourning assemblies whose performances we are permitted to witness owing to the presence of our well-known lady conductor. Ordinarily these assemblages of hired women mourners will not allow the presence of a man, for their demonstrations require the constant exposure of their faces; and to this day the Mohammedan woman of modesty will not expose her countenance to the gaze of a stranger. The period of lamentation varies among the Copts and Arabs, being gov-

DISTANT VIEW OF THE PYRAMIDS.

erned largely by the wealth of the deceased. In the case of the very poorest it is continued without cessation for three days after the burial, and then at intervals of seven days for the next forty days. But in many instances where there is money enough left by the deceased to pay the mourners, it is kept up for a whole year. A widow will expend, and is expected to do so, her whole substance, if she be poor, on hired mourners. The exhibition which we witnessed to-day seemed to be genuine feelings of grief; if not, they were terribly hypocritical; such copious floods of tears, such slapping of faces and dismal howlings and wailings one seldom hears in such combination outside of Mohammedan countries. We were told to-day that these mourning orgies were often carried on with such vigor and long continuance that the participants gave out from sheer exhaustion.

It is Friday, the Moslem's Sabbath, and, as good people should, we make up our minds to go to church and see how the Dervishes worship. The dancers and the howlers both meet in the afternoon within a half hour of each other, and in mosques a full mile apart. We must see both, but how? is the question, which is finally settled by taking passage on the donkey express. There is nothing lazy about these donkey boys when they get a customer astride their animals, and the speed they make through the crowded streets is a constant terror to the rider lest some luckless Arab woman or child get under the feet of his galloping donkey.

Arrived at the mosque of the dancing Dervishes we wait until a number of other tourists, equally as curious as ourselves, assemble, when the sheik of the order comes in and takes his seat at the head of the enclosed circular space. Others of his followers to the number of eleven or twelve, quickly follow and seat themselves to the left of the sheik. In a gallery above are the musicians with flutes and tambourines. The sheik and Dervishes rise and slowly walk around the circle three times, each reverently bowing to the prayer carpet, on which the sheik finally takes his seat. All are again seated until the monotonous music in the gallery commences, when the Dervishes arise, divest themselves of superfluous clothing, fold their arms over their breasts and pass before the sheik, gravely saluting him, and then at a sudden change in the music slide off into a whirling motion, spinning around on the great toe of the left foot as gracefully as a top, with their loose skirts inflated with air. The motion is as precise as possible, their skirts not being allowed to touch each other. The whirling motion continues so long that it becomes monotonous to us, and we leave them at it and post away to where the howlers have already commenced their exercises.

The howlers have their tambourines, drums, etc., in the enclosed space with themselves. They sit in a semi-circle in the first part of their performance, but finally, rising to their feet, bend their bodies slowly back and forth in time with the music. These howlers are long-haired fellows, and as they throw their heads back and forth with the motion of their bodies, which rapidly increases in time with the music, they present a grotesque and wild appearance. From first to last their deep guttural voices are heard waxing louder and louder as the music and the motion of their bodies increase, until the whole performance becomes as exciting as an Indian war dance, several of the Dervishes fainting during the exercises. "If you had to worship as these fellows do," said R—— to H——, as we turned away from the scene, "I imagine your Cairo Paradise would lose somewhat of its attraction." "A fellow's religion to be genuinely healthy must have some physical exercise mingled with it," returned H——, "and I could develop my religious muscle in this way as well as any other."

But we must see the Pyramids. It will not do to ignore these fine old relics of antiquity any longer. They are distant seven miles to the westward of Cairo. We are ticketed by the donkey express, as usual, at a fare of one dollar each. A startling whack on the rear ends of our poor little animals and we nearly lose our heads by the sudden jerk as we start off on a wild gallop through the streets of Cairo. As soon as we can catch our breath, H—— remarks, "These engineers are bent on keeping schedule time by the suddenness with which they let on steam."

At the farther end of the bridge over the Nile we are jammed in with a camel train coming to the Cairo market with enormous loads of green white clover; the passage has been blocked by some camel owner getting his animal out of the train, and we are witness to a scene which would have ended in bloodshed had it occurred in America, where man is not the tyrant nor the servile creature that he is here. A Turkish official applies his rattan most vigorously to the back and shoulders of the stalwart fellow who has by some mischance gotten his camel out of the train and blocked the passage. We watched his black Araby eyes flash as the rod came down on his thinly covered shoulder and back; he was no coward, we could see that, but it was worth his life to lift a hand against his flagellator.

Beyond the Kasr-en Nil—Nile bridge—we turn to the left, following the Nile for a mile or more along a beautifully shaded avenue, past the palace of Geezeh, a summer retreat built by the Khedive Ismail; another sharp turn to the right and we enter a five-mile avenue of Acacia trees leading to the edge of the Libyan desert where the sleepless Guardian of the Nile and the desert—the Sphinx—has kept his unceasing watch for fifty centuries. An Arab sheik living in a village close by controls the territory, and a tribute of two shillings must be paid him for the privilege of a pyramidal inspection. This fee, however, entitles us to a couple of his followers as guides into the chambers, and as assistants in the ascent of Cheops.

There are quite a large number of visitors present who are preparing their candles for a visit to the interior chambers of Cheops; we therefore take our guide's advice and go over to the second Pyramid—Cephrenes—for a similar purpose.

R——, before whose mind floats visions of extinguished lights in these sepulchral chambers by tricky Arabs in order to compel a liberal backshish, hints at dire vengeance if such a thing should occur to us; but we are all assured by the sheik's son that the

ASCENT OF THE PYRAMID.

days of such Arab trickery have passed. There are two entrances on the north side, an upper and a lower, the upper one of which is the one we use in the passage to the interior. The descent is through a narrow passage about three feet in width, at an angle of about 25 degrees for the first 100 feet. At this point a large granite block obstructs the passage, over which we climb and then jump to the bottom of another passage which leads horizontally into a large room called Belzoni's Chamber. As we pass through this last chamber the dust and stifling air, and bats flying into our faces, make us anything but a pleasant experience. Belzoni's Chamber is 46½ by 16½ feet, with a height of 22 feet. It contains a large red granite sarcophagus. There is still another chamber called the Queen's Chamber, to which we made a hurried visit, and then sought the open air.

To get to the top of old Cheops is our next ambition, and for that purpose we go to the southwest corner of the Pyramid. R——, who is not so youthful as he once was, takes a survey of the difficulties of the enterprise and concludes to tarry below whilst the rest of us make the ascent. "These huge old yellow stones were evidently not made for stair steps," gasped H——, as we sat down panting with our exertions a hundred feet or so up the incline. Our Arabs go in advance of us and give a helping hand. At last we have the satisfaction of standing upon the top of Cheops, 451 feet nearer the clouds than we were when we commenced the ascent. There is an area of thirty feet square on the top. We are glad that we have had the hardihood to attempt the climb, for we are amply rewarded by the glorious vision that meets our eye. Southward about eight miles is the Sakkarah group of Pyramids, ten in number, standing on a portion of the Memphis necropolis. On the west nothing but a sand desert; to the east a garden of vegetation stretching up the Nile valley as far as eye can reach. The valley is only about eight miles in width at this point, being bordered on its eastern side by the Mokattam hills, forming the western edge of the Arabian desert. Cairo with its minarets lies spread out before us to the northeast. And down there in the valley is the scene of Napoleon's battle of the Pyramids; and in imagination we think we can see him pointing up in our direction and hear him say to his veterans, "Soldiers, forty centuries look down upon you this day to witness your achievements." When we have satisfied our vision we begin the descent. That horrid jump, jump, from step to step! The memory of it will last as long as the fair vision we had on the top. It was a veritable "rattling of our bones over the stones" which

THE SPHYNX.

well-nigh put an end for several days to any farther sight-seeing around Cairo.

A quarter of a mile to the southeast of Cheops is the Sphinx, whose stony eyes doubtless saw the Egyptian taskmaster in the days of Moses lashing the Hebrew slave to the fulfillment of his task, "That heavenly monarch who his foes defy, like Vulcan powerful, and like Pallas wise," as an inscription on one of the paws says. The body is one hundred and forty feet long; its head is cut out of the solid rock and measures thirty feet from the top of the forehead to the bottom of the chin, and about fourteen feet across. This head was once covered with a wig, a part of which still adheres on either side. The chin was once adorned with a beard, parts of which are now found in the British Museum. At the extremity of the paws, which run out fifty feet from the body, is a temple tomb from which some fine pieces of alabaster are brought us by the two Arab lads who are with us. Between the paws is an altar on which sacrifices were offered before the Sphinx.

We are sitting near the little hotel erected near Cheops for the Prince of Wales' accommodation, watching a gathering storm of wrath among the sheik's followers when R—— puts in an appearance from his rambles. H—— discovers that our friend has been undergoing some sort of a transformation in his absence, which he is not inclined to be very communicative about, and gently removing R——'s hat, reveals the fact that our friend has suddenly grown bald-headed in spots. "I ran across an Arab barber in the village over yonder," he explained, "and concluded I'd have a shave, but before I was aware of what the fellow was doing he had made a dip or two at my cranium, and then he tried his hoe blade on my face with the mutilating results which you see." "I think the fellow understood surgery better than he did the tonsorial art," dryly remarked H——.

The sheik's followers have by this time come to blows with each other, and a pretty lively fight goes on for a few minutes until the bulky form of the sheik puts in an appearance. Too much backshish to-day and dissatisfaction with the sheik's system of distribution lies at the root of the matter. "Where do you suppose that huge pile of stone came from?" queries H——, directing our attention to Cheops. "The best authorities," I answer, "say from the Arabian quarries on the other side of the river, and the remains of the two causeways spoken of by Herodotus as having been built for the transportation of the stone from the Nile would seem to prove the statements true." All the Ghizeh group of Pyramids were originally cased with polished limestone slabs, some of which we still see on the top of the second Pyramid. The two large Pyramids are the work of Khufu and Khafra, Kings of the IV. dynasty, and built undoubtedly for royal tombs. But our donkey boy is ready for the return trip; and so ends our visit to the Pyramids.

A mile from the Esbekiah garden on the right bank of the Nile is Boulak, a wretched looking Arab town, swarming with dogs and half-naked children. But it possesses one great attraction to the visitor in its fine museum of Egyptian antiquities; the wonder is that it is not removed to some more central situation. The Egyptian archæologist might spend days instead of hours here in interesting and profitable study of relics gathered from monuments and ruins in all parts of Egypt.

And now, reader, we have brought you hither with our company to meet a royal personage in whom we all have great interest. He lost his voice over 3,500 years ago when King Death called on him, and he was put away with his ancestors in the royal tombs at Luxor. In 1881 the secret chamber of the Royal Mummies was found, and the Boulak museum is now enriched with the presence of quite a number of the Kings of the XVII., XVIII. and XIX. dynasties. But strip down the shroud covering of that mummy case, and you are looking at the rigid features of the King whose wrath Moses feared when he had slain the Egyptian. A long spare-faced man with high cheek bones and leather colored countenance, with a little patch of auburn colored hair still upon his head. You are skeptical, I see; but it is without question the form of old Rameses II. that lies before us, for the mummy case furnishes proof of it. And here, too, in other cases are the mummied remains of his fathers, Sethi I., Rameses III. and Thothmes II. Another case contains the mummy of a Queen supposed—but without absolute proof—to be that of the Pharaoh's daughter who adopted Moses. The art of mummification reached a wonderful degree of perfection in those days of Egyptian glory when the transmigration theory of the soul's final return to the body was entertained; hence the desire to preserve the body intact for the soul's rehabitation. In one of the rooms we visit is found the famous San stone dug up in 1866 at San, which furnished the key to hieroglyphic reading. With the aid of this stone and the Rosetta one, the Egyptian hieroglyph is made as intelligible as any other of the ancient characters.

"Now that I have been presented to some of the Pharaohs," remarked H——, "I must also see what is to be seen of their once royal city." A railway runs along the west bank of the Nile from Geezeh to Asyoot, a distance of 229 miles. On this we can ride as far as Bedrashayn, fourteen miles above Cairo, and then the donkey express a couple of miles westward to Mitrahenny, and we are then among the mound ruins of Memphis, the capital city of the Pharaohs.

The train goes out early, and we have the misfortune to miss it; but a pair of donkeys make good the loss, and we are off on our twenty-eight miles' ride. For full five miles our donkey boy runs us at the top of our animal's speed until we can endure it no longer and shout for slower time. These donkey boys are a marvel of endurance. Our boy after his five-mile run behind us was as cool and fresh as though he had not gone more than as many rods. "Good donkey," he says, laying his hands caressingly upon the animal I rode; but I, laying my hand upon his brow, answer, "Good donkey boy." A beautiful forest of palm trees extends along the whole way to Bedrashayn, growing in clumps even among the mound ruins of Memphis. This once magnificent city—the Noph of the Bible—is a scene of desolation. So Jeremiah said it should be, and as we pass over its ruinous heaps we see long camel trains with pannier baskets slung over their backs carrying away the dust of the old city to enrich adjacent lands. In the midst of these ruins lies an enormous granite statue of Rameses II., over forty feet in length.

A mile or two farther on in the edge of the desert is the Sakkarah group of Pyramids, the work, it is supposed, of the Israelites during the period of their bondage. The largest one of these is only 197 feet in height. A little farther on is the tomb or Tih, a priest of the Vth. dynasty. The chambers of this tomb are well preserved, and the sculptures on the walls, in delicacy of outline and coloring, are said to surpass those at Beni Hassan. Near to this tomb is the recently discovered Apis Mausoleum, or Serapeum, as it is sometimes called. In this place is a long subterranean gallery with mortuary cells on either side of it containing huge granite sarcophagi measuring on an average 13 by 6½ feet and 11 feet high. In these the sacred bull gods Apis were entombed; there are twenty-four of these most beautiful sarcophagi still in place. A ladder leans against one of them, up which we climb in order to a descent into the sarcophagus. The desert sands concealed this treasure—as it does many others yet undiscovered—until 1860-61.

But we have now taken the reader on the last Egyptian excursion which we shall make together, but we can assure him that we have by no means exhausted the interesting things of this part of Lower Egypt. "The half has not been told him;" let him come and see for himself. As for us—"We must see Jerusalem also."

CHAPTER XIV.

FROM CAIRO TO JERUSALEM.

WE have one regret in leaving Egypt so soon, namely, that we had not so timed our movements and laid our plans that a tour up the Nile as far as Luxor would have been possible.

Such a tour would have cost us much less, and taken up less time, than all authorities we had consulted indicated. The reader who may consult these pages and whose good fortune it may be in the future to see for himself the things whereof he now reads, will do well to remember that a trip up the Nile to Luxor, Thebes, and Karnak, may be made by combining river and railway travel at less than half the cost usually specified by tourist agencies.

Cairo is connected with the Suez Canal by railway a distance of about one hundred miles. Zagazig is the first town of any importance reached. Here a branch railway comes in from Alexandria. On our left, just before coming to Zagazig, are the ruins of the ancient Bubastis, the Pibeseth of the Bible. Its origin dates as far back as the XVIIIth. dynasty; and in the XXIId. it was in the height of its prosperity, becoming the royal city of Sheshonk I.—the Shishak of the Bible. Zagazig is a neat, modern looking town of no special historical importance.

From this point on to Ismailia we have desert sands on our left, the old land of Goshen in the Patriarchal times, whilst

PLOWMAN AND TEAM.

on the right there are evidences of fertility in small groves of palm trees, and a village now and then. Tel el Keber, famous as the scene of Araby Pasha's defeat in 1882, is soon reached. Fourteen miles farther on is Mahsamah, near to which is the recently discovered site of Pithom, one of the treasure cities of which the Israelites are said to have built for Pharaoh. At Nefich, fourteen miles farther, the fresh water canal, along which we have been riding for some distance, divides, sending a short branch to Ismailia, the main canal continuing on southward to Suez. The railway also divides in a similar manner; the short spur of two miles and a half terminating at Ismailia. Lake Timsah, on the northern shore of which Ismailia is located, is supposed to have been the first camping place of the Israelites in their march out of Egypt. The lake makes a convenient point midway between Suez and Port Said for the large ocean steamers making the passage of the canal to pass each other. We pass a night in the neat little town, and take the postal steamer in the morning for Port Said, which is reached after five hours steaming. A half day at Port Said suffices, for there is little of interest to be seen on its sandy streets.

We take our departure from Port Said in a magnificent steamer of the French line, the "Gironde," and coming on deck early in the morning, after a ten hours' steam, we find ourselves lying to in front of Jaffa, waiting for a pilot to enter the harbor. Jaffa's harbor is only one in name, and it is not always that a vessel can land its passengers and cargo by reason of the rocks which lie just hidden in the water, and against which the sea breaks with such violence as to make a perfect foam of the waters along the whole coast fronting Jaffa.

But we are among the favored this beautiful Sabbath morning in finding the sea not yet risen from his slumbers. As we look out from the veranda of our hotel later in the day we realize that we had indeed caught the sea napping in the morning. The classical scholar will remember the story of Andromeda chained to one of the rocks in this low lying reef, against which the sea is now breaking so furiously.

Jaffa will not bear acquaintance. It looks quite handsome from the sea, but on landing, one quickly recognizes the fact that he is in a wretched Arab town, with the usual narrow streets and unlimited amount of filth. We are made to remember likewise that we are now in the dominion of the Turk, whose chief object in existence is to draw from the unwary traveler's pocket all he can. There has come recently into existence a new arrangement in reference to passports. If a traveler comes without a passport he is subjected to a fine of four dollars. We, in common with many others, were not aware of the arrangement and were put to some trouble, as well as a fine of two dollars, on account of our ignorance. Mr. Gilman, our gentlemanly consul at Jerusalem, is endeavoring to have an exception made, in this passport matter, of all American travelers, on the ground of the entire freedom allowed Turkish travelers and all others to land and travel anywhere in America without a passport; he thinks he will succeed.

It will be remembered by the Bible reader that Jaffa has some important events connected with its history. It was here that Peter raised Dorcas to life, and had his vision from the housetop of Simon the tanner. There is an old ruin by the seaside which is known as the house of Simon the tanner; of course we went to look at it. It was from this port that Jonah made his ignominious flight, landing in a port to which he was not ticketed; and thither it was that Solomon brought the timbers for the temple at Jerusalem. But Jaffa is noted for something else which is well calculated to make the modern traveler open his eyes in astonishment and delight; the orange and lemon groves excel anything of the kind that we have ever seen. The trees are hanging full of the splendid fruit. We measured one orange which was found to be 13 inches in circumference; and it was only a fair sample of many that we saw.

"What ghostly looking people those are," said R——, as we noticed a company of white sheeted women in advance of us. "Angelic, rather," returned H——, "for they are clothed in white, and we are now in a land accustomed—in times past at least—to angelic visions." These were Greek women, who invariably envelope themselves from head to foot in these white sheet coverings when they go out on the streets. On every Thursday we find them congregated in little groups in the cemetery to the north of town; they go to visit the graves of their departed friends; to picnic, pray and gossip. They are accompanied by professional praying men, who chant the Koran for a piastre a chapter, and by wailing women who are paid to weep, scream, and otherwise put on the semblance of grief. And so they remain without tiring, in fact thoroughly enjoying themselves, from sunrise to sunset, amid the reminders of their own mortality.

And now we are ready for our journey to Jerusalem. We can hardly credit our senses that we are actually within thirty-six miles of the Holy City, the sight of which has been the height of our ambition since boyhood's days. Some of us take passage in an express wagon—fare one dollar; others of the company in a wheeled vehicle resembling a barouche. The road—a pretty good one as Palestine roads go—leads out past the Dorcas fountain, among fine old orange orchards protected by prickly pear hedges, which few lovers of the lucious fruit would dare to brave in their efforts to acquire. Out over the beautiful plain of Sharon, decked in scarlet by anemone, with the tulip and narcissus giving variety to the floral beauty of the plain. Here are pasture lands, and waving fields of barley and wheat. The implements of agricultural which these fellaheen are using are of the most primitive kind; a mere rooter with one handle for a plow, drawn most commonly by a pair of small heifers or steers. One is reminded as he looks at these heifer teams of what Samson said to the Philistines when they had at last extorted the secret of his riddle from his wife: "If ye had not plowed with my heifer, ye had not found out my riddle." Here and there by the way is an old stone tower, used as a guard house in more troublesome days.

Twelve miles from Jaffa we come to Ramleh, where a half hour's stop is made. Ramleh has no special Biblical importance, as it dates back only to the eighth century. To the westward of the town a little distance are the ruins of an old crusader church, the tower of which—120 feet high—is still standing. This tower is called the White Tower, sometimes the Tower of the Forty Martyrs, with which is connected a beautiful legend concerning the martyrdom of forty Christians who were exposed in a naked condition to the cold of a severe winter night with the condition that if any should abjure his faith in the Nazarene he could come to the guard's fire and live. The faithful band offered fervent prayer, saying: "Forty persons we have entered the arena, let forty martyrs wear the crown." As the night wore on the guard slept, and dreamed that he saw an angel descending with a crown in his hands, which he placed on the head of one of the party; thus he did again and again until he had placed thirty-nine crowns, when he returned not again. Awakened from his dream, the guard discovered the fortieth person at the fire; and convinced by his vision of the righteousness of the cause for which the band suffered, he sought and obtained permission of the authorities to take the place of the recreant, and perished with the rest. Thus the legend runs.

Two miles to the northeast of Ramleh is the Lydda of the Bible, the modern Ludd. It will be remembered as the scene of some events in the life of Peter and Dorcas. About six miles farther on is the Half-way House, where refreshment for man and beast is enjoyed. From this point on we are literally "Going up to Jerusalem," for we have commenced the climb of the Judean Hills. Look at those maidens! Can it be possible that we are meeting some of the descendants of the old Gibeonites, who, as a punishment for their craft in league making with Joshua, were doomed to be wood and water carriers for Israel! We ask for information touching this company of maidens, each one of whom carries on her head a load of small sticks tied in bundles about four feet in length, a load

TOWER OF RAMLEH.

sufficient to tax the physical endurance of an ordinary man. "They are gathering their marriage dowry," the dragoman answers. "It is customary in this country," he continues, "for a maiden to have a hundred bundles of wood stacked up in her father's door yard, before she is considered eligible for marriage;

she does not have to gather any more wood then for a whole year after marriage." "Now, then," said H——, "here is a chance for our matrimonially inclined comrade to pick up a useful wife; he may hunt America over and he will not find one who will do her part better towards earning the daily bread of the household." "And almost any of them would go with the Howadji, for they have heard much about your pleasant land," answered the dragoman.

Just before entering the narrow defile leading into the higher range of Judean Hills, we pass on our left the scene of Joshua's conflict with the Amorites on that memorable day when sun and moon stood still over Gibeon and the valley of Ajalon. A few miles farther on is a very ancient looking town sitting upon a conical hill looking down into a deep wady on the north, the old Kirjath-jearim, it is said, where the ark of God rested for a period of twenty years after its capture by the Philistines. So steep are the inclines and ascents from this on, that we leave our carriages and take short cuts around the wadies, hoping as we ascend to the crest of each hill to get a vision of Jerusalem. But darkness begins to obliterate the landscape so that we are hardly aware of the fact when we are actually entering the long Jaffa street leading up to the western wall of the city. This is disappointing to us; for we would have had our first look at Jerusalem as the setting sun was throwing his gilding rays over it from the top of some of the western hills.

Our hotel quarters are outside of the walls, and it is not until after supper that we go out and, Nehemiah like, take our first view of the walls with a bright moon looking down upon the scene. Our feet stand upon Mt. Zion; no longer the glorious Zion which led the sweet Singer of Israel once to exclaim: "Beautiful for situation, the joy of the whole earth, is Mt. Zion, on the sides of the north, the city of the great King!" No longer the joy, but the curiosity of the whole earth, we come here to see her in her desolation, mindful of what she once was, of what she has seen and suffered, and more than all else, because the King of Kings condescended here to walk and teach, and suffer death. As we walk on past the tower of David towards the valley of Gihon, and turn the corner at the southwestern angle of the wall going eastward, Olivet rises in our front, and our walk is in silence, for the memory is busy calling up the scenes associated with the sacred Mount.

We retrace our footsteps back to the Hotel Fiel, where we are fortunate enough to meet with the very man we have had recommended to us for a dragoman, George Abraham, a young Christian Arab, whom we found in all our after experience to be competent, honest, and reliable in every way. The economical tourist at Jerusalem need not be at an expense of more that $2.50 per day for hotel and guide. When he journeys out through the land he must have tents, cooks, baggage animals and horses, besides a good, competent dragoman, all of which will make his expenses—if he be with a company of at least four or five—about $5.00 per day. All intending tourists to the Holy Land who care to be careful about their expenditures, will do well not to connect themselves with any party for the camping tour until after arrival at Jerusalem; there will be opportunity enough for that at Jerusalem.

It is now the beginning of March and the latter rains may be expected at any time, hence George advises us to make our trip southward to Hebron, and back to the Dead Sea and Jordan valley immediately, reserving Jerusalem to the last for fear of broken weather. We cannot, however, turn away from Jerusalem without giving a day or two to it for general inspection.

"Perhaps," suggested H——, " it would be well to construe literally the Psalmist's injunction to "Walk about Zion, and go round about her; tell the towers thereof. Mark ye well her bulwarks, consider her palaces; that ye may tell it to the generation following." We will make the circuit of the walls then, first, and afterwards make a survey of the interior. Our starting point is the Jaffa gate, the only open gate in the western wall. The Jerusalem gates are not now closed at night, as they were a few years ago. The bulk of the commerce and travel goes in and out at the Jaffa gate. Turning southward by the road which leads down into the valley of Hinnom, our attention is called to a group of people sitting by the roadside; they beseech the Howadji for an alms. But observe them more closely; some of them speak in hollow, gutteral tones, for their palates are gone; the noses of some of them, too, are missing; some of them hold out hands minus fingers, arms without hands. Their skin presents a white scaly appearance. Altogether they are pitiable looking objects; give them a charity, for the God-man, when He walked the streets, was filled with compassion for the poor lepers.

The wall is quite mediæval looking, dating back only to Suleiman I. It is about thirty-five feet in height by ten in breadth. A few of the heavy ordnance of modern warfare would make speedy destruction of such walls. Turning eastward to the southwest corner, we follow a narrow alley leading close under the wall over a portion of the Hill of Zion. A large portion of Zion is now outside of the southern wall. In this region is found the reputed tomb of David. The tomb is covered by a large stone building, on the upper floor of which we find a room 30 by 60 feet, called the Coenaculum, where the Lord instituted the Supper, and visited the disciples on the evening of the Resurrection; it is somewhat apocryphal in character we think. The tomb is jealously guarded by the moslems and no permission is given the visitor to look within. A current tradition is, that long since a woman, filled with curiosity that is said to be natural to her sex, surreptitiously found her way into the forbidden chamber, and came back in a dreadful state of commotion with the loss of sight, hearing and speech. "Those fellows," remarked H——, as we left the building, "must think that we pilgrims from the Occident are a puerile race to credit such stories, to prevent us from indulging a desire to look into the Patriarchal tomb."

An Armenian convent is next inspected, which has nothing more notable in its keeping than the head of which Herod deprived James, and the stone which closed the mouth of the Lord's sepulchre, which the Latins accuse the Armenians of stealing from them. Passing from here down the declivity into Kedron, we follow its dry bed up past the tomb of Zachariah and Pillar of Absalom, until the Bethany road is reached; thence northward close to the wall among the moslem graves, continuing the ramble until we have made the circuit of the walls, a distance of two and a half miles. George says he must have the rest of the day for preparation for our Hebron journey to-morrow, and thus with this slight acquaintance with the Holy City we must rest content until our return.

CHAPTER XV.

OVER THE HILLS OF JUDEA TO HEBRON, DEAD SEA AND JORDAN VALLEY.

LEAVING the Jaffa gate our little company of four take the Bethlehem road en route to Hebron. The morning is as pleasant as a tourist could wish for a ride such as we have before us. Roads are a rarity in Palestine, but the sleepy Turk is waking up a little to their importance, and we are promised a good road as far as Bethlehem; after that "You will see," the dragoman says.

Who would dream that this pleasant valley of Hinnom through which we are now riding had ever had the evil reputation which the Biblical record gives it? And yet it was here that Israel committed the abomination of the Moloch worship, in consequence of which good King Josiah had all the offal and refuse matter of the city carried thither, keeping up a perpetual burning and smoke in consuming it, which came in time to signify to the Jewish mind the place of eternal torment. And this same valley has also seen the fulfillment of Jeremiah's prophecy. "It shall no more be called Tophet, nor the valley of the son of Hinnom, but the valley of slaughter; for they shall bury in Tophet till there be no place." It ran red with the blood of Jerusalem's sons and daughters when temple and nation went down in the great overthrow by Titus.

As we come up out of the valley, on our right are long rows of stone houses which Sir Moses Montifiore has erected for poor Jews. Close along the road runs the old aqueduct, long since out of use, which supplied the Gihon pools at Jerusalem with water from the pools of Solomon, south of Bethlehem. About midway to Bethlehem on our right is the convent Mar Elias, which occupies—it is said—the camping ground of Elijah for one night when he was flying from Jezabel's wrath.

And there is Bethlehem rising in terraced form on yonder hillside, just beyond the olive covered valley at our feet! The city of David, around which clusters so much of sacred interest in connection with his life, and the life of David's greater Lord. Jerusalem lies buried from forty to fifty feet under the modern city, but Bethlehem remains topographically almost the same as when the infant of Bethlehem made his appearance in it. It is sacred ground, and we feel a reverence for the place such as we do not feel for any spot within the walls of Jerusalem.

And here, too, by the way, a ten minutes' walk from the town, is a small white-domed building which Christian, Jew, and Moslem, alike pay homage to—Rachel's tomb. From age to age the occupant of the land, as well as invading foe, has respected the spot and kept some simple monument above her dust in place of the original stone pillar which Jacob reared to her memory. Take a flower, pilgrim, from the spot: it is worth treasuring as a memento of the place hallowed for ages by affection's tender care. Here at our left, as we turn up the narrow stone walled way to Bethlehem, is David's well, from which his three braves brought him the drink his soul longed for when, as a refugee from Saul's anger, he thought of the home in Bethlehem.

The town has a population of about 8,000, an intelligent, but turbulent class, differing in many respects from the common Arabs of the country, owing to the crusader blood in their veins. They are hospitable and kind to the stranger, but fiery in their relations with each other and the surrounding tribes. They are Greek and Catholic in their religion, enterprising and industrious in life, being occupied largely in the making of olive wood and mother of pearl articles for tourist traffic. We dismount in front of the Church of the Nativity, for, let Bethlehem possess what other attractions it may, this, above all spots on earth, save one, perhaps, is the dearest to our hearts. The tradition which makes the grotto over which the church stands the place of the nativity is so old and well authenticated that we can give at once our credence to it, a thing that cannot be done in reference to many other so-called sacred places without the largest stretch of the imagination.

The church itself dates from the time of Constantine, by whose mother, the Empress Helena, it was built. It was reared on the site of a Kahn which, from the days of John, the beloved disciple, was said to be the one where Joseph and Mary sought shelter at the time of the Nativity. In Hadrian's time, A. D. 117-138, the place was so venerated by the Christians that to desecrate it in their eyes Hadrian had a grove sacred to Adonis planted upon it. Jerome in the early part of the fourth century came hither and spent thirty years of his life in a room joining the cave of the Nativity, engaged upon his Latin Vulgate translation of the Scriptures.

The interior is cathedral shaped, the usual lofty nave and side aisle, adorned with a few rather ordinary paintings representing scenes in the life of the Savior. Descending a flight of steps beneath the choir room we reach the chapel of the Nativity, once a rude cave, but now transformed into a beautiful marble cased room 16 by 40 feet, with a height of 10 feet; here hang thirty-two silver lamps. On the right as we enter the chapel is a low arched shrine about four feet in height, in which hang fifteen more silver lamps, the gifts of kings and queens of many lands. In the center of its paved floor is a silver star with this inscription, "Hic de Virgine Maria Jesus Christus natus est"—"Here Jesus Christ was born of the Virgin Mary." It will not disgrace thee, pilgrim, if a manly or womanly tear falls as an offering of sweet affection and reverence in this place of thy dear Lord's Incarnation. Directly opposite this shrine

FIELD OF BOAZ (BETHLEHEM).

is another where the Magi knelt with their offerings. In these shrines the lamps burn night and day; the Turkish soldier with gun in hand watches the visitor's every movement.

> " In Bethlehem the Lord of Glory,
> Who brought us life, first drew his breath :
> On Golgotha, O bloody story !
> By death He broke the power of death.
> From western shores, all danger scorning,
> I traveled through the lands of morning,
> And greater spots I nowhere saw
> Than Bethlehem and Golgotha."

About two miles south of Bethlehem by direct road we reach the Pools of Solomon. An old ruinous fortress built by the Saracens stands at the northwest corner of the Pools, once used for guarding the reservoirs, but now utilized for nothing save, perhaps, as a temporary habitation for some shepherd and his flock. The Pools stand at the head, or western end, of the narrow, wady Urtas. They are three in number, so formed that the bottom of the upper one is on a level with the top of the second, and the bottom of the second on a level with the top of the third. Their dimensions are: upper one, 380 by 229 feet, depth, 25 feet; second one, 423 by 160 feet at west end, but with a width at east end of 250 feet; lower one, 582 by 148 feet at west end, with a width at east end of 207 feet, with a depth of 50 feet. The second Pool is separated from the first by a space of 160 feet, and the third from the second by a space of 248 feet. Thus their united lengths and spaces would extend about one-third of a mile down into the wády. Stone steps at the corners lead down into each Pool. There was little water in any of them at the time of our visit. They receive their water supply from four springs, one of which is found in the old fortress; the main feeder, however, coming from the limestone hill two hundred yards to the west, through an underground conduit. There seems no reason to doubt the truth of the tradition which assigns the construction of these pools to Solomon. They give evidence of the highest antiquity; and the wise man's own words in Eccles. II., 4-6, make it certain that somewhere in the region he built him pools, and in this wady as nowhere else in all the region nature seems to have favored the construction of just such works; but of this more, on our return journey through the wady below us.

And now our journey is roadless; nothing but a narrow bridle path for most of the way, so slippery and rugged that we are in constant fear that a surgeon's skill will be required to mend some broken bones. A road is building which will in the course of time afford a much easier approach to Hebron than that which now falls to our lot. What a scene of desolation meets our eyes from this point on until we enter the valley of Eschol! We travel over hills of solid limestone and through depressions thickly covered with loose stone for a whole half day. The entire territory traversed would hardly keep a herd of goats. But in all this waste and desolation there is left some beauty, for wherever a handful of soil can be found there some flower raises its pretty head as if trying its best to lend a little beauty to the surrounding desolation. The flowers of Palestine are truly many and wonderful.

On a hill top to our left is a little white-domed building which our dragoman tells us is Jonah's tomb. As we enter the vale of Eschol we notice that the grape is still extensively cultivated here; and if the fruit be as large correspondingly as the vines we see, the grapes of Eschol must still be as remarkable as at the time when Joshua sent his spies into the land. Eschol soon joins itself to the plane of Mamre, down which we ride about a mile until Hebron is reached. Hebron contains, we are told, about ten thousand people packed away in their small stone and sun-dried brick houses as thickly as though there was no available space for the living outside of this miserable town. The object of our visit, of course, was to see the Cave of Machpelah, the tomb of the Patriarchs. We leave our animals in charge of the muleteer and make our way on foot through a very narrow and dirty bazar street, followed by a crowd of all ages and sexes whose object is backshish. We are permitted to ascend only a few steps towards the entrance of the mosque that covers the cave. These fanatical Moslems will permit no other than a Mohammedan to enter the precincts of the sanctuary beneath which sleep the fathers of Israel. It would cost a man his life to attempt it. We were obliged to content ourselves with a peep through a chink in the wall made for this self-same purpose.

It is devoutly to be wished that the possession of Machpelah was in some less fanatical hands so that an entrance to the interior might be had by the pilgrim who has come his thousands of miles to visit the sacred shrines. Only three Europeans—royal personages each of them—with a few attendants, have had the privilege of an entrance into the mosque covering the cave within the past century, and that was accomplished by special Firman of the Sultan.

Hebron, known also in Old Testament times as Kirjath Arba, lays claim to the greatest antiquity of any town now in existence. It is said to have a population of about ten thousand, and a more villainous and disreputable looking lot it has never been our misfortune to meet. Although a refuge city in Bible times, we would hardly be willing even to seek a temporary refuge in it now. Its streets, like most of these oriental towns, are narrow and filthy, and afford a variety of perfumery that would surely satisfy the most fastidious. "Surely," suggested R——, "if cleanliness is next to godliness, the Patriarchs, being such godly men, must either have risen above their surroundings or have found a different state of things here from what we now find."

We now ascend the plain of Mamre about a mile to a Russian hospice, where we are to pass the night, almost under the branches of Abraham's Oak, beneath which he entertained the angels on their way to destroy Sodom and Gomorrah. The present "Oak of Abraham" presents a very ancient appearance; it is probably five hundred years old, and will be numbered with

OAK OF ABRAHAM.

the dead oaks shortly. It doubtless stands on or near the spot where the original tree stood. The plain of Mamre can be traversed in all its length in an hour's time. The next day, returning by the same route until the Pools of Solomon are reached, we leave the main road and turn down the wady Urtas. If the current tradition be true, this pleasant little valley is the scene of Jehoshaphat's thanksgiving when he returned victorious from the slaughter of his enemies at Tekoa, and bore the name of Berachah—that is, valley of blessing—from that time on. Solomon found at times a pleasant retreat amid his groves and gardens. Look down into the valley, and we notice even now the finest gardens we have seen since entering the land. About a mile from the pools, and clinging close to the steep northern side of the wady is Etam, Samson's native town.

A stone water conduit bringing water from the Pools follows the upper edge of the declivity to Bethlehem. The valley widens as it approaches the town, and fine old olive groves cover the plain. We are once more in Bethlehem. From here we turn eastward on our journey to the Dead Sea.

We have arranged for a Bedouin escort to the Jordan valley to meet us at this point. It is not safe for a small party to go into this region without first having paid a sort of tribute to the sheik at Jerusalem. The members of the tribe, the wild sons of Ishmael, who inhabited the region at the head of the Dead Sea, recognize the tribute paid in the person or persons of your soldier escort. Our escort, as he takes his place at the head of the cavalcade, does not look as though he would strike terror into the hearts of our enemies. A solitary Arab he is, with an old flint lock gun hanging by a strap over his back, a gun which couldn't be coaxed to hurt anybody. He patters along over the stony way, carrying his sandals in his hand the most of the time to save his sole leather.

We take our noonday lunch in the plain where the angel heralds proclaimed the message of "Good will to men" to the shepherds. It is near the close of the afternoon when we come

THE RIVER JORDAN.

to the deep gorge of the Kedron, and riding along for a half hour on its upper edge we come to the convent of Mar Saba, built right into the rocky sides of the gorge. We are hospitably entertained for the night by the friendly monks. It is a law of the convent to "permit no woman or beardless youth to cross the threshold." The next day at noon we are at the northern end of the Dead Sea. The wind is blowing quite fiercely, and occasional showers of rain are falling. Some writers have described the Sea as waveless and as overspread with a gloomy, hazy atmosphere. We find it in no such condition. The white caps are dancing on its surface, and the waves are rolling in so fiercely that we almost despair of our cherished plan of a bath in its waters; but our ambition in this respect is gratified. It presents much the same appearance of any ordinary lake. The black tents of the Bedouins are visible in every gorge and valley around us.

We arrive at the Jordan River in the midst of a rain, and instead of camping on its banks for a while, as we had intended, we make for Jericho, an hour's ride across the plain from the Jordan. This locality teems with interest to the Biblical student. Here is the scene of Elijah's translation and the crossing of the Israelites when, under the leadership of Joshua, they came into the land to possess it. "Nebo's lonely Mount" rises up behind us just beyond the Jordan, and farther down on the east side of the Dead Sea the mountains of Moab rise into view. In front of us is Jericho, the City of Palms. Not a single palm remains now in all the plain of Jericho, and only a wretched little Arab village and a half-dozen modern houses remain to mark the site of the once opulent city of Jericho.

We tarry here for a night, going out of town a half-hour's walk to the fountain of Elisha, the famous fountain whose bitter waters were sweetened by the Prophet. It is a fine fountain still, the only one in all the region. Here in the edge of the evening we receive our first jackal serenade. From a dozen different quarters their woman-like yells arise, and the answering barks of the dogs of the village make the evening hour in this desolate village one long to be remembered.

The next day we enter the hills where the gorge of the brook Cherith opens into the Jericho plain, and ascend to Jeru-

RUINS OF JERICHO.

salem by the very road of the Savior's parable of the "Good Samaritan." It is still accounted the worst and most dangerous road in Palestine. We pass scores of Russian pilgrims on their way to the Jordan, all on foot, and many of them barefoot, for these poor pilgrims imagine that there is more merit in this painful method of pilgrimage than if they were to make it in a more comfortable manner.

It is about a six hours' ride from Jericho to Jerusalem, or a distance of about twenty miles. The white tower on the top of Olivet is visible all the way.

"Bethany, did you say, dragoman?" Yes, this insignificant looking place is in very truth Bethany, El Azariyeh, the Arabs call it. It is our first view of it, and we tarry long enough to visit a rock hewn tomb said to be the tomb of Lazarus, and the old ruin in the center of the town made by tradition to be the house of Martha, Mary and Lazarus. Hither we shall return again, for the little village will furnish food for reflection, if nothing else, and will repay for a foot journey from Jerusalem.

Rounding the southern slope of Olivet, Jerusalem comes into full view. This is the point from which the Savior viewed it on that memorable occasion when He wept over its coming woes. How glorious must the vision have been at that time! But, alas! its glory has departed, and it sits still with the cloud of an uncertain fate upon it. Not yet repentant, what vicissitudes of peril and suffering are yet before it, only the mind of the Omniscient can tell.

CHAPTER XVI.

WALKS ABOUT ZION.

HOTEL quarters at the "Fiel" have been exchanged for more humble entertainment at the home of our dragoman, and we are prepared to make a leisurely survey of Jerusalem and its environments, with a competent guide to direct us in our rambles. We had planned as a company, a two weeks' stay in the Holy City, but for the writer, at least, this stay is to lengthen out into months. Coming as a tourist only, he stays as a missionary, temporarily in charge of "The Evangelical Mission to Israel," during a short absence of Mr. Joseph, in England. We are glad of the privilege thus afforded us of a more intimate acquaintance with Jerusalem life, and a more thorough knowledge of the topography of a region full of sacred interest.

In Mr. Gilman, our efficient Consul, we find a friend ever ready to give advice, or afford assistance when called on, and to him we are indebted for special facilities afforded us at times for gathering knowledge which, under other circumstances, would perhaps not have been attainable. The Turk, evidently, has been going to school for a few years past; and his knowledge of our great Occidental country is expanding, and his respect for the representative of that country correspondingly increases.

Jerusalem was in its grandeur, in the days when the Herodian Temple crowned the top of Moriah, and the lofty walls rising up at its southeast angle to a height of 180 feet, and shining white in the sunlight as the traveler approaches it around the southern slope of Olivet, in the days when Mt. Zion was adorned with the palaces of the Asmonaean kings; all this gave beauty enough to lead the poet's mind onward to his description of that "Jerusalem the golden, with milk and honey blest." But when we look at its modern representative, and travel through the narrow, filthy, cobble-stone streets, we feel like paraphrasing this poetical description and reading it, "Jerusalem the stony, with dirt and rubbish cursed."

JERUSALEM.

The Jerusalem of the Savior's day lies from forty to seventy feet below the present city. Around the Temple site the ruins of the old city are deepest, for it was here that the work of destruction was most complete, the grand Temple edifice being razed to the ground. The Tyropean, or Cheese-monger's valley, which separated Zion from Moriah, was a narrow gully so deep that a bridge was thrown over it as a means of passage between the two mounts. Seventy feet of ruins have well nigh made a level passage now between Mts. Zion and Moriah. Near to the Jew's Wailing place the top arches of this old Tyropean bridge are yet visible. Moriah is walled in as a separate space, and occupies an area in the southeast corner of the city of about thirty-five acres. The mosques of Omar and El Aksa are the only two buildings in the enclosure. The space is paved, and

JEWS' WAILING PLACE.

here and there growing up out of the pavement are olive and cypress trees, affording a pleasant shade to the lounging Moslem. No Jew is allowed in the enclosure; the Moslem regards it as next to the holiest spot in all the world, and the presence of the heathen, Frank or Jew is regarded as a profanation which he will not brook. It is only a few years since pilgrims from European countries could gain admittance under any pretext;

but now a little backshish will soften the Moslem heart most wonderfully, and gain admittance under certain circumstances. A company of half a dozen or more under the conduct of a uniformed "Cavasse" obtained through a consulate will enable us to see the interior of the Mosque of Omar.

Our dragoman suddenly informs us one day that he has a small company to take to the Mosque and we had better join ourselves to it. We have been waiting for such an opportunity and gladly follow him and his party into the sacred inclosure. A few minutes' contemplation of its exterior shows us an octagonal shaped building with a dome 170 feet above the level of the pavement. Each of its eight sides has a length of sixty-eight feet. We enter on the north side up a flight of steps to a level with the Mosque floor, sixteen feet above the pavement. An iron screen placed between pillars and columns thirteen feet away from the outside wall, runs around the building; and in the center of the room directly under the dome a second iron screen circles around the naked top of Moriah. The name by which the Mosque is oftentimes designated, "Dome of the Rock," is derived from the fact just alluded to.

There are a number of traditions, both Christian and Moslem, connected with this rock. The Moslems believe that it was from this point that Mahomet made his ascent to heaven on his famous steed, El Borak; that the rock, anxious to accompany the Prophet, was detained in place by the angel Gabriel's hand, the imprint of which they show you on the hard face of the rock. It was here, according to Christian tradition, that Abraham prepared to offer Isaac as a sacrifice; here also the place of Araunah the Jebusite's threshing floor, where Bavid erected the altar and stayed the plague; and here the place of the Holy of Holies in the old Temple. These latter traditions may be taken as credible, for there is nothing in them to contradict the Scripture narrative. Underneath the rock is a cave, into which light streams through a circular opening in the roof. There seems yet to be other cavities below the floor of this cave, for

CHAPEL OF THE NATIVITY.

it gives forth a hollow sound when struck. The Moslems say this is an evidence of the truth of their claim that the rock is suspended in midair. Look up at the dome and sides of the great building! but don't do so in obedience to the lounging Moslem's request, else he will call "backshish" on you with an irritating persistency. They glitter in an exquisite beauty of color and mosaics. The Mosque, it is claimed, was built by Abd-el-Melek, between the years A. D. 688 and 693.

Passing out into the paved court yard, we descend by a flight of stone steps at the southeast corner into a vast underground chamber, bearing the name of Solomon's Stables, a discovery made within the last five years. A multitude of enormous granite columns support the roof. How old this cavern is, no one can tell; but rings and chain marks on the supporting columns show that at some remote period it was used for stabling purposes, perhaps by the Crusaders.

As we pass back over that portion of Zion outside of the southern wall we notice that Micha's prophecy is having a literal fulfillment before our very eyes; "Therefore shall Zion for your sake be plowed as a field, and Jerusalem shall become heaps." Yes, the plowman is at work getting the ground ready for gardens.

If we take our way westward of the Joppa gate some six hundred yards we find in the midst of a Mohammedan cemetery the upper one of the two Pools of Gihon. It was here that Solomon was anointed king, whilst the people in their gladness made such noisy demonstrations that Adonijah and his band, who were also having a coronation feast to themselves at En Rogel, heard the jubilations with dismay. From this Pool runs a conduit to the Pool of Hezekiah within the city; both Pool and conduit are undoubtedly the same as those referred to in 2 Kings, 20:20. There is no living water in Gihon; its present function is to catch the water that descends from the clouds in the rainy seasons, and send it off through the conduit to the Pool within the city.

Following the valley as it dips toward Hinnom, a third of a mile, we come to the lower Gihon Pool. Passing this we turn eastward through the valley of Hinnom, having on the right as we pass the Hill of Evil Counsel, which derives its name from a tradition that it was here that the rulers met in the house of Caiaphas and determined to put Jesus to death. Joining it closely is Aceldama, of which a certain guest at a hotel in Jerusalem was heard to say: "I have been this forenoon to see the wonderful field of Aceldama, which Judas sold for thirty pieces of silver."

HOLY SEPULCHRE.

There are a number of rock-hewn tombs at the foot of these two hills. Looking into one of them we found it inhabited by an Abyssinian family, a most wretched looking lot, whom we did not blame for wanting a little backshish.

At this point Hinnom joins the Kedron, and turning south in the brook we come in a few minutes to a very old landmark in these regions, En Rogel, the scene of the Adonijah festivities at the time of Solomon's anointing. The Arabs call it Job's well, for what reason we know not, for it is certain that the man of Uz never had any connection with it. The well is first mentioned in Joshua as the boundary between Judah and Benjamin. It is again mentioned in connection with the Absalom rebellion as the place where the Priest's sons hid themselves that they might gather news for the fugitive David in the Jordan valley. It is 125 feet deep, depending largely on the surface flow into it for its supply of water. When the wells and cisterns of Jerusalem give out, as not unfrequently happens, then come hither the women with their water jars, the men with their large skin bottles, and droves of donkeys, upon which the bottles are loaded and carried to the city, and peddled out, or turned into some one's empty cistern at so much per bottle. Even now as we journey around the city we often meet these water peddlers, crying "Moyeh! moyeh!" for the latter rains are much behind their usual time, and grave fears are entertained of a water famine.

The Jerusalem dwellers appear to regard the rain failure as a special judgment upon them for their wickedness, and one may often hear—during these days—such expressions as "God is angry with us, for He is sending rain upon Galilee and Samaria, whilst we and our crops are parched with thirst. We do not wonder to find these poor unfortunates so ready to trace all their calamities to Jehovah as a result of their own sin, for surely no city or country in all the world has had sadder experience in the school of discipline than Jerusalem and Judea; and it is encouraging to find them so sensitive on the subject.

Returning up the Kedron to a point almost opposite the southeast corner of the Temple area, and on the eastern side of the brook, is a small collection of houses and cave dwellings clinging to the side of a rocky hill; this is Keffer Silwan, or the village of Siloam, built on the Hill of Offense, where the too indulgent Solomon built for his heathen wives idol temples. It was well named the Hill of Offense; and how the good man so lost his head as to fling such a challenge into the face of Him whose presence was signified by the Grand Temple on the op-

HILL OF CALVARY.

posite height, is a mystery incomprehensible. It is a Hill of Offense down to this day; for there are unsavory people and smells in all its habitations.

We are now in a region of bones, graves above and below, to the right and left. The flat stones on the slope of Olivet to the right are Jewish grave stones. Every foot of space is occupied, and the Jew will lie nowhere else, so, when fresh subjects are ready, the oldest graves are opened and a new occupant is laid upon the old. On the west side are the Moslem graves. They will not rest with the Jew, for it is defilement even in death to mingle with them.

Here, as we proceed, are four sepulchral structures lifted up out of the bed of the Kedron and formed in its precipitous eastern side. The first is Zachariah's tomb, although it seems a solid structure cut out of the rock, with no entrance that has ever been discovered. It is pyramidal shaped on top and stands about thirty feet in height. The next is the Grotto of St. James, a series of sepulchral chambers leading far into the rocky hill. It derives its name from a tradition that St. James made it a hiding place after the betrayal and during the trial and crucifixion of Jesus. The tomb of Jehoshaphat comes next, a sepulchral chamber similar to that just described. Absalom's Pillar is next. It is about forty-five feet in height, with a spire-like top. It has a base of twenty feet square. A hole in the north side allows a person to crawl into the interior, but we found nothing but broken stone in the inside. It is a much abused structure, for it is held in abhorrence by the pious Jew, who omits no opportunity of throwing a stone at it, and we find these loose stones hurled at it covering its base to a depth of several feet. It is all because Absalom was a rebellious son and reared the pillar—or perhaps another one on the same spot—to perpetuate his memory, at a time when he thought he would have no sons to keep his family and name alive in Israel. As the Savior passed this way, how often His eyes must have rested upon these four objects we have been describing! They were here, unquestionably, when He was made flesh and dwelt with man. There are few such objects remaining now around Jerusalem, and we view them with all the more interest and reverence when the consciousness is upon us that these identical objects were seen and visited by the noblest Pilgrim who ever trod the rough path of our earthly life.

Let us take this zigzag path leading up out of Kedron and follow it over the steep incline to the Golden gate, for it is an object worthy of our inspection. It is a closed gateway, and has

GETHSEMANE.

been thus closed since about the third century A. D. A tradition is still current that the Christians will yet enter in final triumph through this gate to hold possession of the city. By the Moslems, Mahomet and Jesus are both assigned positions as judges at this gate in the general judgment, which, according to the belief of both Moslem and Jew, is to take place in the Jehoshaphat valley below. The gate is double portaled, and ornamented over the arches by Doric work supposed to be a part of the old gate Beautiful, which gave admittance to the Temple area on the eastern side. It was here, if authorities be correct on the subject, that the gate Beautiful of our Lord's time was situated, and through which He made His triumphal entry during Passion week. And in this connection, may not the prophecy of Ezek. xliv.:2, about the closed sanctuary gate, have a special application to this same closed gate? We think so.

We have promised to see Bethany once more, and we cannot do better than to start from the Golden gate and follow a course leading up over Olivet, which was doubtless taken by our Savior Himself on many of His journeys to the home of His friends in the quiet little village. A ten minutes' walk brings us to the Latin's garden of Gethsemane. Its western wall runs to the Bethany road. The entrance is by a low door in its upper, or eastern wall. The enclosed space is about three-fourths of an acre. In the center of the garden is a paling enclosure, in which the monks cultivate some very fine flowers, which go in large part to the Church of the Holy Sepulchre for its adornment. There are seven olive trees in this enclosure, very old, unmistakably, but scarcely as old as the monks would have us believe; for they tell us that these are the identical trees that were in the garden at the time of the Agony. Even if the olive lived to such an age, there is a fact of history which would prevent us giving credence to the story of the monks. Titus, we are told, cut down all the trees in the locality at the time of the destruction of the city. Around this inner enclosure runs an avenue eight or ten feet in width, with scenes illustrative of the Passion placed upon the wall at intervals.

Is this the true Gethsemane or not? So it has been claimed for sixteen hundred years; and yet three hundred years was long enough to lose all track of the sacred spot. While tradition says yes, reason would say no, to the identity of the place. If solitude was what was sought on that dread night by the sorrowing Savior and disciples, then it would hardly have been sought at that time in that place; for all the region was occupied by the tenting and camping pilgrims to the Passover feast. It seems reasonable, with Dr. Thompson, to look for the true site of

ABSALOM'S PILLAR.

Gethsemane higher up in a secluded vale between the two spurs of Olivet. But what matters it? Gethsemane was a reality, and was somewhere in this immediate vicinity, and it gives a solemn and tender interest to our walk, as we make our way up the stony side of Olivet.

A narrow stone-walled lane, traveled no one knows how many centuries, leads up to the Church of the Ascension. On either side the Mount is terraced, and the almond, fig and olive flourish in soil to which they have been accustomed for ages; without them, Olivet would be only a vast stone heap. The Church of the Ascension dates back to about the fourth century, and marks the place—so says the tradition—where Jesus was parted from His disciples and received up into heaven.

If the Scriptures were in the hands of the people in those first centuries of the Christian era, we can hardly pardon the ignorance which selected such places as are now alleged to have been the scene of numerous events in the life of our Lord. Is it not expressly said in reference to the Ascension that "He led them out as far as to Bethany, and He lifted up His hands and blessed them, and while He blessed them He was parted from them, and carried up into heaven?" Down the eastern side of the Mount over this little knoll we pick our way until Bethany is reached.

How sadly has the little village degenerated since those days when the homeless Son of God found temporary rest and refreshment in the humble home of his friends in Bethany! About forty wretched mud hovels inhabited exclusively by Mohammedans go to make up the village. It is indeed, as its name signifies, "The house of poverty." But the home of poverty may yet be neat, and clean, and restful; and in these respects the Savior doubtless found the Bethany of His day vastly superior to the Bethany of our time. The old Bethany lies here on the surface, and not, as at Jerusalem, fathoms deep under the dust and ruin of several cities. The village occupies a rough limestone plateau, and anciently covered a much larger area on the west than the modern village. Wandering over this space we found many old cisterns long since out of use, as well as a few rock-hewn tombs. The tomb of Lazarus we must look for somewhere on the outskirts of the village, and not where the Bethany people show it, at their very doors. Along the Jericho road a little to the eastward of the town are rock-hewn tombs which would well meet all the requirements of the Biblical narrative. The almond and the fig, with blossom and fruit, growing up out of the scanty soil, take away a little of the barrenness of nature around Bethany.

CHAPTER XVII.

EASTER DAYS IN THE HOLY CITY.

IT has been with mingled feelings of pleasure and sorrow that we have for the last two weeks gone in and out of the Holy City and circled around her on the hills made memorable by past events. The sun rising over Olivet no longer looks upon the glorious city of our Savior's time, for the ages have heaped upon her bosom the debris of the cities built again and again upon the same site. But not so with the everlasting hills which stand like sentinels around her. Here nature is sovereign, and amidst all the strife and tumult of ages past she has suffered but little disfigurement.

Coming out of the Damascus gate on the north, and letting our eyes follow the road for a half mile in its ascent, we see to the right the hill Scopus, over which the army of Titus approached to the final overthrow of the city. Directly in front of us, but a few hundred yards distant, is a hill, shaped much like a human head, the top of which is on a level with the top of the wall; this is most probably the Hill of Calvary, on which the Incarnate God was lifted a spectacle of shame to the witnessing millions. General Gordon, of Khartoum fame, made careful investigation of the subject and pronounced this to be the veritable Golgotha. Of course it is in opposition to the view of the Armenian, Greek and Latin religious organizations who claim that the Holy Sepulchre within the walls is upon the site of the crucifixion and burial; but this is certainly the most foolish fiction of all the multitudes of fictions which we hear daily. The Great Sacrifice was made without the walls, and everybody acquainted with the topography of the ancient city knows that its walls included a greater area than the modern walls do. They extended southward to the valley of Hinnom, taking in that part of the hill of Zion now without the wall and covered in part by an Armenian convent; and northward to an indefinite distance. We find no spot around the city which so well answers the requirements of the sacred narrative as the hill just mentioned. Standing upon its summit we are struck with the fact that the hills of Moriah and Zion both dip down towards our point of view, ending at the Tyropean valley, thus affording the dwellers upon these hills a vision of all that was transpiring on this hill without the walls. It is now covered with graves, and underneath it, hewn from the solid rock, are a number of tombs; together with a large grotto called the grotto of Jeremiah.

Passing eastward along the northern wall we come to the valley of Jehoshaphat, in reality a continuation of the brook Kedron, crossing which we ascend into a vale covered with old olive trees. This vale lies between Scopus and Olivet, and we verily believe would come nearer being the true site of Gethsemane than either of the three sites near the eastern wall shown by the Latins, Greeks and Armenians, as Gethsemane, for the simple reason that the former is away from the public highways, while the latter are near them, and on that account would less likely be selected by the Savior for the travail of sorrow which His soul was to experience that night. But a truce to these questions in regard to sacred sites.

Mt. Olivet is no fiction. What memories sweep over our souls as we stand upon its summit and gaze upon the places which meet our vision! To the eastward overlooking the hills of Judea we see the Jordan valley with its historic river winding like a silver thread northward through its length; and a little to the south lies the Dead Sea, still and glassy looking, as we see it to-day; and we notice likewise a phenomenon which some writers have spoken of—a dull, smoky atmosphere appears to have settled down over the valley and the sea, giving it the appearance of an Indian summer day. Almost at our feet lies the little village of Bethany, whither Jesus often-times resorted for rest and refreshment in the home of His friends.

Facing the Holy City on the west of the mount we see at its foot the Kedron wending its way in a southeasterly direction towards the Dead Sea, while a little to our left rises the Mount of Offense, where Solomon built his idol temples in the very face of the magnificent structure which crowned the top of Moriah. On the side of the Mount of Offense, overlooking the Kedron, is the little village of Siloam, and opposite, just across the brook, is the pool of Siloam. On the eastern edge of Kedron, in this same locality, are Absalom's Pillar and tombs of St. James and Jehoshaphat. In looking at these places we derive a satisfaction in the knowledge that we behold them much as the Savior Himself saw them. From the pool of Siloam runs a water conduit cut through the solid rock a distance of 1,750 feet to the fountain of the Virgin, so called from the tradition that the Virgin used to wash her child's linen at this place. It is a resort for bathers now. The conduit which connects it with the pool of Siloam dates back to Zedekiah's time. Both sides of the Kedron in this locality are covered thick with graves. Here the poor Jew desires to find a resting place in the shadow of the Temple, and thousands of them rest in this locality.

We witnessed rather a peculiar, not to say disgusting, ceremony in the cemetery adjoining the Armenian convent on the southern slope of Zion. It was the ceremony of anointing the dead; the bones of one long dead were taken out, handled and even kissed by relatives, while a priest waved an incense lamp over them, reciting some formula of prayer the meantime, after which a bottle of wine was produced and the skull and other bones bathed with it, and then all placed in a sack and reinterred.

We took a donkey excursion the other day to Mizpeh, the

place where Samuel judged Israel and where Saul was anointed. While here we saw the old style of grist mill in operation. Two women seated upon the floor of their dwelling with a small millstone between them, which they were laboriously turning around on the flat surface of a nether stone, were turning out a grist of barley. Here in Jerusalem there is a slight improvement on this primitive style of mill, there being one steam and several wind mills in operation.

We were the uninvited guests at a wedding ceremony in Bethlehem the other day. Friend R—— and myself made a foot pilgrimage to the village and on arrival met a company of Bethlehem maidens escorting a bride to her husband. Being curious to witness the whole ceremony we quietly turned in at the rear and followed the company until the groom's house was reached. The bride was mounted upon a horse and closely veiled, and the maidens accompanying her were engaged in chanting certain things in her praise. Arriving at the humble stone dwelling of the groom, the bride was conducted into his presence, and the escort of maidens went in to make merry in the dance. Let it be remembered that the sexes do not mingle in the dance in this country. Other male guests are present. These seat themselves outside of the dwelling and forthwith tobacco and wine are produced for their delectation. We, the uninvited guests, unlike the one mentioned in the Parable, being observed are given a very cordial welcome and offered a share of the good things of the occasion. They are not able to understand our prohibition proclivities, and thinking that it is our dislike to the kind of wine offered, a messenger is dispatched who returns with two glasses of ordinary wine, which we have not the heart utterly to refuse and thereby offend their well-meant hospitality. We learned that the festivities would continue for a couple of days.

The sacred sites of Jerusalem have all been visited, and our soul sickened at the amount of superstition and falsities which everywhere abound in the Holy City. Alas! it is a misnomer to call it a holy city. The Moslem, the Greek and the Catholic are all at sword's point with each other; and all of them hate the Jew. It requires the constant presence of the Turkish soldier to keep peace among those calling themselves Christians. The fanatical zeal and hate which dwell in the bosoms of this heathen populace is like a restless Vesuvius, ready without a moment's warning to break forth and overwhelm the community with a deluge of fire and blood. The rightful owners of the soil are thrust out from their inheritance, and are under the necessity of purchasing with large emoluments the privilege of an existence in the homes of their fathers. Look at them as they are gathered at their wailing place on Friday afternoon! With a large price they have purchased the privilege of gathering at the southwest corner of the Temple wall, where a few of the original stones yet remain. There they assemble with their Hebrew Bibles to read and weep over the desolation of their Holy Temple. It is a pitiable sight to see the tears coursing down the cheeks of the young and the old, and witness the fond caresses bestowed upon the poor remnant of their Holy House. Even in this unfeigned grief they are made a spectacle unto men, for the visitor has not "done the city" until he has seen the Jews wailing.

There is at the present time a remarkable movement among the Jews. The Sultan of Turkey has sold to the Rothchilds of London the privilege of sending thither 50,000 Jews, under the condition that they come in companies of fifty at intervals, and dwell in certain parts of the land outside of Jerusalem; and the first company of fifty has arrived since our own coming to the city. By actual government statistics there are not less than 30,000 Jews in and around Jerusalem. The signs are not few which indicate that the days of Moslem rule in Palestine are almost numbered. There is an old tree standing within a ten minutes' walk of our quarters, about which the Moslems themselves have a tradition that when it falls the Mohammedan power in Palestine is at an end. We saw the tree a few days since; it is nearly dead, and the only remaining live limb is supported by a prop; and an iron band around the tree helps to keep in place the large limbs that manifest an inclination to sever their connection with the trunk. Truly, if the tradition be verified, there remains but a few days of grace to Ottoman rule in this land.

As in everything else, so in the observance of the Easter Period the so-called Christian church of the Holy City is divided in opinion as to the proper season for its observance. The Latins inaugurate the ceremonies of their Eastern week, the last of March this year, by a high mass on Palm Sunday, at which the Patriarch of Jerusalem officiates, and by the distribution of palm branches to the pilgrims, who carry them in procession several times around the Holy Sepulchre. A month later the Greeks and Armenians inaugurate their Easter period in the same manner, but with variations in the ceremonies following Good Friday of a decidedly negative Christian character. Sandwiched in with the Latin Easter ceremonies is the Jewish Passover season. During these days the city is given up to holiday enjoyment, most of the shops being closed. The Holy Sepulchre is the place where all the Easter ceremonies are held. From six o'clock in the morning until late in the evening on Good Friday, Palm Sunday and Easter Sunday, the church is thronged with priests, pilgrims and sight-seers. The choral service is performed by two choirs, one of priests and one of young lads in training for the priesthood, the one answering the other in responsive chanting. The choral service is really excellent, but the rest consists in numerous robings and unrobings, and mummeries such as must make the enthroned Savior feel that even now, as of old, His Father's House is turned into a place of evil doings. Beginning with Palm Sunday the priestly exhortations are supposed to be appropriate to the events of each day of Passion week, until the evening of Good Friday, when the whole tragedy of the crucifixion is enacted by the priestly company. A waxen image, blood stained and with a crown of thorns, is fastened to a wooden cross and carried at the head of a procession that slowly moves around the place of sepulture, halting at seven different stations to hear a like number of exhortations delivered in as many different languages. It not infrequently occurs, as on the night when we witnessed the ceremonies, that some altercation takes place between the priests of the three different factions occupying the church, or between the soldiers and others seeking to disturb the solemnities of the occasion. What a spectacle for the Moslem to look upon is this almost daily strife at the Holy Sepulchre! It makes one blush for the name of Christian in this city, where so many abominations are done by those nominally Christian. So great is the strife between the three ecclesiastical bodies in joint occupation of the Holy Sepulchre Church that on all important occasions the presence of the Turk with loaded musket is necessary to keep the peace. We witnessed the ceremonies of Good Friday evening with a file of Turkish soldiers on each side of us.

Some one has said (to whom to credit the wise saying we know not) that "the conversion of the Jew and Moslem to Christianity can never occur until the Holy Sepulchre ceases to exist." Outside of the strife occasioned by its existence are the deceptions practiced by the priesthood upon the credulous, and the idolatrous worship of objects within the church. See that marble slab as you enter the church, with all its silver lamps and gorgeous trappings! It is the stone, we are told, whereon our Savior was laid when taken down from the cross and prepared for sepulture, and there is a constant stream of poor pilgrims who fondly stoop and kiss the stone, while their tears fall thick and fast upon it. Over in that corner about seven yards distant is another so-called sacred spot—the place where Mary Magdalene stood and watched the burial preparations. A beautiful chandelier hangs down over it. In the chapel of the crucifixion, belonging to the Greeks, we are shown an altar beneath which is a hole in the rock where the cross of Christ is said to have stood. At another place we may thrust our hand through a hole and feel the fissure made in the rock at the time or our Lord's resurrection. All of these places, with many others, receive the idolatrous homage of a large class of pilgrims, when the fact ought to be patent enough that the whole locality is a fabrication, so far as its being the site of the crucifixion is concerned.

The Jew of Jerusalem is very punctilious in the observance of all the outward forms and ceremonies of his religion. The Passover Feast is observed during the same week as the Latin's Easter. Unleavened bread in thin, wafer-like sheets is used for a period of seven days following the Passover supper. This is a holy time to the Jew; a seven days' Sabbath in which all manner of work is laid aside. The Passover supper varies a trifle from the old form of its observance. The lamb is no longer eaten; a joint of it only being placed upon the table as a reminder of what once was. Since the destruction of the temple the slaying of the lamb and the blood sprinkling have ceased. A very significant omission it is, too, when considered in connection with the slaying of God's Lamb upon Calvary. During the Passover week the old Torahs, which have been in use since the last Passover, are returned to the chief Rabbi; and if found defaced, or in the least degree imperfect, they are retained and new ones given in their place, each new Torah being carried in procession at night to its synagogue. The book is carried under a canopy supported by four men, women and children bearing lanterns and torches, all singing, clapping hands and shouting in the wildest glee.

Just preceding the Greek Easter ceremonies comes the Moslem pilgrimage to the tomb of Moses. The Latins, Greeks and Armenians have each their Easter festivities and solemn ceremonies, and the Jew his Passover feast, and it must needs be that the Moslems come to the front with something to entertain or attract the public mind during the pilgrim season. Hence the day of pilgrimage to the tomb of Moses. It matters not to them that it is plainly stated in the Scriptures that "God buried Moses, and that no man knoweth of his sepulchre unto this day." Tradition has located the place and erected a tomb over the spot on a height visible from the plain of Jericho. In the early morning, delegations from the various sheikdoms round about are seen coming into the city with several flags in colors of red, blue and green, borne at the head of each delegation. About noon all have collected, and preparations are made for the grand march out of the St. Stephen's gate across the Kedron and around the southern slope of Olivet. In the meantime the eastern wall of the city from St. Stephen's gate southward to the corner, commanding an excellent view of the road as it winds around over Olivet to Bethany, has been covered with a multitude of sight-seers, and thousands of the city's population, as well as multitudes from regions remote, are gathered on the sides of Olivet and the opposite bank of the Kedron. The day is hot and dusty, and scores of tents line the way, in which a portion of the multitude has taken refuge, whilst every olive tree in the region is affording shelter to as many as can crowd beneath it. We view the demonstrations from a point on Olivet very near to the spot where the Savior halted on that memorable occasion when he beheld the city and wept whilst He uttered that pathetic lament over its fast coming doom. As we look over the vast multitude that covers the wall and the slopes of Olivet and the Kedron, we are carried back in imagination to a scene not very dissimilar to the present one, which transpired on these same grass-covered slopes nearly nineteen hundred years gone by, to the Passover scene of Passion Week, which culminated in the dark tragedy of Calvary.

But the cannon planted on yonder hill wakes us out of the sad reverie to a sense of things about to be. The procession is moving out of the city. We hear the distant drum beat, and soon see the waving streamers of the different companies as they descend from St. Stephen's gate into the Kedron Valley. It is a motley crowd of Arabs and Turks; and the music is of a nature scarcely to be imitated in our land of excellent things. The day closes in the city with the firing of guns and the shooting of rockets, much in the same fashion as our Fourth of July evenings close.

For days past the Russian pilgrims have been busy in preparation for the Easter ceremonies. They have been here for weeks visiting the holy places, and wait only to light their tapers at the holy fire to be gone. You see them on the streets everywhere carrying palm branches and bundles of waxen tapers. This holy fire day is the day of days for the Greek and Armenian pilgrims, as well as for the curious visitor from Europe and far America. Through the kindness of our consul we obtain a point of view out of reach of the dangerous trampings and melees so common on this day. Every nook and corner of the church is filled with anxious pilgrims and visitors waiting for the appearance of the mysterious flame.

The Greek patriarch has gone within the sepulchre enclosure, while the Armenian patriarch waits at the door to light his taper from that of his Greek brother as soon as the miraculous fire shall have been kindled. From two holes in the sepulchre enclosure the flame is at length visible. Swift horses stand ready at the church entrance to carry messengers with the holy fire to Bethlehem and Jaffa, that the churches there may receive it; whilst the vast concourse within the church rolls hither and thither in wild commotion in the effort to light the tapers.

It is ludicrous in the extreme to see the ingenuity exercised by some of the pilgrims in getting tapers lighted in advance of their fellows. They are let down in bundles from above by small cords and thus lighted.

These tapers are extinguished in a little while by means of a cap brought for the purpose. The tapers are carried home and given to friends as memorials of the holy fire at Jerusalem, whilst the cap is retained to be buried in. These poor, simpleminded pilgrims of the Greek church actually believe in this monstrous absurdity. But it must be said that the patriarchs themselves no longer claim a holy origin for the fire, when the question is asked them direct by people who think for themselves. The time is near at hand when the holy fire will be a thing of the past in the Greek church, just as it has already become in the Latin church.

CHAPTER XVIII.

THROUGH SAMARIA AND GALILEE.

EIGHT men, twelve horses and mules, and three tents are the alarming amount of impediment which, it appears, has been thought necessary to supply the wants of three modest travelers like ourselves on our journey through this railroadless country. What an amount of backshish these importunate fellows will require, for in this poverty-stricken land, whoever does you the least service must have his backshish, and the multitude who do you no service seem likewise to think that it is a proper tribute to exact from the tourist; the babe in its mother's arms is taught to hold out its tiny hands and say backshish. The latter rains have not yet fallen, and the glare of the sun on the white rocks and roads make vision painful to the eyes; but we have wrapped our hats with fine white cloths to meet the emergency, and we journey in tolerable comfort.

Leaving the Damascus gate, we take our journey northwards over the caravan route between Jerusalem and Damascus. An hour's ride brings us to the ancient Gibeah of Benjamin, where the seven sons of Saul were murdered. Away to the left, sitting upon the top of a high hill, is Mizpeh, or rather the solitary mosque which marks the place where Mizpeh once stood, the seat of Samuel's power and judgeship in Israel. We are traversing the same route which the Pilgrims of Galilee used to travel when they came to Jerusalem to attend the national feasts: and about mid-day, we reach the little Arab village of El Bireh, where, tradition says, the Child Jesus was first missed by His parents on the return from the Passover feast at Jerusalem. It seems a very likely place to discover the absence of the Child, for it would be about a day's journey on foot from Jerusalem, and there is likewise a good spring here, where pilgrims are still prone to halt and refresh themselves, as we ourselves did. The evening of our first day's ride through the land brings us to Sinjil. Our tents had the start of us in the morning and we find them already pitched when we arrive; the British Union Jack floats in peace and harmony with its old enemy, the Stars and Stripes, each from its respective tent.

Our next day's ride is through the territory of Benjamin, and is enlivened by a greater variety of scenery. The naked limestone hills of Judea are left behind, and small valleys, green with growing grain, and terraced hills covered with olive and fig, give the landscape a habitable look. But there is one thing we miss everywhere throughout this semi-civilized country: the tillers of the soil have their dwellings in the villages, and not upon the land they till. The land is houseless, and wears an air of abandonment which it does not in reality possess. During the day we pass over a hill covered with old stone ruins; we halt for awhile and contemplate the situation. This is Shiloh, the hill upon which the tabernacle was first pitched after the conquest, and where the tribes were allotted their inheritances; where Eli lived and died, and Samuel received his call to the prophetic office. And it was here likewise that other sadly romantic little episode occurred by which Shiloh was made to furnish wives to the bereaved Benjaminites. Although figuring so largely in the history of Israel's past, it lies all desolate now; not even a habitation that we could see among the ruins; but numerous calls for backshish made us sensible that there were habitations somewhere in the region. Early in the afternoon of our second day's ride we see the tall form of Gerizim lifting itself up from the valley in our front; and a couple of hours later we are dismounted at the little walled enclosure containing the ruins of an old Crusader church, built over Jacob's well.

When the church crumbled into a heap of ruins the well was hidden from view, and partially choked with the debris; but now the visitor descends into a pit about ten feet deep to the original surface level of the well, and dropping a stone down into its dark depths, ascertains that there are yet about fifty feet of the well's depth unfilled with rubbish. The places throughout Palestine to which tradition, or the Latin church, has assigned some sacred site or event are countless, and many of them are of a doubtful character; but here at this well side one may sit and feel that he is upon sacred ground. Here, while He rested His wearied body, the very Son of God gave to the Samaritan woman the water and bread of life; and here He must have stopped on other occasions, because the well was by the side of a public highway leading from Galilee to Judea, over which He must more than once have passed. The traditional tomb of Joseph a short distance northward is more likely to be the real one than the one at Hebron. Turning westward at this point we ride up the valley between Ebal and Gerizim, and in twenty minutes are at our tents, pitched just under the eastern wall of Nablous, the ancient Shechem.

'Tis a lovely vale we have just ridden through; old olive trees adorn the way, whilst Ebal and Gerizim, with their sacred associations, lend not a little attraction to the way. See yon vast amphitheatre shaped hollow in the side of Ebal! Now look across this narrow valley to a point exactly opposite on the side of Gerizim, and you see a similar shaped hollow. If they had been made by art instead of nature the places could not have been better adapted to the great Biblical event which we believe to have taken place at these two identical places. The whole width of the valley between these two places is not greater than three hundred yards, and the acoustic nature of the place is such that two persons may converse with each other across the intervening space in a still atmosphere. Nablus is said to contain about 13,000 people, largely Mohammedans, and not of the best reputation.

Two soldier guards do duty around our tents during the night. But whilst physical means may be used to restrain the unruly elements in man's nature, it is powerless in the contest with the natural elements, as we found in the experiences of the night, for the wind beat, and the rain poured, and our frail tabernacle came down over our heads. But next morning came to us bright and smiling as though nothing had happened, and we took our way over a new government road—one of the few good ones in Palestine—towards the hill of Samaria, coming in about two and a half hours to the modern village of Sebaste, a miserable little Arab village occupying the hill on which the city of Samaria, once the capital of the ten tribes, stood. The hill rises from the level of the valley surrounding to the height of about three hundred feet, and is nearly three miles in circuit. It is a magnificent site for a city. No wonder that Herod laid hold of it and made it the beautiful city that he did. We counted not less than seventy marble columns still upright, but with their capitals gone, of the original colonnade which Herod built around the city; and numbers of others half buried and prostrate. At the western end of the hill are sixteen more upright columns, all that remain of Herod's palace; and down at the lower edge of the hill on the north side are other buildings of Herodian origin. On the eastern edge of the hill are the ruins of St. John's church, the walls of which still stand from Crusader times. A small dome rises up out of the church which, according to the tradition, covers the remains of the Baptist, Elisha and Obadiah. Casting our vision down into the valley eastward, we can easily trace the course of the frightened Syrians on their way towards the Jordan valley on the night when the Lord fought for poor famished Samaria, and sent her the good news of deliverance by the lepers.

Descending from the hill of Samaria into the plain on the north, we ride through a fertile looking little valley, leaving on our right at the distance of about a mile the ancient Dothan, now only a heap of ruins. Limestone hills alternate with small

RUINS ON THE HILL OF SAMARIA.

green valleys during the larger portion of this day's ride. About mid-afternoon we enter a plain some three miles in length by one in breadth. Evidently Samaria has not suffered so much by the delay of the latter rains as Judea, for the barley and wheat look quite flourishing in the region through which we are now passing. Jenin is reached in time to enable us to ascend a high hill close to where our tents are pitched and take a survey of our surroundings ere the sun has gone down from sight behind the ridge of Carmel. Is it not a lovely vision? We never saw a grander one. There at our feet is the beautiful plain of Esdraelon, stretching from the mounts of Gilboa on the east to Carmel on the west, a distance of twenty-four miles. Level as a table and as green as a garden, it is a picture of loveliness amidst the naked sterility of the country which we will not soon forget. At the foot of the hill upon which we stand is Jenin, supposed to be the En-gannim of Joshua 19:21, one of the cities which fell to the lot of Issachar in the division. This is the utmost northern limit of Samaria. On our right stretches the range of Gilboa mountains, so fatal to Saul and Jonathan. On the far side of the valley fronting us is Little Hermon; looking past Little Hermon on the west, we see the hills of Nazareth, and at the western end of the valley tall Carmel lifts his green ridge up next the sea. In the morning we break camp, ride through the valley to its eastern side and are shown at a little distance down in the valley the fountain of Gideon, where the three hundred men were selected at whose hands the Midianites suffered such defeat. See the silver thread-like stream as it winds its way through the valley in its flow from the fountain! It was just in that locality that the Midianitish host lay encamped. And now our journey lies across the plain a distance of about ten miles to the foot of Little Hermon, or the hill of Morch. The first village in our way is known by the natives as Zerin, but it has a much deeper interest to the traveler when he understands that it stands upon the site of ancient Jezreel, the city made infamous by the wickedness of Ahab and Jezebel, and which was the scene of the last tragic act in the lives of this pair of evil-doers. Many stirring scenes have taken place in this immediate locality. The wild Prophet of Carmel has traversed this ground, bearing messages of coming woe to wicked rulers; armies, both ancient and modern, have met in the shock of deadly combat. In this immediate locality Kleber held the army of the Turks at bay until his little handful of soldiers was reinforced by the arrival of Napoleon. We come after a few minutes' ride to Sulim, the Shunem of Elisha's time, where he found such kind hospitality at the hands of a certain lady, and where, as the course of events rolled around, he brought back to life the dead son of his kind entertainer. We find here a nice fountain in the midst of a lemon grove, and take our mid-day rest and refreshment under the shade of the lemon trees. Passing around over the left shoulder of Little Hermon, we enter an arm of Esdraelon; and following the road leading along the base of the mountain on the north side, we are soon at the village of Nain, noted in our Lord's life as the place where He restored to life the only son of the poor widow. Farther on a half hour's ride and we are at Endur, the Endor of King Saul's time, where the witch is said to have conjured up the form of the dead Samuel. Crossing this arm of the Esdraelon plain, which extends in a northeasterly direction to Tabor, which may be seen from this point, we are among the Nazareth hills, and an hour of slow up hill riding brings us in sight of Nazareth.

We rejoice at the sight as though we were looking at the face of a long absent friend; for years have flown since the desire first took possession of our soul to look upon the places made sacred by our Lord's youth and manhood, death and resurrection. Nazareth is a modern looking city; the red tiles on the roofs of so many of its buildings give it quite a cheerful look from a distance. It is hill-encircled on all sides, and tries to climb by terraces the highest hill on its western side. Later on we are shown the place on one of these terraces near to where the present English Orphanage building stands, from which the attempt was made to hurl our Savior by His ungrateful townmen. We are likewise shown the workshop which Joseph and Jesus are said to have used. It appeared to us wondrously fresh and whole for so old a building. Near to it is shown the Synagogue in which Christ preached and offended the Nazarences at the time when they led Him forth to cast Him over the hill. The house and kitchen of Mary were visited; they look like caves hewn out of solid rock. Of one thing we are sure, the modern American housekeeper would think her lot in this world a very hard one if she had to carry on her domestic functions with no better house accommodation than tradition assigns to Mary. There is an old and very copious fountain adjoining the places just mentioned, to which, doubtless, both Mary and Jesus have often gone for water. It is the only fountain in the town and is constantly thronged with the maidens and women of the town who have come thither with their water jars for water. It is marvelous with what skill these women carry the water jars on their heads. The rain falls again in torrents during the first night of our stay at Nazareth. May Judea also share in the blessing which Galilee is now receiving in these rains, for her cisterns are most woefully in need of replenishment. There is an excellent institution for the education and training of Arab girls in Nazareth; it is under the care of the English Episcopal church. At present there are eighty girls under training. These schools are the real efficient missionary agencies in this land. Let the homes have Christian mothers, and Christ will soon be known and reverenced throughout the land from which He is as yet practically excluded.

We leave Nazareth with the rain still falling at intervals in light showers. We ride into Cana of Galilee dripping with the almost constant rain-fall since leaving our tents. We take refuge in the Latin Convent, visit the church, erected, it is said, over the spot where occurred the miraculous change of water into wine. The village of Keffer Kenna—the modern name of Cana—is an indifferent little Arab place, with nothing to make it noteworthy save the one traditional fact above alluded to. We are not a little surprised and amused by a little Arab boy, almost an infant, who, coming up to where we were standing and innocently looking up into our face, commenced to sing in his infant's English, "Jesus loves me, this I know," etc. Some-

SEA OF GALILEE.

body is keeping the light burning here, we thought. After lunch in the Convent we take our departure from Cana; and about the middle of the afternoon we are passing the Horns of Hattin, where, according to tradition, Christ delivered the Sermon on the Mount. The plain around it, over which we are passing, is the scene of the last great battle between the Crusaders and Saracens. Here on the field of Hattin, Saladin struck a death blow to the power of the Crusaders in the Holy Land.

An hour's ride from this point brings us to Tiberias and the beautiful sea of Galilee. No wonder the Savior loved it. It is calm as a summer morning when we reach its shore. The Bedouins are bringing their flocks from the neighboring hills to water them from the lake. It is the Jews' Sabbath when we arrive; and the Jews, largely in the majority in Tiberias, are dressed in their Sunday best. Tiberias is a dirty, ruinous old place, with a population of about 5,000. Our tents, by an unfortunate management, are pitched within the walls; and we soon discover that there is a large population, of which, doubtless, the census makes no note, but which are likely to tent with us during the night. As the sun is about to sink behind the western hills, we discover what we have been eagerly searching for during half of the afternoon; grey old Hermon has cast aside the light cloud veil which has obscured his tall form during the afternoon, and now stands revealed in all his majesty. We spend the Sabbath by the seaside.

The Scotch Free Church some time ago established a medical mission at Tiberias, of which Dr. Torrence now has charge, lately reinforced by Rev. Mr. Ewing and wife. We had the pleasure of meeting with them in their Sabbath service, and also of meeting a son of the famous Dr. Guthrie, of Scotland, a barrister from Edinburgh who, like ourselves, is a pilgrim in the region. It was pleasant to join with these brethren in a service of worship on the shore of this beautiful lake, so fraught with memories of the Incarnate God. He loved to linger on its shores. Here He uttered some of His most wonderful discourses, on its shores found four at least of the Apostles, and gave healing to multitudes of diseased bodies. Surely these dwellers by the sea lacked not evidence of His Messiahship in the wonders He wrought in their sight and hearing! And yet those awful woes under which Capernaum, Bethsaida and Chorazin have withered into nothingness, were all deserved; for they believed not, in spite of the evidence which His works furnished of His Messiahship.

What a melancholy contrast between these shores as we see them now and as they were in the Savior's time. Then, there were nine populous towns on the shores of the sea, and its waters were alive with fishermen's boats and boats of commerce. Whole fleets of war vessels in the time of Josephus used to cut its waters, and engage in deadly strife upon it. But now you look in vain for its towns. A few scattered columns and boulders, almost hidden by tall thistles, at Tell Hum, are supposed to belong to Capernaum. Magdala—the modern Mejdel—is a squalid little Arab village. Tiberias, a new town and the residence of Herod when the Savior taught upon the lake shores, is only a shattered ruin. An earthquake in 1837 threw down its walls and killed the half of its population. On the eastern and southern shores nothing but ruins are found. About a dozen small boats are now found on the lake. Did not He who spake as never man spake say it should be so? and need we any other evidence of His divinity than this, that the history of these shores was spoken by His lips long years before the events themselves which go to make up the history were actual occurrences?

About a mile south of Tiberias, past the ruins of the old Herodian palace, are the Tiberias Hot Springs, famous for their health-giving properties as far back as the time of Josephus. Whilst our tents are striking on Monday morning we ride down the shore of the Lake to investigate them. The water stands at the high temperature of 144° Fahrenheit, and is brackish in taste. It reaches the bath house from four different springs,

THROUGH SAMARIA AND GALILEE. 213

having their source somewhere in the heights above. The bowels of the earth appear to be in a dreadfully disturbed condition all along this western shore of the Lake. There are caves in the cliffs back of Tiberias so hot with steam vapor that they cannot be explored.

FISHERMAN CASTING NET—SEA OF GALILEE.

Our tents are to be pitched at Nazareth to-night, and they have gone on by a direct course, leaving us to pursue the route to Mt. Tabor, and thence over the hills to Nazareth. Four hours' riding over a broken country brings us to the foot of Tabor on the northern side. Thus far we have found the country treeless, save those of a fruit-bearing variety; but around Tabor we find the terebinth and carob growing quite profusely. Tabor is a pretty mount to look upon; separated from neighboring heights, it rises up alone fourteen hundred feet above the level of Esdraelon. We are an hour in making the ascent over the zig-zag, stony way on its northern side. The scrubby terebinth oaks cling to its side two-thirds of the way up. The top is a broad plateau, large enough for a good-sized town to stand upon. There is a Latin monastery and Greek church on the top near the eastern end, with the ruins of an old Crusader church, for which the Russian pilgrims seem to have a special reverence, for we found scores of them, men and women, down on their hands and knees digging and scratching away among the ruins for some relic to carry away with them.

On the top of Tabor one has the finest view of Palestine scenery he can get anywhere in the land. Little Hermon with Nain and Endor a few miles to the southwest, the mount of Gilboa to the south, eastward the continuation of Esdraelon and the Jordan, westward the whole stretch of Esdraelon—the old valley of Jezreel, or Plain of Megiddo—with the bold Carmel promontory, and to the northward the Nazareth hills with the town nestling in among them at a distance of about six miles. Such a vision of a region around which clusters so much of Biblical interest is one greatly to be coveted and enjoyed. The inner man is refreshed on the top of the Mount and we journey on towards Nazareth.

Our tent stakes are pulled again the following morning, and we make the last stage of our journey between Nazareth and Carmel; Mr. and Mrs. Ridpath going up the coast by way of Tyre and Sidon to Beyrout, and the other pilgrim, with an attack of Syrian fever upon him, taking a steamer down the coast to Jaffa, thence back to Jerusalem.

CHAPTER XIX.

FROM JERUSALEM TO ATHENS, VIA BEYROUT, SMYRNA AND EPHESUS.

OUR Pilgrim days are over in this Land of the Bible; pleasant ones they have been, too, albeit there have been sorrowful reflections in the presence of things that cast a gloomy shadow over the past. But our knowledge is increased, our faith in the Book or Revelation fortified and our love for the Man of Calvary intensified by having wandered over the stony paths, climbed the limestone hills and ridden over some of the fertile plains of Palestine.

Our fellow-pilgrims who accompanied us thither have gone on their way homeward weeks ago, and left one solitary pilgrim to find his way back as best he can. But one is hardly ever alone in such a pilgrimage as we are making; and thus it happens that at the very outset we have an agreeable companion in the person of an American minister, who so feels the infirmity of his years that he is glad to have some more youthful energies to rely upon.

It is now the early part of May, and the latter rains which have fallen quite abundantly since the middle of April have put a cheerful look on things generally. As we pass over the plain of Sharon on our way back to Jaffa, we notice the fellaheen gathering in the harvest. "Strange it is," remarked Father L——, "that the machinery-man from our side of the waters has not penetrated the Orient with his labor-saving steel and iron. See those people! reaping with the hand sickle, just as they have done during all the centuries since Father Abraham's time." "And just as they will continue to do," I answer, "until something is invented to take the stones out of their way, and when the stones of Judea are gathered up there will not be much left of it." Too rough for wheeled vehicles, they use camels and ropes to get the sheaves to the threshing floor; this primitive floor was made, we cannot tell how many years ago, by smoothing off the rock.

A day of waiting on our steamer at Jaffa gives us opportunity to visit the Mission schools under the care of the Church of England, see once more the strange mixture of wailing and pic-nicing in the cemetery north of town and take a last ramble among the beautiful gardens, lemon and orange orchards of the town. It is night-fall when our Turkish steamer weighs anchor and starts on her journey up the Syrian coast.

Next morning when we go on deck we find ourselves just opposite Sidon, the snowy Lebanon mountains raising their tall summits in the background. Two or three hours more of steaming and we round the sandy point on the northern slope of which is situated Beyrout. There are no docks in any of these Oriental harbors at which an ocean vessel may land passengers and cargo; she must anchor out in deep water and make all transfers by means of small boats. There is the usual confusion and wild scramble for passengers among the Arab boatmen.

From information previously obtained, we had decided on the Hotel Victoria, whose boat—we had been told—would meet the steamer. We hail the man whose boat bears the yellow ensign of the "Victoria," and are soon proceeding with him to the landing. Fearing lest we had made a mistake, we ask our man, who is an Italian, if the rates per day at his hotel are five francs, holding up five fingers as we do so; he assures us that is right, and we subside. But wary as we have been, a few days later when we come to settle our bill we find that we have been taken in, and our bill doubled, and no amount of plain English could make the rascally Italian landlord understand the moral defects of the transaction. There is another hotel "Victoria," a more modest and honest affair, on whose reputation our Non capisco man makes gain for his house; reader, beware of him when you go to Beyrout! And pass not by—turn around him if you can—the mercenary Turk who sits at the receipt of customs; for a little backshish he would sell his best mother-in-law.

Beyrout is pleasant, rather neat appearing town, as Turkish towns go; and if there was any government in the land there would be nothing to hinder it from becoming an important commercial seaport. But under the present regime the Turk is not able even to run his own post-office, for here at Beyrout we find half a dozen different nations keeping post-office for him.

Our hotel is surrounded by gardens with a bright array of geraniums of all hues, and groves of palms, orange, lemon, mulberry and pomegranates are scattered out over the city, giving the dull stone buildings an air of beauty and cheerfulness. We enjoy a quiet Sabbath visiting the large and prosperous mission of the Presbyterian Church. The first service in the morning is in Arabic, and we are present only to see how much of a hold the mission has taken on the Arabic mind. We were greatly surprised to find a large church well filled with a good, attentive congregation. An English service followed the Arabic, conducted by an Episcopalian clergyman.

The mission Press, scattering its millions of pages of religious literature in the Arabic language far up the Bosphorus, southward to Egypt and out into the plains of the Euphrates and Tigris, is a mighty factor in the great seed sowing of gospel truth among the Arabic races. But this is not the only axe that is being laid at the root of Moslem fanaticism and ignorance. The work of education at Beyrout and elsewhere is training up native teachers and preachers, from whose mouths the native population more readily receive the truth than from foreigners. The Presbyterians have a well established college and theological seminary in the city under the care of the Jessups. There is also a well conducted and patronized Ladies' Seminary which is doing a good work.

Leaving Beyrout by the Austrian Lloyd steamship "Minerva" on the evening of the 7th, the next morning at daybreak we are abreast of Cyprus. The regular fortnightly steamer lies too a day at this Island, but being a special, we pass it without a halt. Barnabas hailed from this Island. It is now in the possession of the English, and unless the interior is more fruitful than that portion of it which we see along the southern coast, it must prove a barren possession; but it is doubtless held as a check on the Dardanelles. Another twenty-four hours' steaming and the Isle of Rhodes looms into view in our front. We give it the cold shoulder likewise, although its pretty town, shining white amidst olive trees, make us wish that we might step ashore for a while. Its harbor is noted as the place where the Colossus of Rhodes once stood. Steaming along its northern coast we have on our right, but a mile or two distant, the mainland of Asia Minor.

During the next twenty-four hours' steaming we have isles to the right and isles to the left; a constant succession of barren, rock upheaved isles of varying sizes, many of which are noted in Grecian song and legend. One above all others has a peculiar interest to us. Most fervently did we wish that we might not pass it in the night, and in this particular we are gratified. Southward a distance of four or five miles, lifting its ragged top high above the sea, is the Island home of the banished John. Patmos, ever sacred in the Christian's memory, and gladdening to the pilgrim's eye! How we longed to step ashore and ascend to the castle and town which show so prominently on its top. With our glasses we see that its sides are deeply rent in places, forming gorges wild and lonely. The whole Isle cannot be more than 20 miles in circumference. Looking out from his sea girt prison over the waters to the near shores of Asia Minor, and thinking of his persecution-tossed brethren at Ephesus and elsewhere, we do not wonder that the Apostle, longing to be present with them, and thinking of the impassable barrier of the sea, says of the new heaven and earth, "And there was no more sea."

Samos soon comes into view, and is passed on our right. It is celebrated in heathen mythology as the birthplace of Juno; there the Grecian Philosopher Pythagoras was born, and for a long time the historian Herodotus resided on the Island and composed, it is said, the major portion of his celebrated history here. Another night of restful slumber passes whilst our vessel pursues her way through the quiet waters of the Ægean, and we wake to find ourselves in the Smyrna harbor.

We have planned a visit to Ephesus for this day, and as we desire to go and return on the same day by regular train we lose no time in getting to the railway station. A ride of two hours over a plain covered with vineyards, fig and olive trees, all looking bright and fresh in their early spring attire, brings us to the little station of Ayassalouk, near to which are the ruins of ancient Ephesus. The first object that attracts the attention on leaving the train is the tall supporting columns and arches of the aqueduct which supplied Ephesus with water. But what are those things standing like sentinels on the top of each of these columns? They are storks, watching at the sides of their mates as they sit upon their nests. No one seems inclined to harm them, and they are as tame as doves. But to the stranger's eye it seems a weird and fantastic sight to see those birds of the swamp in sole possession of these remains of ancient greatness.

But there are other evidences still of the desolation that has overtaken the once magnificent city of Ephesus. There are forests of thistles all around you as you try to make your way by some narrow foot-path to the tombs and columbaria scattered around. By dint of climbing and dodging the thistles by the way, we reach the ruins of the church of St. John. A large congregation is gathered within the ruinous walls of this old church, which, being disturbed by our approach, come swarming out of the sashless windows and up from the roofless top in black clouds. The rooks are in possession; and again a sense of desolation and abandonment comes upon us as we contemplate the old ruin and remember what it once was. Tradition says that the Apostle of the Apocalypse ended his days here, so also Luke, and that a large church was erected and dedicated jointly to their memories; likewise, that when too feeble to walk to it the aged disciple was carried into it, and tenderly addressing his little flock as "little children," exhorted them "to love one another." Still continuing our climb up the hill we reach the spacious ruins of an old castle of Genoese origin. It crowns the top of a conical hill quite conspicuous to your right as you approach the station from Smyrna.

Descending again to the plain we take the beaten track a mile or more out from the station until we come to the mass of ruins where once stood Ephesus proper. Recent excavations, conducted by Mr. Wood, have brought to light the real site of the temple of Diana, the magnificent theatre, capable of seating twenty-four thousand persons, the Odeum, etc. The cave of the Seven Sleepers, and St. Luke's tomb, are also pointed out to the visitor. But all save the last two are a mingled mass of shapeless ruins.

How completely has the unrepentant Ephesus experienced the fulfillment of the Apocalyptic message in the removal of her candle-stick! Not a habitation is to be found where once her people moved in countless numbers. But a far different state of things meets us at Smyrna. It is a city of over 200,000 people, half of which are Greek Christians, with a fine port frequented by the vessels of all nations. True, there are some narrow, crooked and dirty streets, but, all in all, it is the most handsome of the cities where the miserable Turk bears rule that we have yet seen. It climbs the gradually ascending slope of Mt. Pagus until its very top is reached; there a castle, the walls of which still stand in tolerable order, occupies a large area. In the central ground of this castle are underground arches and chambers of an old Christian church, which may possibly be the one where Polycarp once ministered, the second one in the order given of the seven churches of Asia. Only a few minutes' walk to the westward brings us to a tall cyprus tree beside which is the stone mausoleum of the martyr Bishop of Smyrna. All through the ages the Christian church of Smyrna has treasured and kept careful watch of the spot where the ashes of Polycarp were deposited. The tall cyprus that stands by the side of his mausoleum is a prominent object from the harbor.

The Smyrna people we find to be a pleasure-loving lot. Theatres and cafes along the quay are always thronged; while bands of music are giving forth their harmony of song to captivate the ear and draw the piaster from the pocket. Under anything like an equitable government Smyrna would soon rise into the rank of the first commercial cities of the world.

The "Minerva" is bound for Constantinople, and has on board a large number of pilgrims returning from the Holy Land, for the special accommodation of which she has remained at anchor in the Smyrna harbor for a day whilst the pilgrims visited Ephesus. Father L—— continues his journey in the "Minerva," and I am once more alone with my face set toward the Grecian coast.

At noon on the 12th the Austrian steamer "Galatea" bears us out of the harbor en route to Athens. Once more we are out among the Grecian Isles. Mytilene, the ancient Lesbos, once the rival of Athens in literature and the arts, "Where the Burning Sappho loved and sung," is passed on our right, and swinging around a point of the mainland to the southward we have Scio in our front. Here we halt to land and take on passengers and mail. Scio is called the "Paradise of the Levant," and its appearance from the deck of our vessel justifies its title. The town of Scio spreads itself over much of the eastern face of the Isle; olive trees sprinkled all over the town give it an inviting appearance. Seven years ago it suffered the misfortune of a severe earthquake, several thousands of its citizens losing their lives; no paradise without its serpent. Sabbath morning finds us rounding the southernmost point of Greece. The white columns of a ruined temple crowning the top of a small rock island near the shore is an intimation that we are approaching the land where in ages past the devotees of the multitudinous gods and godesses were wont to lavish their means in the erection of magnificent marble structures, remains of which are to be seen in many parts of Greece to-day.

As Piraeus, the port of Athens, comes into view, remembering our experiences with the mercenary Turk "At the receipt of customs," and with the vociferous boatmen who each and all want to set us upon terra firma, we gird our loins for the ordeal, and see that our passport is in the proper pocket. But our anxiety is all useless, for the friendly Greek, who proves to be an officer of the royal household, and whose chance acquaintance we had made on the vessel, took us under his protecting wings and the officials looked on with supreme indifference. It is with a feeling of relief that we recognize the fact that our wanderings in the land of the half-civilized Turk are at an end, and that now we are to move among a civilized people. Piraeus is a thriving port of entry, with a present population of about thirty thousand. A railway connects it with Athens, trains running every half hour. A fifteen minutes' ride through a succession of olive groves, and we alight in the capital city of the Grecian Kingdom.

CHAPTER XX.

RAMBLES AROUND ATHENS AND CORINTH.

AT THE Hotel Royal we find neat and comfortable quarters at a moderate expense. Our landlord is a Greek, and although in our college days we acquire some knowledge of the classic language, yet it avails us nothing in converse with the modern Greek. He has made a new dictionary since the days of the classic writers, and while retaining the same alphabet and many of the words, the language of the modern Greek would hardly be understood by the literati of the classical period. But here as everywhere else we find those who comprehend us in the use of English, if we do not understand them in the use of the native language; so we get along nicely with our landlord through the medium of a clerk who speaks some English.

Athens is not to be compared to the cities of the Asia Minor coast which we have been visiting, in its lack of progressive spirit or cleanliness of look; nor, on the other hand, can it be compared to the average of European cities, in its commercial activity, and rapid strides in the arts and sciences of an advanced Christian civilization. It occupies a mean between the two extremes. Not satisfied with the stolid and non-progressive character of its neighbors across the Ægean, and yet partially hampered by them in its movements, Athens is to be admired for her rapid advancement towards the higher perfection of art and scientific attainment of her European rivals.

Famed in past ages as the center of civilization, of the highest renown in the arts and sciences, whence originated poets, orators, historians and philosophers, such as other lands could not produce, she may yet recover her old position of eminence among the nations.

When the visitor has looked over the magnificent ruins on the Acropolis and elsewhere, which have come down in hoary age from the Athens of Paul's day to remind the Athens of the present day what grandeur is yet unattained by it, he will readily pardon the pride of one of its ancient citizens when he thus apostrophizes it: "Oh thou, our Athens, violet wreathed, brilliant, most enviable city." Some of our guide books describe the streets of Athens as most wretchedly dirty and crooked; we found them neither, generally speaking. There are some streets both narrow and crooked; but the main thoroughfares are of average width, well paved and clean. But this guide book inaccuracy only shows the lack of recent revision. The cities of Greece, like those of Italy, have been undergoing vast changes during these later years. A tidal wave of prosperity seems to have flowed in upon them; railroads and canals are connecting them by rapid transit with the rest of Europe, and they are feeling the quickened pulse of the times in a marvelous manner.

In traversing the streets of Athens one is reminded of his college days when he used to pore for hours over his Homer or Odyssey, for he sees Greek signs confronting him everywhere. Instead of the Italian Via or the French Rue, he sees the familiar Odos. Looking up for the names of the streets, he reads on one corner Socrates, on another Sophocles, on another Demosthenes, etc. At the eastern end of the city is a conical mountain overlooking the city as well as the Acropolis beyond. This is Mt. Lycabettus, with a little white church sitting on its summit; and thither we make our first visit as an advantageous point to study the city from. The toil of the ascent is well repaid by the glorious panorama of the city and country adjacent. We imagine that few worshippers ever find their way to the lonely little church of St. George on the hill top.

Athens, like Rome, takes a special pride in preserving the ruins of the older city; and as we pass through portions of the city where new buildings are being constructed, or levelings made for new streets, we notice marble busts, and great pottery jars that have been freshly unearthed, and vessels which the Athenian housewife of centuries past found a use for, all laid out with care, ready for transit to some of the city's museums of antiquities.

Athens has few public squares that present any attraction to the visitor; the Pl. de la Constitution, or Palace square, being perhaps the only exception. The principal hotels of the city surround it on the north and the west, the Royal Palace and gardens being on the east and south sides. One has a good opportunity to see the Athenians in a festive mood if he visits this square in the afternoon of any pleasant day in early spring or autumn, for they gather here around small tables to indulge in games, gossip, and to listen to the military band that daily furnishes some excellent music. The Greek's musical attainments are far superior to the Turk's. The grounds adjoining the palace are tastefully laid out and abundantly supplied with tall cypress trees, which, with their dark green mingled with the lighter hues of the pepper and other trees, give a pleasing tone of color to this part of the city, otherwise treeless. Here the nightingale, under queenly protection, sends forth his morning song with many to enjoy but none to molest him.

Modern Athens, apart from the ruins of her more brilliant ancestor, has little to detain or interest the visitor who has first made the tour of the continental cities; but in the gigantic marble ruins which cover the Acropolis hill, and a few old temple and theatre ruins which surround it, she has an attraction which is not excelled even in Rome itself. Let us take a day around the Acropolis in communion with old Athens; and as we jour-

THE PARTHENON.

ney thither it will be well to approach it on the north side and inspect some other antiquities equally as interesting as those that crown the top of the hill.

Here is an old temple in a wonderful state of preservation, when its age is considered. It is the Theseum, justly considered the most perfect specimen of architectural beauty in existence. It was built 469 B. C. by Cimon, son of Miltiades, for the reception of the bones of Theseus when they were brought from Scyros. It antedates the Parthenon by about thirty years. It is built of Pentelic marble in the Doric style of architecture. Thirty-four columns, each 3 feet 4 inches in diameter and 19 feet high, surround the building, making a covered portico the entire circumference of 298 feet. Earthquakes have shaken the columns, throwing parts of them a little out of joint; and the Turk has left his destroying marks upon it; but when viewed at a little distance these imperfections are not noticeable.

Continuing our ramble around to the west side, we mount a flight of old stone steps cut in the rock and stand within a very few yards, in all probability, of where Paul stood when he made his memorable address to the much perturbed Athenians concerning the "New Doctrine." Mars Hill, or the Areopagus, is a low rock hill on which the highest judicial court of Athens was accustomed to hold its nocturnal sessions. The Athenians of Paul's day, and long before his day as well, were accustomed in their genial climate to out of door meetings. Not only was this true of their judicial gatherings, but it was likewise true of their religious meetings, and places of public entertainment, as we shall have occasion to notice. We are interested in this place, and cannot forbear imagining an Athenian audience just below and ourselves the orator of the occasion; and in this effort we can assure the reader that we had rapt attention; not the least disrespect was shown us by our grey-headed audience. And was it not even so in Paul's time? Here the most weighty decisions in matters pertaining to religion and the state were given; here criminals of the highest order were given their trial and received their sentence. "There was everything," say Conybeare and Howson in their Life of St. Paul, "in the place to incline the auditors, so far as they were seriously disposed at all to reverent and thoughtful attention. Whether we contrast the intense earnestness of the man who spoke, with the frivolous character of those who surrounded him, or compare the certain truth and awful meaning of the Gospel he revealed with the worthless polytheism which had made Athens a proverb on the earth, or even think of the mere words uttered that day in the

ATHENS.

clear atmosphere on the summit of Mars' Hill, in connection with the objects of art, temples, statues, and altars, which stood round on every side, we feel that the moment was, and was intended to be, full of the most impressive teaching for every age of the world."

Striking the carriage way that winds up the western face of the declivity, we follow it until it gives way to the footpath which leads us up to a vaulted Turkish gateway; passing through this tunnel-like entrance we find ourselves upon a terrace with a number of buildings and gateways, through which we pass to steps leading up to the Propylae or grand entrance to the ruins on the summit. To give a description of this grand gateway that would do it justice would require a chapter by itself; suffice it, therefore, simply to say that it was built of Pentelic marble and extended across the whole western end of the Acropolis, 170 feet; begun in 437 B. C., it was finished in five years. Five portals still remain, and until the 14th century the whole remained in a good state of preservation. Marble blocks and columns lying in one mingled mass of ruin over a large area now meet our gaze.

At the northeast angle of the ruins are the remains of the Parthenon. Look and admire, for you will see nothing like it in the wide world; "The finest edifice on the finest site in the world." Here was attained the highest perfection in architectural art; and the sculptor's art, as well, reached its culminating point under the hand of a Phidias in the adornment of this Minerva temple; finished in 438 B. C., it remained in good preservation until the Venetian siege, about the middle of the 17th century, when the explosion of a powder magazine tore off the roof and left the grand temple only a mass of ruins. The temple was 243 by 108 feet, with 46 supporting columns of pure white marble 36 feet in height with a diameter of $6\frac{1}{2}$ feet. Within it stood the gold and ivory statue of Athenæ Parthenos—Minerva —47 feet in height, the work of Phidias. The British museum has enriched itself to a considerable degree by a large portion of the frieze which once adorned this most magnificent temple.

There is an Athenian tradition concerning the Lyccabetus hill which the cloud of ravens that we have disturbed in our visit to the Parthenon brings to remembrance. Athena was bringing the rock to Athens to form a bulwark for her citadel, when a raven caused her such sudden surprise by announcing the birth of Ericthonius that she dropped the rock where we see it now, and in resentment for the bird's officiousness, forbade his race to roost on the Acropolis; but now, in defiance of the goddess' prohibition, the bird would be sole master of the situ-

230 FROM OCCIDENT TO ORIENT.

THE ACROPOLIS, ATHENS.

ation, if it were not for the hawks and kestrels which dispute possession with him. The Parthenon, situated on the eastern edge of the rock hill, occupies the highest point of it, 300 feet above the level of the city. The walls which encircle the top edge of this rock precipice are as old as the time of Miltiades and Themistocles, with later repairs by Venetians and Turks. We might well tarry much longer on this interesting hill to examine other temple ruins of note, but there are yet several objects of interest at the southern foot of the hill that will claim attention, so we had best make our way down to them.

Descending to the foot of the Acropolis on the south side, we find the well preserved remains of two theatres, the Odeum of Herodes Athicus, with seating capacity for six thousand persons, the theatre of Dionysus, with seats for thirty thousand spectators. The seats in this latter theatre are well preserved, the lower tier being marble settees intended for the priests, with a central chair for the priest of Dionysus. This theatre was completed by Lycurgus about 340 B. C.; and we see the same seats, occupying, doubtless, the same position as they did in the time of the builder. It seems incredible that a poor pilgrim of the 19th century should seat himself in the same identical seat that an idolatrous priest of the 4th century B. C. had occupied; but we are certain that he did. Within a few minutes' walk of the theatre stand fifteen columns belonging to the temple of Zeus Olympus; one other column lies prostrate, being overthrown by a gale in 1852. This temple was begun in 530 B. C., but owing to frequent interruptions was not completed until 135 A. D. One hundred and twenty columns, each 64 feet in height by $7\frac{1}{4}$ in diameter, originally surrounded the structure; and the columns that remain, of the Corinthian order, still retain their capitals.

Turning our steps now in a southwesterly direction, a walk of half a mile brings us to an old monument which, from its prominent position and height, has doubtless awakened our curiosity while we were upon the Acropolis; it is the monument of Philopappus, erected to the memory of a Syrian of note, somewhere between 105-115 A. D. It is in a ruinous state, and king Time is likely to get the better of the old structure before another century passes. In the eastern side of this Philopappus hill is the so-called prison of Socrates; whether real or fictitious we know not. It is a triple-celled grotto cut in the face of the hill, and, judging from its general contour, more likely to have been a rock-hewn dwelling than the prison of Socrates. In this immediate region there are remains of a large number—about eight hundred—of rock-hewn tombs and dwellings which are, by some authorities, supposed to have formed a part of the primeval Pelasgic city.

Near to the prison of Socrates on the north is the hill Pnyx where the Athenian orators used to address the multitudes. Here we find a smooth rock platform capable of accommodating seven or eight thousand persons. These assemblies of the Athenians, as also on Mars Hill and in the Dyonysian theatre, were all in the open air. The Bema and stone steps leading up to it are still in place; indeed, they can't well get out of place, for they are cut out of the rock itself.

We have made hasty visits to most of the antiquities of Athens, and ere we leave Greece we are desirous of visiting the Isthmus of Corinth to see what may be seen of old Corinth. We are sorry now that we did not plan a little better in reference to our journey back to Italy. Instead of going round the southern coast of Italy by steamer from the Piraeus, we might have taken train from Athens by way of the Isthmus and Gulf of Corinth to Patras, and thence by steamer to Brindisi. In this way we could have visited Corinth without retracing our steps back to the Piraeus; but circular tickets purchased at Rome will compel the longer sea journey. Let other travelers make note of this; for tourist agencies usually consult their own profit more than the traveler's convenience and economy.

Taking an early morning train, we are off for a day's excursion to Corinth, distant forty-four miles. We soon reach the

Pass of Daphni, with Mts. Poikilon on the right and Ægaleus on the left. Emerging from the Pass, our route leads us along the northern shore of the Elusinan Bay. Looking southward, our eyes fall upon the waters of Salamis, and, at the left, the point of Ægaleus, where once

> " A king sat on the rocky brow
> Which looks o'er sea-born Salamis,
> And ships by thousands lay below,
> And men and nations—all were his !
> He counted them at break of day,
> And when the sun was set, where were they ?"

Here it was that Xerxes witnessed the memorable battle of Salamis, when he sought to crush the Athenian fleet by the multitude of his vessels which filled the Bay; and noting each valiant deed that was performed by individuals of his fleet, he would inquire who they were, and where they lived, who did such valiant deeds, that he might properly reward them when the victory was won. He did not dream that "The battle is not always to the strong," and that at the close of the day he would be despoiled of the fine fleet that he deemed invincible.

The ride along the edge of the cliffs looking down into the sea is truly a most enjoyable one. Below us about one hundred and fifty feet, are the clear blue waters of the sea lying on this calm spring morning in perfect quietude. We are soon crossing the isthmus separating the Gulf of Corinth from the Bay of Elusis. A canal, over which we pass, is now in process of construction, which, when completed about two years hence, will very considerably shorten the sea route from Athens to the Italian coast. Three hours of ride and we are at the modern village of Corinth. Westward about two and a half miles we observe a steep rock mountain rising 1,700 feet above the plain level, encircled on the summit by an old wall. This is the Acro-Corinth; and at its base on the northern side lie all that is left of old Corinth. A miserable little village at the base has grown up among the ruins. Seven columns of an old temple constructed about 500 B. C., standing erect, are the most noticeable of all the ruins. Corinth, it is said, once had a million of people, and the whole plain round about was covered with the city.

The city is of special interest to us because of its associations with Paul's life. He toiled at his craft of tent making here for eighteen months, preaching the gospel of the Crucified One to the wicked Corinthians. They were wicked, exceedingly so; for we find the Apostle in the letters he afterwards wrote them making reference to things done among them that were a shame even to name; and the history of its people, as we gather it from profane sources, goes to prove that Paul had reason enough to write of them as he did.

It is just harvest time; and the Greeks, men, women and children, are gathering in their harvest, reaping with the primitive hook sickle. But we wonder, as we look at the rock-strewn soil, at the fine fields of grain growing upon it. We are ambitious to climb the huge rock of the Acro-Corinth, for we are told that the vision from the top is not excelled elsewhere in Greece, but we have been guilty of a little piece of imprudence, which we warn others who visit the place not to commit, in wasting our time and strength in walking to the place from the station at new Corinth, so that when we are partially up the steep incline we find ourselves lacking in the two particulars mentioned. We content ourselves with a refreshing draught from a fine spring that comes flowing out of the side of the rocky citadel, and in pantomimic conversation with some of the harvesters who take their noon day lunch at the spring.

There are some very unique costumes among the Greek peasantry. Here are men with short skirts coming down to the knees, much after the fashion of the stage actress's dancing costume. These skirts are of a white cotton or linen texture, apparently of half a dozen folds in thickness. A long sock and heavy shoes complete the attire to the extremities. Were it not for the masculine countenance of the wearer, it would puzzle us oftentimes to tell male from female, owing to the similarity of dress.

As we turn away from Corinth with a lingering look at the huge rock that we have not been able to surmount, Byron's "Siege of Corinth" comes into remembrance with a renewed interest:

> " Many a vanished year and age,
> And tempest's breath, and battle's rage,
> Have swept o'er Corinth; yet she stands,
> A fortress formed to Freedom's hands.
> The whirlwind's wrath, the earthquake's shock,
> Have left untouched her hoary rock,
> The keystone of a land, which still,
> Though fallen, looks proudly on that hill,
> The landmark to the double tide
> That purpling rolls on either side,
> As if their waters chafed to meet,
> Yet dance and crouch beneath her feet.
> But could the blood before her shed
> Since first Timoleon's brother bled,
> Or baffled Persia's despot fled,
> Arise from out the earth which drank
> The stream of slaughter as it sank,
> That sanguine ocean would o'erflow
> Her isthmus idly spread below ;
> Or could the bones of all the slain,
> Who perished there, be piled again,
> That rival pyramid would rise
> More mountain-like, through those clear skies,
> Than yon tower-capp'd Acropolis,
> Which seems the very clouds to kiss."

CHAPTER XXI.

FROM ATHENS TO LONDON, THROUGH NORTHERN ITALY AND THE ALPS.

YES! we are glad that we have paid a visit to the land of the Greek, even if we have seen it to a limited extent only. We have tasted of the delights of his land in sufficient measure to whet our appetite for a more thorough acquaintance with it at some future time—when it can be reached by an air line passage through the clouds—perhaps. We carry away a friendly feeling for the Greek, for he has treated us kindly and given us full value for all our money. He does not keep a horde of beggars on his streets to make life miserable for his tourist friends. Not a beggar have we seen in Athens during our stay of nearly a week. Unlike his Turkish neighbor who regards you with a scowling countenance even while he is drawing his daily sustenance from you, he greets you with a pleasant smile, which we may receive as his speech of welcome.

These reflections upon the Greek character are noted down as we sit upon the deck of the "Taormina" watching the preparation for departure. The "Taormina" is an Italian vessel, and not as good as some others of the same line that we have voyaged in. Her crew are Italians, and there is not a man on board who speaks any English save the first mate and chief engineer, both of whom seem desirous to make the voyage as pleasant as possible to the solitary American passenger.

All goes well until we have passed over the Saronic Gulf; but as we round Cape Malea at the southern point of the Peloponnesus, a hurricane of wind strikes the vessel on the starboard side and sends her over on her port side at a very uncomfortable angle for one who wants to stay on deck. The Cape is well named Malea, for from of old it has had an evil reputation, whence arose the proverbial saying among the ancient Greeks, "After doubling Cape Malea, forget your native country." Just to our left at this point is the island of Cythera, the first one of the Ionian Islands among which our course now lies.

The large island of Zante stands directly in our front as we go on deck on the morning of the second day out. The town of Zante stretches for a mile and a half along the shore of the semi-circular bay on the eastern side of the island. The Italian calls the island the "Flower of the Levant"; and it does wear an island beauty of no mean character as we view it in our passage. An hour's steaming brings us abreast of Cephalonia, the largest one of the Ionian islands, having a circumference of over one hundred miles. It is an island of convents, there being over twenty of them, holding about one-sixth of the cultivated land of the island. Opposite the northern portion of the island, with a narrow strait betwixt, is the Island of Ithaca, so celebrated in Homeric song. It is a small, rocky island not more than seventeen miles in length by four in breadth. Homer well describes it as—

"Horrid with cliffs, our meager land allows
Thin herbage for the mountain goat to browse."

Santa Maura—the Lucadia of ancient times—Paxo and Antipaxo, and Corfu, are passed on the second day from Athens, and in the early morning of the third day, the Sabbath, the white stone buildings of Brindisi are in sight. The vessel lies here all day attending to cargo, and we improve the opportunity of a ramble through the old town. No place of worship could be found, save the cathedral, in which we have not learned to feel at home. Brindisi is the least interesting place for a tourist to visit of any place we have seen.

Pulling anchor again at ten o'clock p. m., Bari is entered early the next morning, where another halt is made long enough to enable us to look the town over. It is an overcrowded town, with no attractions for the visitor save an excellent harbor and a lively port; eight ocean steamers are at anchor, busy loading and unloading cargo, as the "Taormina" comes in. A brief halt is made at Ancona, and we have the open sea before us until we end our voyage at the Queen City of the Adriatic.

The dangers of the Adriatic are safely passed after a five days' steam from Athens, the last one of which upsets the stomachs of our passengers most completely. How the foaming sea did dash its huge waves up over the deck! We are glad when the tall spires and towers of the City of Waters comes into view. We tarry a couple of days to see what new thing under the sun can be found in this most unique of all European cities. She seems to rise right up out of the waters, for her hundred isles on which her foundations are laid are all hidden by the solid masses of buildings.

One would think that Venice must be a very unhealthy city by reason of the large lagoons which lie around her on all sides save the sea side; but the water being salt, no malarious influences are felt. The tall tower of St. Mark's Cathedral and the Campanille are conspicuous from a long distance seaward. As we come in from the sea and steam up the grand Canal we begin to observe the peculiarities of the city. The long black gondolas are shooting around through the waters everywhere. There are said to be over four thousand of these water carriages in Venice. One looks in vain for horse or carriage, street car or bus. Not even a dog to break the silence of the night with his endless bark. What a blessed relief this is, too, to one fresh from Oriental cities; for there he learns to hate a dog if he never did before! The Oriental canine

GRAND CANAL, VENICE.

sleeps all day and wakes up at nightfall to join in the chorus of barks that everywhere make night hideous. Little narrow canals cut their labyrinthine way between rows of dark houses in every direction. These are crossed at intervals by steep little bridges for foot passengers. Venice is not without its streets, exceedingly narrow though they be. The Venetian can wander around in his gloomy city wherever he pleases without having to resort to the gondola; but none but a Venetian should undertake it, for the stranger will most assuredly lose himself.

We have found our way by the aid of a Venetian to our hotel quarters at the "Lena," near to St. Mark's Square; but we are very sure that the feat could never have been performed by ourselves, uninitiated as we were in the intricacies of the narrow, tortuous streets of this water-logged city. The narrow stone ways squeezed in between the canals and lofty buildings lead us at all angles through the city, suddenly coming to an end at times, and passing us over a small arched bridge to the opposite side of the canal. The situation is unique, novel beyond description; but the novelty soons wears off when we find that we dare hardly venture beyond the limits of our surroundings without getting lost. That would not be so much of a mishap if we could accost the first man or woman we met and have our bewildered faculties readjusted; but when each and all answer "non-capisco" we realize that we have about as much hope of deliverance as the man in the woods who has again and again made a complete circle only to be confronted by his own track, when he thought himself making a bee line for home; yes, reader, we know how it feels from personal experience!

Perhaps it isn't just the right thing to say in print, about a city for which so much admiration is expressed by others, but we shall be rash enough to ignore the fashion and say that the walls of a prison in our own roomy country would present just as attractive a home to us as to be immured in

ST. MARK'S, VENICE.

the heart of sunless Venice and be compelled to stay there. What object the original founders of Venice had in building it out upon the waters we cannot imagine, unless it was for defense; and if this was the reason they planned wisely, for the weapons of primeval or mediæval times would have proved powerless against her, unaided by strategy. But for modern warfare, when she could be shelled from the mainland, she is as much at the mercy of her enemies as if she occupied a coast position.

But there are some interesting things to be seen around Venice; so let us see them, and be gone. St. Mark's Square is one of the few places in Venice where an unstinted measure of sunlight may be enjoyed; and thither the Venetians resort in great numbers in the afternoon and evening to listen to the excellent brass band which nightly furnishes music, or to sit under the arcades of the palatial buildings which surround the square on three sides, sipping coffee, reading newspapers or enjoying a general tete-a-tete. Here the visitor may see the elite of the Venetian society, in rich and fashionable attire—for even the Parisian could not pay stricter attention to fashion than do these Venetians—and they appear to enjoy life about as well as the people of the more brilliant city of fashion.

As we stand on this Square, between one and two o'clock p. m., we are witness to an interesting little circumstance which may be seen on almost every afternoon of the year. Clouds of dun-colored doves collect on the cornices and portico roofs of the surrounding buildings for their regular two o'clock feeding. The visitor on the Square at the time above mentioned is most generally prepared with some grain which he holds out in his hand, and so tame are these doves that they will flock down and alight upon his head, shoulders and arms, until he is literally covered with the birds, so eager to feed out of his hand that they alight one upon another, knocking each other off in the effort to get the grain. But note the fact that when the great clock in the tower close by strikes the hour of two the doves are all gone in an instant back to the cornices and portico roofs; for this is the hour of their regular feeding by the city. The people of Venice cherish a tradition that six hundred years ago a certain admiral gained a signal victory through the medium of carrier pigeons, and those we have seen fed on the Square are a sort of pensioned descendants of the admiral's birds, whom the people feel a pleasure in preserving and feeding.

The cathedral at the eastern end of the Square is one of the principal attractions of Venice. It was built early in the tenth century, in the form of a Greek cross, its greatest length five hundred and seventy-six feet, with a width of two hundred and sixty-nine feet. The mosaic work of the interior, wrought into pictures, covers an area—it is said—of about fifty thousand square feet. The entrance is under an archway of antique columns, mounted here and there upon the capitals of each other. Over the entrance you will also see the only horses to be found in Venice; they are of gilded bronze, however, instead of flesh and blood, said to be the work of some Roman of the time of Nero. They have seen a great deal of the world in their day, having traveled to Constantinople in Constantine's time, and to Paris in Napoleon the First's time, and back again to their present position in 1815.

The Palace of the Doges is the pride of Venice, and it contains enough of art and architecture to keep the visitor in-

BRIDGE OF SIGHS, VENICE.

terested for hours. Just at the back of the Palace is another object in which we are interested, the poet's "Bridge of Sighs," which ties into a sort of marital relation the Ducal Palace and the old Prison. The natural surroundings of the place as well as the recollection that many a poor fellow took his last look of the outer world from that air suspended passage way, between what might be fitly termed the connecting link between hope and utter despondency, has a tendency still to make the heart sad. Lord Byron, it is said, tried a dungeon in the old prison long enough to impart somewhat of the prisoner's feeling to him, which he puts into verse as follows:

> "I stood in Venice on the Bridge of Sighs;
> A palace and a prison on each hand;
> I saw from out the wave her structure rise
> As from the stroke of the enchanter's wand:
> A thousand years their cloudy wings expand
> Around me, and a dying glory smiles
> O'er the far times, when many a subject land
> Looked at the winged Lion's marble piles,
> Where Venice sat in state, throned on her hundred isles!"

Leaving Venice we take our way westward over the beautiful Lombardy plains, just now in all their vernal freshness, and in seven hours we are in Milan. A handsome city Milan is; the more so when we put it in contrast with Venice. Beautiful parks, equal to almost anything that we find around London, adorn the outer edges of the city; one in particular would make a very fair heaven upon earth if sinless creatures alone walked 'neath the shade of its beautiful chestnuts, or lounged beside its running waters, lakelets and cascades. Here the beauty, wealth and chivalry of Milan are wont to show themselves in the early evening. But the incomparable excellence of Milan is its wonderful Cathedral. Nothing like it have we seen in all Europe, in its richness of exterior. As we stand on its roof and contemplate it, we marvel at the ingenuity of the brain that devised it. A perfect forest of marble pinnacles rises from its roof. Some five thousand statues and statuettes spring up from pinnacle, roof and sides, and there are places for several thousand more; and all this is marble. Viewed in its interior it scarcely equals St. Peter's; but, all in all, it is the monarch of Cathedrals. To describe it so that the reader may get an adequate idea of its magnificence is a hopeless task. Its erection was commenced about five hundred years ago, and it is still receiving additions from year to year. From its tower, which rises three hundred and sixty feet above the level of the street, one of the most magnificent views in all Italy may be enjoyed. The visitor is permitted to ascend.

Northward next we take our way, and in a little less than two hours we are at Como. Now we are leaving the beautiful in art, and coming to the beautiful in nature. We take a little steamer in waiting and glide out upon the placid waters of the lake to enjoy to the full the magnificent mountain scenery. Backward and forward across the narrow lake, scarcely more than $1\frac{1}{2}$ miles wide in its broadest part, our little steamer goes to drop off and take on passengers at the numerous villages lining each shore. Some fifteen miles up the lake we, in our turn, drop off at the town of Menaggio and take a train in correspondence, and in three-quarters of an hour we are at Porlezza, on Lake Lugano. Another steamer is in waiting, and twelve miles' ride down the lake betwixt snow-crowned mountains, down whose furrowed sides come the waters of the melting snow, falling in cascades into the lake, and we arrive at

MILAN CATHEDRAL.

the town of Lugano, where we halt for a quiet Sabbath day's rest. Well may the tourist afford to spend a day or two in this most charming region in communion with nature, for it is refreshing to both soul and body.

On Monday we take our departure over the St. Gothard route, passing for a whole day through the grandest of Alpine scenery. Now we are whirling along the ridge of some lofty mountain, looking down from a height of several thousand feet into a valley through which winds a silvery stream, now rushing out of some dark tunnel to enter an iron bridge spanning some deep gorge in the mountain's side; now a rapid run and a snake-like twist down the mountain side, emerging sometimes from the mouth of a tunnel which, seen some little time from our mountain height, was deemed to belong to some other line of railway running below us, now down in the valley looking up at the white mountain tops from five to eight thousand feet above us, and watching the cascades, small and great, as they pour their foaming waters over dizzy heights; thus varied is the journey we make this day, a constant delight to the lover of natural scenery. We are twenty minutes in passing through the famous St. Gothard tunnel, nine and one-fourth miles in length. Fifty-six tunnels in all were found necessary in the construction of this railway, the whole a marvel of engineering skill.

At Basle we make a day's halt, but finding little to interest us, take our departure for Strasbourg on the following day. We visit the Cathedral, which is noted chiefly for having the tallest church tower in the world, and the most wonderful clock in existence, which is at the same time a self-acting theatre, the whole scene of the denial of our Lord being presented at twelve o'clock each day, and a complete astronomical apparatus, all the motions diurnal and annual, of the heavenly bodies being observed in a perfect clock-work movement. We make the passage of the Rhine across the pontoon bridge to Kehl, from which the Germans bombarded Strasbourg, and return to view the fortifications, which have the reputation of being—with the one exception of Gibraltar—the strongest in all Europe. We have reserved this visit until the last, and events yet to be narrated proved the wisdom of so doing, for we were in too ill a humor with Strasbourg hospitality after the occurrence of said events to pay any farther attention to it.

It will be remembered that Strasbourg is a city acquired by the Germans from the French in the struggle of '71; its former possessors being as determined to win back the lost province of Alsace and Lorraine as the present ones are resolved to keep a firm and abiding grip upon them. And thus a jealous vigilance is maintained on the border which bodes no good to those who wilfully or inadvertently tread upon the Dutchman's toes.

It is six o'clock in the evening when we stroll forth from the hotel "Victoria" to look over the fortifications, preparatory to a leave-taking the next morning. A small squad of soldiers is visible at a point ahead of us where the road leads through the earthworks; but it is not the soldiers we have come to see, and taking a footpath that leads by a zigzag course up the ramparts we soon have the satisfaction of knowing that we have scaled the ramparts of this Gibraltar-like fortress without the loss of a single man, and we are in the quiet enjoyment of our victory when a single company of German infantry charge up the hill and demand a surrender; considering the superiority of the force thus suddenly thrown upon us, it is deemed the better part of valor to haul down our colors. As a prisoner of war we appear before an officer at the gateway which we have but a few minutes before shunned, who appears to be in an inquisitive mood, although we understand not a question he asks. The fact of the matter is, he and all his subordinates are Dutchmen, whilst the prisoner is an American, and each knows nothing of the other's language. Happy thought! why not try him in French? they think; "Parle vouz France?" they ask; "non parle France, uno Anglaise," we answer, perversely. A messenger is dispatched for some one who speaks English, who, after fifteen minutes of waiting, puts in an appearance; but his English is about the size of our French, and the fact that a passport is wanted is about all that we can make out of the Dutch-Englishman. We seize on that fact and sling our yah, yahs at him until we start forth, as we suppose, for the hotel "Victoria," where the passport is to be found in a valise. But alas! it's before another pompous Dutchman that we appear, who will not be convinced that we are not a gentleman of linguistic ability, and who, in high dudgeon because we will not answer his questions, in either German or French, leads us off through a dark hallway, turns a key in a door and ushers us into prison quarters for the night.

Horrid the stench of that room! It will remain in our nostrils for many a year to come, if we live so long. Loathsome that piece of crawling humanity lying on a board platform on which we are expected to rest for the night! We are in a generous mood at this moment, and we mentally yield him the whole, broad, hard platform for the night. Yes, and he can have the whole of the room, too, if it shall lie in our power to be so generous. A note to the landlord of the "Victoria" is hastily prepared, and given into the hands of the turnkey, who is summoned by a rap on the iron window. He says, "Yah, yah," when we try to make him understand that it is to go immediately to the "Victoria." An hour passes; Oh, joy! deliverance is surely come, we think, as we hear the key turning in the lock; but it is only another bedfellow, a filthy tramp who rejoices in being able to get in out of the rain. The two Dutchmen are quite at home, apparently, and are soon in the land of dreams; but, reader, the other fellow wasn't at all sleepy, and so he tried first to make himself think that he was on guard duty over the Dutchmen, and put on a very martial air as he paced to and fro in his narrow cell. But the imagination would break once and awhile under its load, and the awful fact that he was a soldier who warred not with carnal weapons against flesh and bood, but with spiritual weapons against the rulers of darkness, etc., and a preacher of righteousness, behind the bars as an evil-doer, would obtrude itself and take possession of the whole man for a time.

And so the hours wore on as he marched and counter-marched through his cell, until midnight, when he sank from sheer exhaustion upon the corner of the platform, where his two fellow-prisoners were happily oblivious of all worldly cares, and in a moment was with them in the land of dreams. But there were emigrants on the persons of his friends who improved the opportunity to take a "stow away" passage on the American pilgrim's neck, which fact soon came to the consciousness of the pilgrim, and placed him once more on guard duty, which position he held until eight o'clock the next morning, when a proper investigation of affairs revealed to the humiliated Germans the mistake they had made in taking an American clergyman for a French spy. How they did apologize for the blunder! but it was hard to mollify our wrath, especially at the turnkey, who failed to deliver the note to the landlord of the "Victoria" until the morning. Our host quickly came to our relief when he found out the situation, and to his friendly interest in no small measure we owe our prompt discharge.

We are glad to say good-bye to our German friends at the earliest possible moment; and it is a fact which the pilgrim is not loth to put on record that he cares not whether he ever sees any portion of the Dutch Empire again or not. Belgium and Holland receive only a passing glance as we hurry on to Antwerp. A day is passed in this pleasant and prosperous city, when we take our departure across the dreaded Channel to Harwich. Our fears in regard to the Channel prove groundless, for we have a pleasant passage occupying a night, and a couple of hours by rail in the early morning lands us once more in London.

CHAPTER XXII.

RAMBLES AROUND GLASGOW, EDINBURGH, AND STIRLING.

LONDON again! It seems an age since we left the city on our rambles through the Orient, so much ground has been covered, and so many things seen that were new to the Occidental eyes, that it seems scarcely possible that all could have been done in the eight months of our absence. True it is, that we are longer lived than the ancients, when life is measured by what is accomplished in it rather than by its years. We have performed a feat in these months that would have required as many years for the traveler of even a century ago to accomplish. The world is being wonderfully tied together by bands of iron, waterways across desert sands, and the swift-moving monsters of the deep, which have little to fear from either wind or wave.

A few days' stay in London before entering Scotland enables us to make a visit to Windsor Castle, not in the hope of seeing the Queen, for it is the fact of her absence that gives the ordinary visitor access to the Castle and grounds around it. For this reason we could not make our visit to it last autumn when we were in the city. The Queen is now at the Balmoral Castle in Scotland, and Windsor is open to visitors on certain days of the week. The Castle is about an hour's ride by train from the city; the little town of Windsor nestling close under its protecting walls. The Windsor trades-people tell us that they are glad when the Queen goes away, for then

HOUSES OF PARLIAMENT, LONDON.

they have a tourist trade which is not possible when she is at home. From the Round Tower within the Castle walls may be had a very fine and extensive view of the surrounding country. Just across the Thames, northeast from the Castle, is Eton college, with its finely laid out grounds, and the old William Penn mansion; and farther on in the distance is a church spire which marks the place where "Grey's Elegy in a Country Church Yard" was written. The Castle itself is a massive pile of grey stone buildings, interesting as a royal residence for many centuries. In St. George's Chapel we find some very handsome marble memorials of the Prince Consort, Duke of Albany, and others of the Queen's household. The Chapel now known as the Albert Memorial Chapel was once Cardinal Wolsey's tomb-house; but Cromwell despoiled it of its wealth, and in recent times it has been refitted in royal style, and is now the Chapel where the Queen worships, when she is at Windsor. A visit to the royal stables, where the little white horse which the Queen drives herself is quietly enjoying his vacation, is made, and a ramble through the stately forest of Windsor ends our visit to the Queen's Castle.

We take our journey into Scotland by the London and Northwestern railway, which closely follows the western coast all the way. The journey of four hundred and twenty-five miles is made in nine hours of daylight riding, and we enter Glasgow in time to seek our friend A——'s suburban residence in Rutherglen before his good wife has cleared off the family board. We are among friends once more, and our tour through this Land of Romance and Song is to have the additional profit and pleasure of our friend's company in many of the delightful rambles which we have planned to make.

Since boyhood's early days our heart has turned lovingly and longingly towards the land where fearless Knox and faithful Covenanter have given a deathless testimony to "The truth as it is in Jesus." We are especially fortunate in the time of our visit, for the Glasgow Exhibition is open; and it is to be presumed that the best the Kingdom affords in the realms of the fine arts and industrial manufactures will be visible here at this time. Our first visit is, therefore, to the Exhibition, and the Bishop's Palace is our first attraction. This is a sort of an antiquarian's museum, beginning with the very architecture of the Palace itself. Here are collected together relics of the feudal age, of Scotland's civil and ecclesiastical history, of men and women who fell in noble strife for the right, as well as those of a more ignoble character, the sad fates of many of whom have touched the world's heart with pity for them. Here are relics of Mary Queen of Scots, a lock of her hair, some autograph letters and other mementoes of the unfortunate Queen. Yes! and here is a relic we would travel a long distance to see— a Bible once owned by Scotland's Covenanter Prophet, Alexander Peden, of whom we shall make further mention in the next chapter. And here is another relic which carries us back into Covenanter days, the original parchment of the "Solemn League and Covenant." That document, signed with the blood of many whose names appear upon it, and which gave the most of the heroic band that signed it martyrs' crowns, is one well worthy the pride which the Scots feel in its possession and preservation.

A second visit gives us an entire day in the main Exhibition building, where a nation's arts and industries are well represented. The ship building industry, for which the Clyde is so justly famous, makes an attractive exhibit. Models of ocean steamship yet to be built, of mammoth proportions and superior to anything yet afloat in point of speed, gather admiring crowds around them. When one sees the Cyclopean shafts of these ocean Leviathans laid bare, as we have a chance to do in the Machinery Hall, he is astonished at the power necessary to drive a steamship at the rate of speed attained by some of the best of the Atlantic liners. No wonder is it when, plunging like a war horse in her battle with the waves, she throws her stern clear up out of the water, exposing the screw, that the great vessel trembles from stem to stern with the shock of the liberated screw.

Glasgow is second to none in the United Kingdom as a manufacturing city, and all branches of manufacture are well represented in the Exhibition. It is a good place for boasting Jonathan to spend a few days. He will have the good sense to see that though he may excel the sturdy Scot in the inventive faculties, he is no equal to him when it comes to putting invention into material form, more particularly when that form requires the steel and iron rolling mills to put it into shape. Glasgow may not be called a pretty city, when placed in comparison with other cities of the United Kingdom, but it is one of the busiest cities we have visited. Its tall smoke stacks rise like a forest of dry and topless trees out of city and suburb. Almost every line of manufacture is carried on in the community, and in some instances the manufacture is of vast proportions.

To see Scotland at its best one would need to visit it in the month of June or July. Its sea-girt situation gives it a damp, chilly atmosphere at other seasons, not at all agreeable for the many pleasant tours that may be made in the summer season over ground that is full of historic and romantic interest. It was our own plan to make Glasgow the center of our tourings; for it has the advantage of water and rail communication with most points of interest to the tourist; and we know not, after having tried the plan, what better course to advise those to take who may hereafter visit Scotland with a view of seeing it thoroughly and economically. In an economic point of view, one may see more for the least money in Scotland than in any other part of Europe or the Orient that we have passed over in our journeyings. If the reader will give us his company now, we will take him on an excursion through the Highlands and Trossachs, and he will see how much can be accomplished in four days.

One may reverse the tour we are about to make—that is, take one of David MacBrayne's elegant little excursion steamers at the Broomielaw in Scotland, descend the Clyde to the entrance of Loch Long, continuing on up the Loch to Inversnaid, thence by coach to Loch Katrine, and thus on to Edinburgh, and return to Glasgow, all this in one day, if he choose to pass Stirling and Edinburgh so hastily.

Going to the Caledonian railway station, we purchase a second class ticket, fare for the round trip $4.15, and take an evening train for Edinburgh, distant forty-seven miles. It is Saturday evening, and we shall spend the Sabbath in this handsomest of Scotch cities and observe what attention the people give to the Fourth Commandment. Edinburgh is a city of churches, furnishing one for every 1,700 of her population, or 155 in all, 104 of which belong to the different bodies of the Presbyterian organization. Our first visit is to the historic old St. Giles, where John Knox, the Elijah of the 16th century, stood in fearless defense of the truth, and hurled his fierce anathemas at the Godless occupants of Hollyrood. The spirit of the stern Reformer would fire up at the High Churchism of the place at the present time, were it permitted to reenter the old Sanctuary. It was here that Jenny Geddes so sadly disturbed the composure of the Dean by hurling her stool at his head, when he commenced to read the Ritual. Jenny was righteously indignant, for she mistook the Liturgy for the Mass, and she had seen enough of Prelacy and Popery to show her the hollow formality of such worship. St Giles' is the oldest sanctuary in Edinburgh, originating some time in the 14th century. It has passed through a number of transformations until we find it in its present shape, under the control of the Established Church of Scotland. On the south side of the church is a simple square stone slab sunk in the pavement, with the initial letters, J. K., 1572, on it, marking the spot where rests in peace from all polemical strife Scotland's great champion of religious truth and freedom, John Knox. A little distance eastward on High street is the John Knox house, the old home of the Reformer with some modern renovations. It is owned by the Free Church, and kept as a sort of shrine for the pilgrim's visit; and well worth our while it is to enter and contemplate the home surroundings of the Reformer. The old study, finished in heavy panelled oak, is kept as nearly as possible as Knox used and left it.

A Free Church and a Y. M. C. A. service in the afternoon and evening close a quiet Sabbath in a city whose foundations are evidently laid in righteousness, for its equal in a Sabbath keeping point of view we have never yet found. The principles of the great Reformer, clung to so tenaciously and at the price of much blood by the Covenanting people of Scotland, have taken deep hold on the nation's life, and given it a strength and power truly healthful and beneficent. Well did England's historian remark "That the principles which Knox created saved Scotland."

Monday also we devote to sight seeing in Edinburgh. Scarcely three-fourths of a mile distant from the Knox House, at the foot of Canongate street, is old Holyrood Palace. It is open to the visitor. The Palace has a history running back to 1128 A. D., which would be interesting for us to read up in connection with our visit; but our interest in it lies largely in its connection with the life of the unfortunate Mary Queen of Scots. Sad memories come up to us in our rambles through its halls and rooms. The Queen's apartments were on the second floor on the northern side of the Palace; and here we see her bed, with its coverings falling to pieces from age. Here also are chairs covered with embroidery, the work of her own hands and those of her maids of honor. See those dark stains on the floor just outside the door of the Queen's Chamber! It was here that the murderous daggers of Ruthven and Darnley, with their minions, drank the life blood of Rizzio, the Queen's favorite; a bloody piece of work which undoubtedly cost Darnley his life at the hands of his Queen. Could these old chambers we are traversing speak of what they have seen, what a record of tears, hopeless sighs, plots, and deeds of blood, would they unfold! There is a long gallery, 27x150 feet, filled with portraits of the Scottish kings, which, however, possess but little of artistic merit, and we hastily pass through it and out into the roofless Chapel at the north side of the Palace. In this Chapel Lord Darnley and Queen Mary were wed. In

EDINBURGH CASTLE.

a vault beneath the south aisle lie the remains of David II., James II. and his Queen, James V. and his Queen, and their second son, the Duke of Albany, and Lord Darnley. Solemn and stately does the old Palace of Holyrood stand, a monument to dark deeds and an unfortunate Queen.

Edinburgh is not specially noted for its monuments, but the Scott monument on Princess street is doubtless one of the handsomest reared to poet or novelist; and its beautiful park surroundings lend it attraction.

Our next visit is to the Edinburgh Castle. All the history of the city is more or less intimately connected with the Castle. This huge rock fortress has been used for defensive purposes from a period more remote even than the beginning of the Christian era. It has been the birth-place and residence of kings and queens, the scene of many a bloody encounter. It has been captured by assault and strategy, burnt and dismantled, times without number. Poet and novelist have woven it into song and romance, until it would be hard to find a school boy or girl in the Kingdom unfamiliar with its history. Admittance is freely given to visitors, and if we come within the hours specified for the purpose, we can visit Queen Mary's room, and the Crown room, where the Scottish Regalia is kept. On the outside, on the loftiest edge of the northern cliff is situated the King's Bastion. Here we notice a famous specimen of medieval ordnance, the great gun called Mons Meg. It measures twenty inches in the bore, and is composed of long pieces of hammered iron held together by coils of iron hoops. It was used at the siege of Norham Castle in 1497; but it uttered its last roar in 1682 in a salute to the Duke of York, when it was burst in the discharge. This is the best portion of the citadel to view the city surroundings from. Yonder at the northeast corner of the city is Calton Hill, with the Burns monument showing in the foreground. The Scots are trying to make this hill an imitation of the Athens Acropolis, and have begun a National Monument modeled after the style of the

Parthenon, but which has come to a halt in the building from a lack of funds. Eastward is Arthur's seat, with the Abbey and Palace of Holyrood at its northern base. Below the Castle Hill to the northward is the deep ravine which separates the new town from the old. Art and Nature are here combined in rendering this ravine an attractive spot with prettily laid out gardens.

Descending from the Castle Hill eastward until we come to St. Giles, and then southward on George IV. street, we come to the Greyfriar's Square, a spot ever memorable in the history of the Reformed faith in Scotland. In Greyfriar's Church was first produced "The Solemn League and Covenant," and after a sermon by Alexander Henderson it received the signatures of the Congregation, and was then passed out to the multitude assembled in the church yard, and signed, as we are told, "On the flat monuments, amidst tears, prayers, and aspirations which could find no words, some writing with their blood." Near by rests the preacher of that occasion, and near to him the Covenant's restless enemy, Sir George Mackenzie, with many of the worthies who bled for their attachment to the Covenanting cause. A pleasant city is Edinburgh; and as we say good-bye to it, we cannot find more fitting language to express our own admiration for the queenly city than that of Christopher North, who says: "Weigh all its defects, designed and undesigned, and is not Edinburgh a noble city? Arthur's Seat! how like a lion! The magnificent range of Salisbury Crag, on which a battery might be built to blow the whole inhabitation to atoms! Our friend here, the Calton, with his mural crown! Our Castle on his cliff! gloriously hung round with national histories along all his battlements! Do they not embosom him in a style of grandeur worthy, if such it be, of a City of Palaces?"

" Ay, proudly fling thy white arms to the sea,
Queen of the unconquered North."

From Edinburgh we take an early morning train for Stirling, passing through Falkirk, the scene of some noted battles in the time of Robert Bruce. At Stirling one may put in a busy day in visiting the Castle, field of Bannockburn, the Wallace monument on Abbey Crag, and Cambus Kenneth Abbey. Around the Castle centers many a stirring scene in the lives of Wallace and Bruce. On the way up to the Castle we visit the Chapel in which Queen Mary and her son, James II., were crowned; then passing through a cemetery once used as a tournament ground, we observe a number of memorial statues of noted Covenanter leaders, James Renwick, Andrew Melville, Eben. Erskine, John Knox, and others. But most interesting and touching of all is a pure white marble group enclosed in glass, erected in memory of two young Scottish maidens who suffered death by drowning in the Solway rather than deny their faith in the Lord who bought them. We copied the following inscription from the monument, which tells its own simple and pathetic story: "Through faith, Margaret Wilson, a youthful maiden, chose rather to depart and be with Christ, than to disown His holy cause and covenant, to own Erastian usurpation and to conform to Prelacy enforced by cruel laws, bound to a stake within flood-mark of the Solway tide, she died a martyr's death, 11th of May, 1685." A younger sister, Alice, suffered with her for the same cause. The monument presents in clear white marble two gentle sisters in youth studying the Word of God. By their side kneels a lamb, while behind them is the form of an angel with the laurel in hand ready to place it upon the brow of the maidens.

Passing on into the Castle grounds, we notice another pyramidal monument to the memory of the martyred Covenanter. A fine statue of Robert Bruce also adorns the outer yard; his face turned toward Bannockburn battle field, and eyes and features all expressive of the keenest interest in the result of the struggle which he is supposed to be watching. It would seem as though the battle ground itself, only about a mile distant, was the place for this monument, but the laird who owns the ground refuses to give it room, and hence its position on Stirling hill. In the Castle the visitor is shown the room where James II. treacherously slew William, Earl of Douglass, because he could not persuade him to break faith with his friends; it is called the Douglass Room.

Northward a mile or more across the Forth, on Abbey Crag, stands the lofty Wallace Tower, a reminder that here at Stirling Castle, Wallace and his men did what was deemed impossible for men to do in scaling the lofty walls and taking the Castle out of the hands of its English masters. From the Castle we proceed to a Tower, which stands on a height overlooking the surrounding country. When, in addition to the height on which the Tower stands, you mount up several hundred steps higher to the top of the column, you will find yourself in possession of a most superb view of the Forth in its windings through the valley. From this position we locate the tower of the old Abbey of Cambus Kenneth, and forthwith direct our steps thither. The Abbey was founded in 1147 by David I., and has been the scene of many stirring events in Scottish history. Only the tower is left standing; some of the remains of the foundation wall are yet visible, enabling the visitor to trace the circuit of the original walls. Near the tower, and within the space once occupied by the Abbey, is the tomb of James III. and his Queen, restored by Queen Victoria. Miss Porter in her "Scottish Chiefs," has made the Abbey the scene of some most interesting events.

A visit is made next to the field of Bannockburn, twice fought on by Wallace and Bruce. A tall flag staff marks Bruce's position during the battle. So end our wanderings around Stirling. A night at a quiet little hotel in Dunblane, a station or two farther on, where a change of cars for Callander is necessary, and we are ready for the Trossachs' tour.

CHAPTER XXIII.

THROUGH REGIONS FRAGRANT WITH MEMORIES OF POET, NOVELIST AND MARTYR.

AFTER the first of May, the excursion arrangements for the Trossachs tour are so complete that we find coach, steamer and train all in close connection. Leaving the train at Callander we find the coach for the Trossachs in waiting. This coach is a sort of mongrel breed among vehicles; like nothing else we have ever seen, peculiar to this region, we think, and as convenient and comfortable as could well be devised. The seats are all arranged on the top of the vehicle, and will accommodate about sixteen persons; a happy medium between the omnibus and wagon in height, it is neither so top heavy as to alarm the passenger when it lurches over, nor so low as to make him wish that he had a higher point of observation for the beauties that surround him.

Our vehicle is loaded down when we leave the station; but our four fine horses make an easy job of it. The river Teith is soon crossed and following the course of a southern branch of the Teith for a couple of miles we come to Coilantogle Ford, famous as the scene of the conflict between Fitz James and Roderick Dhu.

> " See here, all vantageless I stand,
> Armed like thyself with single brand;
> For this is Coilantogle Ford,
> And thou must keep thee with thy sword."

Our way now lies along the north shore of Loch Venachar, a pretty little sheet of water about four miles in length by three-fourths of a mile wide. At the upper end of the lake is the spot where, at the whistle of Roderick Dhu—

> " Intent through copse and heath arose
> Bonnets and spears and bended bows;
> On right, on left, above, below,
> Spring up at once the lurking foe,
> From shingles grey their lances start,
> The bracken bush sends forth its dart."

It is a bright, beautiful June morning, and as we enter the woods where little streams wind their way down the hillsides through leafy ways which almost conceal them, where the birds are making the morning melodious with song, we cease to wonder that Poet and Romancer found in this delightsome region so much of inspiration, an inspiration which has clothed the whole region in a garment of imperishable glory. Loch Venachar is passed, and a mile farther on we reach Duncraggan, which, in "The Lady of the Lake," is made the first tarrying place of the messenger of the "Fiery Cross:"

> " The lake is past,
> Duncraggan's huts appear at last."

At the head of Loch Achray, which we soon reach from this point, we come to the famous "Brig of Turk," where the Knight of Snowdon discovered that in his zeal in the chase he had outstripped all his attendants—

> " And when the Brig O'Turk was won,
> The headmost horseman rode alone."

After passing the little Loch Achray we enter the Trossachs. How wild and wierd the scenery for the next few miles after passing the Trossachs Hotel! The name "Trossachs" means a "bristled" or "bristling region," and well indicates the character of the region. Wordsworth says of the place:

> " There's not a nook within this solemn pass
> But were an apt confessional for one
> Taught by his summer spent, his autumn gone,
> That life is but a tale of morning grass withered at eve."

At the head of Loch Katrine, which is reached on emerging from the Trossachs, we leave our coach for a steamer in waiting which convey us down the lake to Stronachlahar. How beautiful the prospect now before us! On the right rises the tall form of Ben Aan, 1,800 feet above sea level, whilst on the left Ben Venue climbs skyward a thousand feet higher than his brother peak on the right. As we glide out on the waters of Loch Katrine, "Ellen's Isle" quickly comes into view, and the little steamer is kind enough to circle around a little to the north and bring us close to the romantic little Isle which Scott has endowed with a peculiar interest in his "Lady of the Lake." Did Scott weave out of his imagination solely the incidents which he localized here on the little wooded Isle? or is there a historical foundation for them? History would appear to warrant the supposition that it was to this identical retreat that the heroic Ellen Douglass conveyed the Knight of Snowdon while his gallant dogs followed in the wake of the fairy skiff; and it is this incident that the Poet describes in the following lines:

> "Fast o'er the lake the shallop flew;
> With heads erect, and whimpering cry,
> The hounds behind, their passage ply,
> Nor frequent does the bright oar break
> The darkening mirror of the lake,
> Until the rocky Isle they reach,
> And moor their shallop on the beach."

Loch Katrine is equal to any of the Italian lakes in its own natural beauty, lacking only their villas and towns to take away its loneliness; but perhaps this lack is more than counterbalanced by the fascination of romance and song which attaches to it. Glasgow draws its water supply largely from this lake. All the lakes thus far passed on this tour are connected by small streams, and find a final outlet in the river Teith.

Ten miles on the lake brings us to Stronachlahar, at the western end. Once more we find our coach in readiness for another ride of four or five miles to Inversnaid, on Loch Lomond. Here we have time for dinner and a little sight-seeing before the steamer from the head of the lake calls for her passengers. The Inversnaid burn pours its foaming waters from a height of some thirty feet into the lake at this point, making a very pretty cascade, which is crossed a few rods above the point of its fall by a rustic bridge. It was at Inversnaid that Wordsworth saw the "Sweet Highland Girl," whom he has celebrated in one of his poems:

> " Sweet Highland Girl, a very shower
> Of beauty is thy earthly dower!"

Loch Lomond is called the "Queen of the Scottish lakes;" and it appears to deserve its reputation. Its length is about twenty-one miles, but its average width can scarcely exceed two miles. Around its shores are laid many of the scenes in "Rob Roy;" and two miles north of Inversnaid is " Rob Roy's" cave, "A deep, gloomy hollow in a rugged and precipitous rock." Here "Rob Roy" was accustomed to collect his followers and prepare for his desperate forays. Here also, it is said, Robert Bruce found an asylum after his defeat at Dalree.

Leaving Inversnaid the steamer bears down the lake a mile or two, making a landing on the opposite side at Tarbet. Steamer is exchanged for coach again at this point for a short ride of two miles to Arrochar, on the northeastern corner of Loch Long. Twenty-four miles of steaming down this pleasant lake, with frequent landings at points along the shore, and we enter the Clyde, up which we can go on our steamer as far as Greenock, when we must leave it for train back to Glasgow. We have time yet for a ramble around Greenock and along its busy quays, where the commerce of the Clyde is handled by vessels small and great of many nations. Greenock's docks are large and extensive, and many of the best vessels that cross the ocean were built in them. It is worth while to pay a visit to the ship building industries of Greenock. On the opposite side of the Clyde from Greenock is Hellensburgh, a pretty town in a fine location, and the habitation of many of Glasgow's business men and retired merchants. Taking a train at Greenock we are brought back into Glasgow before darkness obscures the vision around us.

And thus, reader, we finish the four days' tour which we commenced in the last chapter, asking you to note how much might be accomplished in so short a time at the nominal fare we specified. Of course to this is to be added about four dollars for expenses by the way; and then we have made one of the most enjoyable trips imaginable, through a region redolent with song and romance, and which gives us such variety of scenery as can be found nowhere else in Scotland.

And yet we have another region to visit, less attractive in natural scenery, perhaps, but one, nevertheless, around which the glamor of a Poet's life is shining, a Poet whose song finds inspiration in the life and rural aspects of the hills of Ayrshire. The tour from Glasgow to Ayr and the land of Burns is easily accomplished in one day. An hour and a half by rail brings us to the town of Ayr, in the immediate vicinity of which the poet Burns was born. The town has a population of about forty thousand people, and outside of the Poet has little to interest the visitor. We may visit the old Inn where Tam O'Shanter and Souter Johnny were accustomed to sit too long over their grog, and where Burns himself lost much of the manly virtue which, had it been possessed in greater degree, would have given him brighter fame and a more loving remembrance. The inn is still the rendezvous of spirits too convivial. We may visit also the "Auld Brig," which figures in Burn's poem of "The Twa Brigs." The old stone bridge has verified the prophecy the Poet made it utter when it replied to the chaffings of its newer rival, "I'll be a brig when ye're a shapeless ruin," for the old still stands without alteration, while its neighbor has been rebuilt.

Passing out of the town a couple of miles we come to the Burns cottage, the Poet's birthplace. It is a low, one-story thatch roofed building, unoccupied by any family, but in charge of a keeper, who lives in a house joining it on one end. It is kept as a sort of Burns museum; and here we may see the bed in its niche in the wall where the Poet first lay on the bosom of maternity; here also the table, clock, chairs and other relics of the Burns family, with an autograph copy of Burns' "Tam O'Shanter." On a little farther to the right of the road is the "Auld Alloway Kirk," where Tam O'Shanter, full of grog, saw the ghostly revels which filled his soul with terror and sent him on in headlong flight over the "Brig of Doon:"

> "Tam skelpit on through dub and mire,
> Despising wind and rain and fire."

The "Auld Kirk" is now roofless, and the little bell hangs silent in its stone frame. In the churchyard in front we read the inscriptions on the stones which stand at the head of the graves of Burns' father, mother and sister. The Burns monument stands on the opposite side of the road from the Kirk in a nicely kept garden. In a chamber of this monument we are shown a number of mementos of the Poet, among other things, the Bible in two parts which young Burns gave to his "Highland Mary," together with a lock of her hair. A few rods distant, in a sort of grotto, are two sitting granite statues of Tam O'Shanter and his boon companion, Souter Johnny. They are the work of an amateur and comically expressive. Tam is in the midst of a hearty laugh, whilst Johnny, who has occasioned it by one of his stories, is slyly looking sideways at Tam to observe the effect of his tale. In close proximity to the monument is the "Auld Brig of Doon," across which Tam and his flying steed were hotly pursued by the ghouls. The whole region is redolent with memories of the Poet's life. Sad it is to contemplate that a genius so capable of leaving its impress upon a people's life and literature should so early find an end to its powers in the ruin of a dissolute body. But it were but a simple charity to hope that in the end Burns cheated his destroyer, as he promises to do in the following lines:

> "And now, Auld Cloots, I ken ye're thinkin',
> A certain bardie's rantin', drinkin',
> Some luckless hour will send him linkin'
>   To your black pit;
> But, faith! he'll turn a corner jinkin',
>   And cheat you yet."

With two fellow-travelers we leave Glasgow one pleasant morning for a trip to Lanark and the Falls of the Clyde. It is to occupy but one day, and to be made at a cost of $1.30 for both rail and coach fares. This is one of a series of fine excursions arranged by the Caledonian Railway Co. An hour by rail and we are at Lanark. It will be remembered by those who are familiar with the Scottish struggle for independence under the leadership of the brave Wallace and gallant Bruce, that Lanark was the scene of the initiatory struggle led by Wallace. It was here that he killed Hazelrigg, the English governor, whose bloody cruelty had robbed him of his wife. The country round about keeps the Chieftain's memory fresh in song and tradition. Taking our seats in a small wagon we commence our trip to the Falls of the Clyde. About a mile from Lanark the river is crossed, and another mile up the river brings us to a point where we leave our vehicle for a walk through the woods of Corehouse to the Cora Linn fall, a beautiful cascade which throws itself over a cliff eighty-four feet in height. The water descends into a narrow chasm with perpendicular walls of rock one hundred and twenty feet in height on either side, fringed on the top with a leafy growth which almost hides the roaring stream. Retracing our steps we regain our wagon and drive back a couple of miles for a visit to the Crags of Cartland, where an old Roman bridge hangs over a deep chasm of the Mouse water, a hundred feet or more in depth. Just above this bridge is Wallace's Cave, where he found a refuge after the killing of Hazelrigg. It is reached by a path on the left side of the chasm, which only those steady in nerve and head would do well to try to follow. The cavern is small, and but for its historical associations would scarcely interest the visitor. A mile farther on down the Clyde and another halt is made to enable us to visit the Stonebyres fall, even yet more beautiful than the Cora Linn, by reason of the broader expanse of waters that pour over the cliffs.

Our way now lies through a country of strawberry vines just in bloom, until we reach Carswell station, where our coach journey ends. From here a foot journey brings us to Craignethan Castle, of interest to the readers of Scott's "Old Mortality," for it is the "Tillietudlem" of his romance. It is situated on a steep promontory washed by the Nethan, a tributary of the Clyde. It is surrounded by a high wall of solid masonry which is in a fair state of preservation. Two towers of the Castle still stand, crowned by a thick overgrowth of mountain ash, hazel, brier and hawthorn. A large vaulted room known as the Queen's Room is shown, said to have been occupied by Queen Mary either a few nights before or after the fatal battle of Langside. At Tillietudlem station, a short distance from the Castle, we take train back to Glasgow, having had a very pleasant day's ramble; my two traveling companions being equally as delighted with the tour as myself.

In coming to Scotland we were influenced largely by the motive of visiting those regions where so many of the children of the Covenant wandered over the Moorlands and hid themselves in the deep glens to escape the fury of the human bloodhounds that pursued them. Our friend, whose pleasant hospitality we have been enjoying during these days of our pilgrimage in Scotland, being familiar with these localities, becomes a companion in our travels. Bothwell Bridge, the scene of one of the conflicts between the Covenanters and the royal army, is reached by a short railway journey from Rutherglen. The old bridge has undergone many modifications since the days of that sanguinary conflict, so that the modern bridge bears little resemblance to its predecessor; but it is deeply interesting, both historically and by reason of its own beautiful surroundings. Scott has found a place for Bothwell Bridge in his "Old Mortality." As we stood on the bridge with the noisy, shallow waters of the Clyde rolling underneath us and contemplated the picturesque surroundings, we were carried back in imagination to that fatal day in June, 1679, when the Covenanters under Balfour of Burley, Hackston and others, faced the army under the Duke of Monmouth and his savage lieutenants, Claverhouse and Dalzell. They fought well, those sons of the Covenant; but they were not equal to the task of successful resistance before an army of well drilled and disciplined soldiers, and they fell like grass before the royal troopers, until four hundred of them lay stretched upon the ground; twelve hundred more surrendered, and thus ended bloody Bothwell for the Covenanters.

But it was the Shires of Dumfries, Lanark and the two Galloways that saw most of the silent suffering and bloody wrongs of those dark days in the history of the Covenanting people, known in the history of the Scottish Church as the "killing time." In company with our friend we make a two days' tour through this region.

Leaving the train at Abbington we are met by a relative of friend A——'s, in whose cart we take passage for a twenty-five mile ride. It is one of the most pleasant of June days, and the air is filled with a balmy fragrance which causes both bird and man to feel the joy of the occasion. Arriving at Sanquhar we visit the place, now marked by a granite column, where was twice proclaimed, by Renwick and Cameron, the "Solemn League and Covenant." Leaving Sanquhar we soon come to the Crawick Glen, where many of the persecuted found a safe hiding place. Passing on through the Home Walks of the Duke of Buccleugh we follow up the wild little stream of the Crawick Waters as it makes its way between perpendicular cliffs of rock, covered with shrubbery and young trees, until we come to a point where Conraik Burn gushes out of a narrow little glen, just here godly Alexander Paden found a hiding place which served him day after day as a secure retreat from the bloody dragoons of Lagg and Claverhouse. It bears the name of Peden's Glen, and is a spot hallowed by many a prayer and hymn of praise.

For a couple of hours our road lies along the Crawick Waters, passing on the way the old home of the shepherd poet, Hyslop, the author of "The Cameronian's Dream," and other poems. "There," said my friend, indicating a certain spot by the way, "two Covenanters were shot and buried in their bloody garments where they fell." On a short distance farther, pointing up to some hillside spot, he would say: "There the troopers overtook another son of the Covenant and sent him home for his martyr's crown." Once and again did our friend indicate places where, overtaken by the merciless dragoons, faithful witnesses for the truth laid themselves down in bloody graves. The blood of the slain Covenanter so plentifully poured out in these deep glens and on heathery hillsides has brought forth in Scotland a rich harvest of doctrinal purity and adherence to the Christian faith. Long may she hold herself as pure and as sound in the Faith as she now is!

And now our journeyings through the land of the Covenant, the bard and the romancer are at an end. Pleasant memories do we carry away with us of our two weeks' wanderings here and there in it, and a half resolve that, sometime in coming years, we will return, for a more perfect acquaintance is formed as we say our good-byes to our kind friends, and turn our pilgrim feet towards the Emerald Isle as our next objective point of travel.

CHAPTER XXIV.

WHERE PAT LIVES—OBSERVATIONS IN THE EMERALD ISLE.

AFTER nine months of continuous tramping we begin to realize that our travel appetite is failing us; and we turn with longing to the home and friends on the other side of the water. Our feet have grown weary under us during the last two weeks, and whilst the friends at home have been busy cultivating their crop of Indian corn, we, too, have been busy, in our way, cultivating a corn crop which has yielded us an abundant harvest of grain, constantly reminding us of the unlucky moment when we let our sympathies run away with us at Bari, and bought a pair of narrow, box-toed shoes of an Italian shoemaker, who boarded the vessel and persisted in declaring that there was neither bread nor macaroni for himself or family, until he could sell the shoes. Of course we did not want to return to America with a feeling that our parsimony had let a poor Italian family starve to death, and so bought his shoes, and commenced to raise corn which we can find no market for, even if we are in Europe. If that shoemaker only had our corn crop we would feel a great deal better now in the anticipation of a farther sojourn on Irish shores.

At noon on the 22d of June we leave Glasgow for Greenock, where the "Hare," one of J. C. Burns & Co.'s staunch little steamers, is taken for our trip over the North Channel to Belfast. Four shillings only are charged for deck passage to Belfast, a half day's voyage; and voyage never had a more pleasant experience on the sea than fell to our lot on this pleasant, sunny afternoon in June.

Belfast is reached at eight o'clock p. m., and having made the acquaintance of a warm-hearted Irish farmer on the way over, he introduces us to some friends of his, who are glad to afford a modest but comfortable entertainment to the pilgrim at seventy-five cents per day. Our intention is to journey northward to Portrush, on the northern coast, before seeing the sights of Belfast. At 6:30 on the first morning after our arrival we are all ready for the steam horse to take us northward on our tour to the Giant's Causeway. The compartment is filled with some Irish workmen, from one of whom who sits next to us, we try to get some information touching home rule in Ireland; but a warning gesture and some whispered words awake us to the startling fact that free speech is too much of a luxury to be enjoyed in that crowd. Our friend is a Protestant, whilst the most of our traveling companions are Catholics; and so combustible is their make-up—so our friend informs us—that it would require but a spark of opposing sentiment to make things more lively than an Indian war dance. What conversation we have is carried on in an undertone when the rattling of the train makes it inaudible to our companions opposite. What a luxury to be a citizen of so goodly a land as that which we hail from! The more we see of other lands the greater grows our pride in our own freest, best of all lands.

A three hours' ride brings us to Portrush, on the northern coast, and thence a half hour by electric train and we are at the Giant's Causeway. Running the gauntlet of guides we proceed across meadows, all blooming with a variety of flowers, until the edge of the perpendicular cliffs skirting the sea is reached. It is well worth the tourist's while to make this somewhat wearisome walk along the upper edge of these cliffs for a mile or more that he may take in the beauties of the scenery which are a part and a parcel of the wonderful phenomena of

GIANT'S CAUSEWAY.

nature lying at their feet. One looks over a sheer precipice of from 800 to 1,000 feet, the sides of which in some places look as though they were formed by driving innumerable square stone spiles side by side, so much do they resemble a work of art rather than one of nature.

Finding a path known as the "Shepherd's Path," we descend to the Causeway itself. Here again we find the rock formation to resemble that of driven spiles like the cliff sides, with this difference, that, instead of all being square, they are likewise octagon and hexagon, and so closely fitted together as to make the whole thing to appear rather a work of human skill than a natural formation; and the only serious objection to so considering it is the enormity of the labor required to so construct the entire work. The building of the Pyramids would be a simple task in comparison.

A few hours later in the day of our ramble along the cliffs a serious mishap occurred to a Belfast clergyman wandering along the upper edge of these same cliffs. Seeing the ground on which a friend was standing beginning to slip beneath his feet, he made a sudden spring to save his companion, and in doing so precipitated himself over the cliff, falling nearly a hundred feet in broken falls before he could succeed in stopping himself. He saved his friend, but became himself a subject for the surgeon.

Returning to Belfast we spent a quiet Sabbath at Dr. Hanna's church. From the Doctor as well as from others of a humbler class, we gathered some information relative to the much-discussed question of home rule for Ireland which very materially changed our views in regard to it; and although it is not designed to enter the field of politics to any extent in these pages, yet we feel constrained to make a statement or two in regard to the situation in Ireland touching home rule and its bearings upon the Protestant Church of Ireland. The question is in reality more of a religious than a political one. The north of Ireland, as every intelligent person knows, is almost exclusively Protestant, whilst the south is Catholic. The Protestants of Ireland are almost to a man against home rule, whilst the Romanism of the country is equally as clamorous for home rule. Put this in a nutshell and it means simply this: Home rule in Ireland means Catholic rule, for the home Parliament would be about two-thirds Catholic, and Catholic rule means to-day just what it did in the days of the Irish persecutions. For proof of this statement see the situation in Belfast at the present time. The city is two-thirds Protestant, and yet in spite of this fact a Protestant Sabbath school may not go in procession through its streets with banners and music without being mobbed; and even without these accompaniments, the protection of the police force is necessary when they go in procession to the depots to take trains for excursions into the country. Dr. Hanna's own Sabbath school of over twelve hundred children was going on the Saturday following our visit by train into the country for a picnic, and both banner and music must be left out in their march to the depot; and last year this school was forced to abandon its usual picnic by reason of this same bitter hostility. Men who talked to us of the situation as we were traveling spoke in whispers lest their conversation should reach Catholic ears. Now imagine a Catholic home Parliament making laws for the Protestantism of the country.

It is Irish agitators who, for the sake of personal, political and mercenary motives, are keeping Ireland in a state of ferment over the question of home rule. They go like firebrands among the ignorant Catholic population proclaiming that if home rule was once inaugurated the vast estates upon which they are now only poor, oppressed tenants would be broken up and each of them would have a little farm of his own. Great as the discontent is now in Ireland, when these promises would fail of verification under home rule the rampant Irishman would paint things a redder hue than they are now. The ejections and lawless deeds of blood that we frequently hear of now, take place where the tenant, inflamed by firebrand orators scattered through the land rises up in rebellion against his landlord and refuses to pay his rental. The north of Ireland is contented and prosperous and almost unanimously agreed against any change in the government. Why should not middle and southern Ireland, possessing equally fertile regions, be equally prosperous and content? Protestant Ireland cries out against home rule Parliament because it needs the protection of the Imperial Parliament in the enjoyment of its civil and religious liberties.

The General Assembly of the Presbyterian Church of Ireland, recently in session at Belfast, declared itself as opposed to home rule. The Irish Loyalists number about 2,000,000, and Irish Protestants about 1,200,000; all these are arrayed in opposition to home rule. It may be asked, then, "Why is it that 86 out of the 106 members of Parliament that Ireland sends to St. Stephen's are demanding home rule for Ireland?" Simply because that the Irish Loyalists are not concentrated in separate provinces in such numbers as to carry their candidates and thus be represented at St. Stephen's. The existing representation is therefore a gross injustice to the Loyalists and Protestant people of Ireland. If the representation in the Imperial Parliament was in accordance with the real sentiments of the Irish people it would stand about 43 Loyalists to 63 Parnellites. For the sake of the Protestant people of Ireland, its peace and an equitable rule, it is to be hoped that the Church of America will not commit the foolish blunder of the last Republican Convention in Chicago in endorsing home rule in Ireland; for it means more to the distressed Island than most people at a distance imagine. Ireland is infinitely better off under the protective rule of the mother country than she would be under any home rule of her own.

A day is given to the sights of Belfast, but there is little else besides city to see, and after we have spent a half-day riding around on the tops of tram cars, and the other half-day around the docks, we feel as though we had exhausted our tourist interest, and was ready for another stage of the journey. Belfast seems to enjoy a thriving trade; her ship building docks especially are the center of a vast amount of noise and confusion as the busy hammers of thousands of workmen fall with deafening clatter on the great iron and steel planks of the sides and bottoms of new ocean steamers. But we are sure that we are not slandering the denizens of Belfast when we say that their city is one literally soaked in whiskey. Here the women claim equal rights with the men in the matter of whiskey drinking and tippling; and nowhere in all our rambles have we seen as much of this vile and beastly habit indulged in by both sexes as here in Belfast. Pat must cease to cry want and hard times in our ears as long as he finds so much to spend in gratifying an appetite which makes him inferior to the long-eared animal that we find so abundant in his country.

Our passage is taken for Dublin on a small trading steamer that pulls anchor about seven o'clock in the evening and puts out to sea. An old tub of a vessel she is, too, that would have taken us to the bottom of the sea rather than into the port of Dublin, if old ocean had roused himself into storm fury; but the sea is in one of his most placid moods, and we come without mishap into Dublin harbor early the next morning. Our luggage goes on to the railway depot, and we are left for a day's ramble around the Irish capital.

Phœnix Park, the Irishman's pride, gives us occupation for half-day. You would arouse the Irish in a Dublin native if you were to tell him that there was anything better in the shape of a park in the world than his Phœnix Park. And yet it is true that it is little better than a well-kept 1,700-acre wood lot, having in it seven or eight hundred deer. Its chief attraction lies in its shade, quiet and roadways, on which the Dublin aristocracy may display their roadsters and take a constitutional in country solitude. In the western part of the Park is the scene of the Burke and Cavendish assassinations, a spot which the visitor is sure to have pointed out to him by the Park policemen, and which will doubtless ere long be marked by some suitable monument.

Dublin, like Belfast, is given over to the vice of drunkenness. The more we see of the situation in Ireland, the more we are convinced that a good dose of Iowa prohibition would be of infinitely more value to the Irish than home rule.

WHERE PAT LIVES. 279

Dublin can boast of one of the best educational institutions of the kingdom—Trinity College—where we spend a portion of a day an interested observer of the sports and dress of Trinity students. It is to be hoped that the American college student will not adopt the head-dress of the Trinity student, which is a black cap with a square flat top like a mortar board; a good thing, perhaps, in the capacity of a sun shade or umbrella, but ill adapted to the comfort of the wearer in a prairie wind.

Taking train at nine o'clock a. m. in Dublin we move on southward to Queenstown, where we are to meet the "City of Rome," on which our homeward passage is to be made. At three o'clock p. m., in the midst of a pouring rain, we reach Queenstown; where a night of rest is enjoyed whilst our vessel is ploughing her way over St. George's Channel from Liverpool. Here we have the satisfaction of again meeting our fellow-traveler R——, and of comparing notes with him on the question of home rule, which the reader has already had the benefit of in this chapter.

CHAPTER XXV.

HOMEWARD BOUND.

A BRIGHT morning this 28th day of June, when the glad news is announced that the "City of Rome" is lying to just outside the Queenstown harbor, waiting for her Irish passengers. There are one hundred and thirty of us, nearly all Irish, crossing the sea to find permanent homes in the States, to go aboard the tender for conveyance out to the steamer.

What amusing phases of the Irish character we see as we take a stroll along the quay among the busy crowd! Most of them have taken steerage passage, and are intent on getting together sundry articles which they think they will need on the voyage, pans, tin cups, bedding, and not a few are hunting remedies for sea sickness. Here an old Irish woman, illiterate in every other respect, but a graduate in the school of flattery, beseeches us for the Lord's sake to leave her a sixpence or a shilling for the poor starving family, in the meantime plastering her speech freely with wishes for heaven's choicest blessings to rest upon us during the voyage, as well as at every other point of our existence; but, behold! when, taught by our observations that the grog shop instead of the grocery man will come into possession of our gratuity, we tell her that she is too late in her application, for the hungry Italian and backshish-loving Arab has taken all we have to spare, she turns on us a volley of curses that would grace the speech of a fiend from the bottomless pit.

Our tender shoves off with her load of passengers, and we are soon scrambling up the gang stairs of the "City of Rome." "This vessel's prow is turned in a direction exactly to my taste," remarks R——, as we make the tour of her lengthy promenade deck, and the other pilgrim looks out westward over the wide waste of waters, longingly, as though he wished the vessel's prow was three thousand miles nearer the sun setting than it is at the present moment. The steamship "Celtic," of the White Star Line, follows us closely when, about 10 o'clock, the "City of Rome" puts out to sea.

About 3 o'clock p. m. the Irish coast is cleared, and we say good-bye to land for the next seven days. A tour of the steerage deck reveals the fact that our Irish passengers are having a most uncomfortable experience in a first attack of sea sickness. We heard some of them say, when going out on the tender with them, that "They knew they were going to be sea sick right away," and so of course they must be, in order not to disappoint expectations, for there is certainly no other reason for it, with the monster steamer, and smooth sea that we are favored with on the first two days of the voyage.

On Saturday, our third day out, there are evident signs of a coming tempest. The night is a wild one, and our fine vessel rears and plunges like a war horse in the midst of the angry billows. The morning brings no abatement of the tempest. The passengers are nearly all sick; no sun to look in upon us with a smile of hope; all is gloom, and as the Sabbath advances the tempest increases. A giant wave strikes the vessel on the bow about 12 o'clock, raking the hurricane deck fore and aft, nearly sweeping us off our feet into the sea. A protecting cabin against which we are leaning, firmly grasping a hand rail attached to it, saves us doubtless for a more expensive funeral. Captain Young is interviewed by an "Evening Sun" reporter when we come into New York harbor, and in the next day's issue of the "Sun" we find the Captain's account of the storm as follows:

A high tidal wave struck the steamship "City of Rome" on July 1st, after being out three days and while in longitude 47.50 and latitude 38.22. The steamship arrived at her dock, pier 43, North River, last evening, with passengers, crew and cargo safe and sound, although those on board had a pretty lively experience and one a good many do not care to repeat. She carried on the trip 1,201 steerage passengers, 119 first-class and 112 second-class passengers. The "City of Rome" is the largest steamship crossing the Atlantic. Her regular tonnage is 8,415, and she is considered a very stanch craft.

Her commander, Captain Hugh Young, was seen this morning by an "Evening Sun" reporter. He said that about noon of July 1, almost without any warning, a stiff westerly gale sprung up, closely followed by an immense tidal wave, which struck the steamship full on the bow, and swept over the forward deck with great violence. The force was so tremendous that the boom was carried away, and stove in the railing of the bridge. A seaman was knocked down and badly cut about the face and head. He is reported to have recovered from his injuries and will be able to resume work on the next trip.

Captain Young says the wave dashed over them so suddenly that none of the cabin passengers were aware of what had occurred until it was over. There was but the single wave, and all commotion was over inside of five minutes.

The steerage passengers were pretty well shaken up, but none were reported injured. The "City of Rome" has been on the Anchor Line for five years, and this is the second experience of the kind she has had. The last time was about two years ago, and then, like this occasion, the steamship pulled through all right. It will take several hundred dollars to repair the damage done the steamship by the angry waves, but she will sail for Europe all the same on the morning of July 11 as per schedule.

A rather singular circumstance in connection with the mishap was recalled by a sea captain this afternoon. It seems that just about a year ago at this time the "Umbria," of the Cunard Line, had her decks swept with a tidal wave, which shook the vessel from stem to stern, and while considerable damage was done, none of the passengers were injured. The accident occurred nearly in the same latitude and longitude as did the one to the "City of Rome."

STEAMER "CITY OF ROME."

But forty hours of gale are at last safely ridden through and our dangers are over, we trust, for the rest of the voyage. In the midst of our greatest peril we were confident of two things; first, that the watchful eye of the Eternal was over us, and that the raging billows must hush their fury, if His mandate went forth for that purpose; if not, all was well, for we were still in His keeping. We were confident, in the second place, of the storm-breasting qualities of our grand old steamer, for she holds first rank among the great travelers of the deep.

The morning of Independence day dawns bright and fair on ship board, giving opportunity to our sea-stricken voyagers to go on deck and enjoy a day of sunshine and pleasant converse. As the passengers come straggling up on deck after breakfast, the fire alarm is suddenly sounded, and officers, deck hands and stewards are seen hastening up to the forward part of the hurricane deck. "Can it be possible," we say to a friend with whom we are in conversation at the time, "that we have escaped the storm only to fall a prey to the devouring fire?" Surely it must be so! for the fire buckets are passing, and the life boats are being got ready. Blanched faces appear at cabin doors, and anxious questions are asked of all who are supposed to have any information. Those are anxious minutes that pass before we learn that it is simply a fire drill of the crew!

And now our noble ship is getting down to business in fine style, making about eighteen knots an hour. It is the expectation to finish our voyage to-day, the 5th of July. Outward-bound vessels are quite numerous, and our flag is dipped in salutation oftener this day than during all the rest of the voyage. It is 6 o'clock in the evening before the Long Island shore is sighted, and a little later when Sandy Hook promontory comes into view. We cannot tell you, reader, of the joy that this vision of our native shores brought us. If there is a spark of true native-born American love in the bosom of him who leaves our happy shores for a period of wandering in European and Asiatic lands, the pilgrim will return with it magnified an hundred fold; for he has had an opportunity to make comparisons which, with all due allowance for inborn patriotism, still leaves America far in the van of nations.

It is sundown as we enter the North River; too late to pass the customs' and doctor's inspection, so our vessel comes to a halt opposite the Statue of Liberty and waits for the morning. How beautiful the river scenery is to-night, as we sit on deck watching the passenger boats gliding up and down all aglow with electric and colored lights! The shores, too, are all bespangled with lights of many hues, and a little belated patriotism is indulging itself at various points in a shower of rockets. Our passengers, too, are making the evening lively on deck with song, drink and social intercourse. And thus ends the record of our wanderings; and with a few general notes on the ways and means, economical and otherwise, of making such a tour as we have just finished, we will take our leave of the reader, wishing him the pleasure of a similar experience.

The first sine qua non of travel is taste for it. If the natural fondness for travel amounts to a passion, so much the better, the profit and pleasure of the tour will be so much the more enhanced. Months of continuous travel are likely to grow monotonous and, like an over feed of good things, to turn even into nausea if there be not some hidden spring of fondness for it in the nature of the tourist to feed the vision and stimulate the waning energies of the body. Another requisite of travel is companionship. One good, agreeable companion whose tastes correspond in large measure with your own, is better than more. With this kind of an outfit, not forgetting to place in our breast pocket a letter of credit for about $700, we are ready for our ocean voyage, and a trip such as we have taken.

What kind of a ship, and what class of passage shall we take? The larger the vessel the more comfortable the passage is likely to be, for there is less of sea motion in proportion to the size of the vessel, and that means less liability to sea sickness. The traveler who finds himself prostrated after his first meal or two by this bugbear of ocean travel is likely to feel somewhat like the Frenchman who, after he had paid his tribute to Neptune, remarked with a ghastly grin on his face, "For plaiser I cross the ocean never." One may cross the ocean, if he has any natural fondness for it and manages himself judiciously, without knowing experimentally what sea sickness is. Notwithstanding our experience of about thirty-five days on ocean and sea, we have not had more than fifteen minutes of sea sickness all told, just enough to enable us to sympathize with others less fortunate.

The class of passage will depend on circumstances. If we are economically inclined a second cabin, or intermediate on a good-sized vessel, will afford us all the comforts necessary: If we are crossing in summer, and are gentlemen, a steerage passage will answer us very well. A steerage ticket will cost us but twenty dollars, while a second cabin on a vessel like the "City of Rome" will cost us thirty-six dollars; with little difference so far as food is concerned. If a French vessel be taken from New York to Havre or Marseilles, second cabin is as good as anybody but an autocrat need desire. Let there be no box luggage to look after; take nothing but hand luggage, and an endless amount of worry and trouble, besides expense, will be saved. The tourist abroad, be his motive health, pleasure, or knowledge, or all in combination, will find his pleasure enhanced by making all the use he can out of his legs; and then it makes that $700 letter of credit do so much more for him. But if he have a box or trunk to look after, he finds it making sad inroads on his time and plans of economy.

For a visit to Europe we would sooner take the early fall months than the midsummer ones, for the reason that cool weather is better than hot in any country for touring purposes. If it is the grand scenery and quiet rest of the mountains of Italy and France that are sought, the summer months will do very well. But another reason still for fall touring is that you do not fall in with the fashionable multitudes from our own side of the water that have emptied themselves out into all the principal cities of Europe. Hotels, boarding houses, and pleasure resorts are all crowded to their utmost capacity, and rates are correspondingly high. London is one of the most interesting of all cities, and can be seen to best advantage in the early fall months when it is comparatively free from fogs. Of the two seasons we visited it in, spring and fall, we have a decided preference for the fall. Apartments for two or more persons by the week may be had for about three dollars each person, with or without board. Two, or even three, weeks are necessary to see the objects of interest in and around London.

If one makes the tour of the principal cities of Europe in this leisurely manner, his whole expenses per month, including traveling expenses, need not be more than seventy-five dollars. Railway travel in Great Britain should be third-class; second-class coaches are withdrawn by some of the roads, being so little patronized. The third-class coaches are cushioned and are in every way as comfortable as the first-class. On the continent, especially in Italy, the travel should be second-class, as the third-class cars are more like cattle pens, and are used by the lowest class of people. Look out for the French cabman; you will find nothing worse in his line, go where you will. Make a bargain with him before you use his vehicle or he will charge you two or three prices. The same advice will do for the Italian cabies. In Italy the pest of your life will be the beggar. Give him the cold shoulder, for his history is that he eats the bread of idleness because he has conceived the idea that you have more money than you know what to do with and that you are traveling on purpose to find some means of its disposal, and he is doing you a favor to place himself in your way. He is too much of an aristocrat to stoop to the menial task of earning his daily bread when it can be had from you simply for the asking.

One may live very comfortably in Rome or Naples on 80 cents a day. If you are going on to Egypt and the Holy Land do not get frightened at the idea that you are going among a lot of wild animals and must have a company to go with for safety's sake. We had the misfortune to throw away about thirty dollars by adopting this idea, and joining a personally-conducted party at Rome. Avoid Cook, Gaze, Jenkins, and all other tourist agencies, and journey on independently. You will never be without company, and never out of the reach of English-speaking guides, and much better terms can be made at the places you intend to visit than can be made at a distance; and in addition to this you are a master of your own movements. If sickness or any other calamity overtakes you, you are at liberty to stop or return as you may find it necessary. One of the most prolific sources of dissatisfaction that met us everywhere on the soil of the Orient was this hampered condition of tourists under the personal direction of some tourist agency, and the advantage that was taken of their ignorance in the matter of fares.

The Arabs of both Egypt and Palestine are, as a rule, glad to see the pilgrims coming and will afford them all the assistance in their power—for backshish. It is necessary always to make bargains with them beforehand, for they are great lovers of foreign coin and will take all they can get of it. Although quarrelsome among themselves, it is very rare that they offer any violence to the traveler. Only the wild Bedouins think of this. In Jerusalem the pilgrim will find plenty of good accommodation at rates more reasonable than in any part of the more civilized western world. It is only when one comes to travel through the land with tents, dragomen, muleteers, and the whole paraphernalia requisite for comfort on the lengthy tour through waste lands, that he finds himself involved in more than the ordinary expense. This portion of the trip must be made at an expense of about five dollars a day. And if ladies are in the party who are not inured to long rides in the saddle, palanquins will be found necessary, which will increase the expense to about seven dollars per day. The tenting tour through

Palestine is a hard one at best, and should not be undertaken by ladies who are not stout and rugged.

As to clothing, take but little of that with you; a simple change of underclothing, with a traveling suit of some light-colored material which will not show the dust. Buy as you go, for in most of the markets of the old world clothing is cheaper than on this side of the water. These suggestions are for travelers of limited means, who want to make their little go as far as possible.

THE END.

www.ingramcontent.com/pod-product-compliance
Lightning Source LLC
Chambersburg PA
CBHW032104220426
43664CB00008B/1123